10.00

THE CULT OF
INFORMATION
■

THE CULT OF INFORMATION

■

A Neo-Luddite Treatise on
High Tech, Artificial Intelligence,
and the True Art of Thinking

■

THEODORE ROSZAK

University of California Press
Berkeley • Los Angeles • London

University of California Press
Berkeley and Los Angeles, California

University of California Press, Ltd.
London, England

First edition copyright © 1986 by Theodore Roszak
Second edition copyright © 1994 by Theodore Roszak

Library of Congress Cataloging-in-Publication Data

Roszak, Theodore, 1933–
    The cult of information : a neo-Luddite treatise on high
tech, artificial intelligence, and the true art of thinking /
Theodore Roszak.
      p.   cm.
    Originally published: New York : Pantheon Books, 1986.
    Includes bibliographical references and index.
    ISBN 0-520-08584-1 (alk. paper)
    1. Information technology.   2. Artificial intelligence.
  I. Title.
T58.5.R67   1994
004—dc20
                                         93-37189
                                           CIP

Printed in the Unites States of America

9 8 7 6 5 4 3 2 1

The guilty may fear but vengeance he aims
At the honest man's life or Estate,
His wrath is entirely confined to wide frames
And those that old prices abate.

These Engines of mischief were sentenced to die
By unanimous vote of the Trade
and Ludd who can all opposition defy
Was the Grand executioner made.

Let the haughty no longer the humble oppress
Then shall Ludd sheath his conquering sword,
His grievances instantly meet with redress
Then peace will be quickly restored.

Nineteenth century Luddite song quoted in E. P. Thompson,
The Making of the English Working Class.

CONTENTS

■

ACKNOWLEDGMENTS

■

This book has required a great deal of help from principled hackers, conscientious librarians, and experts in many fields. Those I want to thank especially are: Sanford Berman, John Buschman, Judy Clarence, Douglas Ferguson, Evelyn Greenwald, Earle Lane, Thomas Mann, Charles Piller, Martin Schiffenbauer, Gordon Smith, Jim Warren, Bill Woodcock.

PREFACE

■

The little boy in the fairy tale who blurted out the embarrassing truth that the emperor was wearing no clothes did not necessarily mean to say that the emperor deserved no respect at all. The poor man may have had any number of redeeming qualities. In his vanity, he had simply weakened to the appeal of an impossible grandeur. His worst failing was that he allowed a few opportunistic culprits to play upon his gullibility and that of his subjects.

This critique of the computers in our lives, and especially in our schools, has much the same limited scope. It is not part of my purpose to dismiss the computer as worthless or malevolent. I would hardly be in the position to draw that conclusion. The manuscript for this book was typed on a word processor; at numerous points, the research for the text made extensive use of electronic data bases. I approach this study with a healthy respect for the many helpful things computers can do, and not from a position of doctrinaire technophobia. I do, however, want to suggest that the computer, like the too-susceptible emperor, has been overdressed in fabulous claims. Further, I believe these claims have been deliberately propagated by elements in our society that are making some of the most morally questionable uses of computer power. The glowing promises with which they have surrounded that power need to be challenged if the computer is not to be delivered into the wrong hands.

As this should make clear, my interest in these pages is not in the technology of computers, but in their folklore: the images of power, the illusions of well-being, the fantasies and wishful thinking that have grown up around the machine. Primarily, my target is the concept to which the technology has become inextricably linked in the public mind: *information*. Information has taken on the quality of that impalpable, invisible, but plaudit-winning silk from which the emperor's ethereal gown was supposedly spun. The word has received ambitious, global definitions that make it all good things to all people. Words that come to mean everything may finally mean nothing; yet their very emptiness may allow them to be filled with a mesmerizing glamour. The loose but exuberant talk we hear on all sides these days about "the information economy," "the information society," is coming to have exactly that function. These often-repeated catchphrases and clichés are the mumbo jumbo of a widespread public cult. Like all cults, this one also has the intention of enlisting mindless allegiance and acquiescence. People who have no clear idea what they mean by information or why they should want so much of it are nonetheless prepared to believe that we live in an Information Age, which makes every computer around us what the relics of the True Cross were in the Age of Faith: emblems of salvation.

Information has had a remarkable rags-to-riches career in the public vocabulary over the past forty years. It was surely among the least likely candidates to achieve the exalted status of a godword, but so it has become, and not by accident. Beginning with its esoteric redefinition by the information theorists during World War II, it has come to be connected with a historic transition in our economic life, one which unites major corporate interests, the government, the scientific establishment, and at last draws in the persuasive rhetoric of advertisers and merchandisers. If only as a unifying theme that holds so many powerful social forces together, the concept would be worth critical attention. But the Information Age has now entered the educational curriculum in an aggressive and particularly insidious way which could distort the meaning of thought itself. That is the special concern of this study.

Two distinct elements come together in the computer: the ability to store information in vast amounts, the ability to process that information in obedience to strict logical procedures. Each of these will be taken up in turn in Chapters 5 and 6 and explored for its relationship to thought. There we will see how the cult of information fixes upon one or the other of these elements (sometimes both) and construes its intellectual value. Because the ability to store data somewhat corresponds to what we call memory in human beings, and because the ability to follow logical procedures somewhat corresponds to what we call reasoning in human beings, many members of the cult have concluded that what computers do somewhat corresponds to what we call thinking. It is no great difficulty to persuade the general public of that conclusion since computers process data very fast in small spaces well below the level of visibility; they do not look like other machines when they are at work. They seem to be running along as smoothly and silently as the brain does when it remembers and reasons and thinks.

On the other hand, those who design and build computers know exactly how the machines are working down in the hidden depths of their semiconductors. Computers can be taken apart, scrutinized, and put back together. Their activities can be tracked, analyzed, measured, and thus clearly understood—which is far from possible with the brain. This gives rise to the tempting assumption on the part of the builders and designers that computers can tell us something about brains, indeed, that the computer can serve as a model of the mind, which then comes to be seen as some manner of information processing machine, and possibly not as good at the job as the machine.

The burden of my argument is to insist that there is a vital distinction between what machines do when they process information and what minds do when they think. At a time when computers are being intruded massively upon the schools, that distinction needs to be kept plainly in view by teachers and students alike. But thanks to the cultlike mystique that has come to surround the computer, the line that divides mind from machine is being blurred. Accordingly, the powers of reason and imagination which the schools exist to celebrate and strengthen are in danger of being diluted with low-grade mechanical counterfeits.

If we wish to reclaim the true art of thinking from this crippling confusion, we must begin by cutting our way through an undergrowth of advertising hype, media fictions, and commercial propaganda. But having done that much to clear the ground, we come upon the hard philosophical core of the cult of information, which is as much the creation of the academies and laboratories as of the marketplace. Gifted minds in the field of computer science have joined the cult for reasons of power and profit. Because the hucksters have enlisted so many scientists in their cause, there are tough intellectual questions as well as political interests that need to be examined if we are to understand the full influence of the computer in our society. In a very real sense, the powers and purposes of the human mind are at issue. If the educators are also finally swept into the cult, we may see the rising generation of students seriously hampered in its capacity to think through the social and ethical questions that confront us as we pass through the latest stage of the ongoing industrial revolution.

The so-called information economy may not be what its major boosters would have us believe. It is not the futuristic utopia so long prefigured by science fiction. It is, however, a significant and exciting transition in our industrial history. No technology has ever unfolded its potentialities as swiftly as computers and telecommunications are doing. It is understandable that those of us who are witnessing this whirlwind transformation should find ourselves dizzied by the rush of innovation, the sudden influx of new technical powers. But we have seen too many technologies of the past go wrong to let our critical attention be misdirected by the computer enthusiasts. Information technology has the obvious capacity to concentrate political power, to create new forms of social obfuscation and domination. The less prepared we feel to question the uses to which it is put, the more certain we are to suffer those liabilities.

Ultimately, this book is as much about the art of thinking as it is about the politics and technology of information. There is an obvious humanist agenda running through the critique. I work from the assumption that the mind—and not only in the form of human intelligence—is as close to being a wonder of nature as any miracle revered by the religions of the world. To reflect on the powers of the mind, to probe its secrets, these are among the time-honored pursuits of philosophy. It is quite another matter, however, to teach children and tell the public that the secrets have all been revealed and the powers harnessed—and to offer a collection of semiconductors in a metal box as proof. Measured against that claim, even the most ingenious computer is bound to look ludicrously inadequate in the eyes of thoughtful people—more of a joke than an achievement. As critical as this book may be at many points in challenging the status of the computer in our society, it includes among its purposes that of saving this remarkable invention from the inordinate claims that its enthusiasts are making for it. Unburdened of vainglorious ambition, dressed in more modest but palpable working clothes, the computer, like the emperor in the fairy tale, may yet become a reasonably valuable public servant.

IN DEFENSE OF THE NAKED MIND

■

INTRODUCTION TO THE SECOND EDITION

THE COMPUTER AND GENERAL LUDD
■

There are computer enthusiasts I have met who will hear no evil spoken of the machine they hold dear. They tend to regard every critic they encounter as the latest species of "Luddite," those notorious machine-wreckers of the early industrial revolution who are remembered in the textbooks as mindless enemies of progress. For example, one reviewer of the first edition of *The Cult of Information* declared in *Business Week* that the author's views would appeal to "closet technophobes and incipient Luddites." It is a book, he said, that "caters to their hidden fears and biases about what the computer is doing to their lives."

The Luddites have come to play a peculiar role in technological history. They are usually invoked as convenient whipping boys whose function is to squelch critical discussion of machines and their uses. Once the label "Luddite" has been attached to you, the inevitable next question is, "How would you like to go back and live in a cave?"

Historians now tell us that the original Luddites may have taken a bad rap. The hard-pressed weavers of northern England who rallied around the mythical General Ludd appear to have had no grudge against technology in and of itself; their grievance was with those who used machines to lower wages or eliminate jobs. General Ludd's "army of redressers," as they named themselves, never attacked one of the new power looms unless its owner had violated the workers' interests. Though they were desperate men fighting to feed their families, their hostility was carefully targeted. They asked how the machines were being used, by whom, for whose benefit—and then normally tried negotiating a better deal with their employers. Only when that effort failed did they feel forced to resort to violence. But to begin with, theirs was essentially an appeal for justice and humane treatment.

I am quite willing to have this book seen as a "neo-Luddite" treatise in just that sense. It belongs to that same tradition of passionate but, I hope, measured criticism. In this respect, I count myself an ally of all those serious students and users of information technology who hold a reasonably balanced view of what computers can and cannot, should and should not, do. Many of those who read the first edition of *The Cult of Information* recognized that the book, far from being a wholesale rejection of high tech, sought to discriminate between the use and abuse of computers. For example, in an on-line conference convened in 1986 on one of the country's most respected electronic bulletin boards (The WELL, operating out of the San Francisco Bay Area), there were some contributors who saw the book as nothing more than an outburst of "technophobia"; but others were sympathetic to the effort. One participant said in the author's defense,

> I'm really puzzled about why this book pissed you off so much....He attacks the hype and the misuses of the technology, not what most of us are trying to do....Those of us who are working on what we consider humane, democratic, decentralized projects should welcome critiques which make the public more skeptical....In other hands, with only slight variations, it could be centralist and propagandist. And the

myth that surrounds it—which is the true target of Roszak's critique—will determine how people will react.

Lest there be any misunderstanding, then, let me preface this edition with a clear statement of my admiration for this remarkable technology. Like all the works of *homo faber,* high tech, this latest chapter in humanity's ongoing industrial saga, deserves to be honored as a manifestation of the astonishingly inventive genius of our species. I use a computer to earn my way as a writer; I might even qualify as a highly proficient user. I marvel each time I boot the machine at the cunning that has found a way to translate so much of human culture—numbers, words, graphics, music, three-dimensional design, animation, fractals—into simple digital symbols that can be read as electrical signals. I am astonished at the speed and compaction that has been achieved by computational devices in little more than a generation. I can even understand how some might (though mistakenly, I think) identify an accomplishment of this magnitude as an incipient form of superior intelligence.

If there were not thousands already applauding the skill of those who have fashioned this technology, I might be the one to do it. But there are more than enough who stand ready to praise; indeed, one of the things that worries me most is the great number who are handsomely rewarded for doing so. The "data merchants," as I call them, find their careers or their investments tied to the extravagant promises that attach to computers; they have every reason to believe that there is nothing computers cannot do and should not be doing. The result has been the creation of a mystique of information that makes basic intellectual discriminations between data, knowledge, judgment, imagination, insight, and wisdom impossible.

Again, so that I will not be misunderstood: as a writer and a teacher, I admit to having a healthy appetite for information. I value having plenty of data readily available as much as the next person. *Unless,* that is, the next person happens to be a computer manufacturer, a software mogul, an advertising executive in charge of the IBM account, or an Artificial Intelligence expert under contract to AT&T. Whenever I hear vested interests like these speaking of information as if it were *all* the human mind needs to think with, I begin to feel as if I might have strayed into some strange sect where all about me I find people worshipping light bulbs. No question but that light bulbs are useful devices; I would not want to live without them. But I never would have thought of them as objects of veneration.

So too with information. The cultlike status it has attained both bewilders and troubles me. The eagerness some enthusiasts (as well as many academics, intellectuals, and journalists who should know better) display to globalize the word until it covers all the cultural ground in sight seems to me blatantly wrong—especially when it comes to teaching the young. If they had their way, they would flatten the natural hierarchy of the mind until people cannot tell the difference between the telephone directory and Homer's *Iliad*. So in these pages I raise a small protest on behalf of the naked human mind, its creative powers, its animal resiliency, its undiscovered evolutionary potentiality, its deep enigmas of aspiration and self-transcendence. I seek to remind readers of the obvious that so often goes unobserved. There have been works of genius, indeed whole golden ages of culture—many of them the creation of peasant peoples and tribal folk—based upon nothing more than human speech, imagination, and memory. The heights of intellect and vision have been scaled by people gathered around campfires to tell stories, by poets scratching away with a quill by candlelight, by scribes bending over a sheet of parchment, by inspired painters working on the wall of a cave. There is, of course, no reason why we should not, in our time, look for other, more expressive media of communication, but I find it important to recall that mind has never been dependent on machinery to reach the peaks of achievement.

Though that reminder is not meant as a rejection of machinery, which is itself a glory of our species, I am sure some will see it as a typical humanist response to the overweening claims of the technician. Well, perhaps it is. But where high tech is concerned the disposition of forces ought to be obvious to anyone who has as much as a passing acquaintance with the shape of the global economy. High tech is the biggest thing going in the world of financial and political decision; it enjoys the unstinting support of governments and great corporations. Billions of dollars stand behind every computer chip. There is not the least chance that the most extreme humanistic critic of these machines and their makers will register as more than a minor annoyance to economic power of this magnitude. The computer establishment is the Goliath in this confrontation; before it even the most militant critic stands like David without his slingshot.

HOW ARTIFICIAL CAN
INTELLIGENCE BE?

■

Since the first edition of *The Cult of Information* there have been some noteworthy changes in computer technology, as well as many wrenching transformations in the high-tech industries. Whole new waves of innovation have crested and subsided; the price of just about everything on the market has dropped; major corporate players are passing through a period of drastic restructuring. The mighty IBM has suffered setbacks that were unthinkable in the early 1980s; the long-standing Kulturkampf between elite Big Blue and populist Apple has ended with the two rivals looking more and more like partners sharing a troubled and uncertain market. In the eyes of some, the printed page is a more endangered format than ever before—and happily so; one still comes across people for whom there is no distinction between *culture* and *computer.* Yet book publishing continues to thrive as a business, and people in all lines of work continue to regard "hard copy"—print on paper—as the "real thing." As a society we are still paper bound and paper based. A decade after the front cover of *Time* magazine substituted the personal computer as "machine of the year" for its usual "man of the year," home computers, now cheaper than ever, have still not penetrated more than a third of American households. And most of those who own the machine struggle to find any more interesting use for it than typewriting, record keeping, and game playing.

Where these changes touch upon the thesis of this book in some significant way, I have sought to bring things up to date; the more important of these developments are catalogued and discussed in this introduction. But little of what has happened during recent years in the computer industry and its economics affects my main concern, which has to do with the philosophical status of information and the art of thinking, issues that contextualize the technology, in much the same way that what we take "health" to be contextualizes the practice of medicine, or what we take "sanity" to be contextualizes the practice of psychiatry. Information is what information-processing technology processes; but if we have no clear idea what information is and what it is not, what questions it can and cannot answer, what its relationship is to other intellectual faculties—

indeed, if we are not certain as to whether there *are* any other intellectual faculties besides the processing of information—then we can have no clear idea what authority this technology should hold over our lives.

One change that does relate to a major concern of the first edition has to do with the general orientation of cognitive science and research in Artificial Intelligence. As long as it was believed that "thinking" was merely some form of rapid data processing, it seemed reasonable to assume that faster machines accessing ever-greater amounts of data would one day surpass ordinary human-headed thinking. In the mid-1980s inordinate claims were still being made for the future of machine intelligence, despite the fact that all the predictions made along those lines in the past had fallen flat. Even Marvin Minsky of MIT, one of the most unrestrained proponents of Artificial Intelligence, has come round to a far more complex model of mentality. In his book *The Society of Mind,* the mind is no longer the "meat machine" he once took it to be; it has become a sort of United Nations bureaucracy, a collection of autonomous "agencies" that represent the variety of knowledge and somehow manage to form working coalitions among themselves to produce intelligent behavior. The all-important "somehow" remains far from explained.[1]

As our understanding of human intelligence deepens, one hears somewhat fewer predictions about how soon the computer will equal or surpass the mind to become the inevitable next stage in intelligent evolution on our planet. Since the human mind remains the baseline for measuring progress in the field of Artificial Intelligence, one still comes across extravagant claims about the prospects of developing near-substitutes for real intelligence—especially among those who see the best hope for AI in neural networks, a form of nonprogrammed machine learning that copes remarkably well with pattern recognition and natural language. But all the more ambitious predictions about the future of AI are being placed farther off in the future and have a more guarded ring to them. Marvin Minsky continues to tell us that we can expect to see the invention of "artificial scientists, artists, composers, and personal companions"—but it will be "over the next few generations." (Technological prognostication that extends beyond the lifetime of the prognosticator is always a safe bet.) But he concedes that AI has come upon what may be an insurmountable barrier to its effort to unlock the mysteries of mind. It is called "common sense." I noted this point in the first edition; now I would emphasize it even more.

Almost in spite of itself Artificial Intelligence research has taught us a significant truth about human thought. We have learned that computers that can rival grand masters at chess do not have enough sense to come out of the rain. Literally. The newspaper-in-the-rain situation task I describe in Chapter 6 continues to plague AI research —to the point of finally looking like an insurmountable barrier, rather like the limit imposed in physics by the speed of light. If so, that would be a discouraging conclusion for those who regard the mind as a "barrier" that needs to be "surmounted." Simple matters like this turn out, under close analytical scrutiny, to be not quite so simple after all—at least not for a computer. Similarly, programs that are intended to master the hidden intricacies of a child's daily routines—going to school, buying candy, raiding the refrigerator, making a jelly sandwich, playing with others—continue to fail miserably. As Minsky puts it, "Experts are simpler than novices!... Whenever...children speak or play, they combine a thousand different skills." It is primarily because of the stubbornly elusive nature of common sense that the philosopher Hubert Dreyfus, one of the keenest critics of Artificial Intelligence, calls the field a "degenerating research program," a once promising paradigm that now yields fewer and fewer useful results.[2]

It seems the context for the seemingly humble mental talent we have named "common sense" is a sprawling, lifelong blur of cumulative, largely ineffable personal experience that defies formal representation. A consensus may at last be forming that true intelligence embraces the entire bewildering pattern of learning and behavior called "being human." As baffling as that pattern may be, most students of AI would now agree that it has something to do with being born, and having a body, and growing up in families, and belonging to societies, and walking around in the real world, and meeting people, and doing things, and (for all we know) having "intimations of immortality." Farther back still, intelligence may, as John Searle believes, have something to do with the basic biological constitution of the brain, an indispensable evolutionary element that eludes machine simulation.[3] In any case, there are fewer and fewer computer enthusiasts who still believe this messy, fluid field of living experience can be turned into the sort of computational "data" a machine can understand.

Though some continue to try. Bart Kosko believes that "fuzzy logic," which seeks to express the vague, grey-scale tones that lie between black and white, may one day come closer to capturing common sense.[4] Doug Linnat at the Microelectronics and Computer Technology Corporation in Austin, Texas, has similar hopes for project Cyc, one of the longest-running and most expensive AI programs ever undertaken. Cyc seeks to corral the seemingly infinite ambiguities of human language by the brute-force method of identifying and anticipating all the possibilities of machine misunderstanding. Cyc programmers are out to contextualize every connotation of every word in the English language, so that their computers can tie into an ever-expanding web of common-sense scenarios. But what Cyc may actually be proving is how unbridgeable the gulf is between human and electronic mentality. Program all the known biographical details of Abraham Lincoln's life into one of Cyc's computers and the machine comes up asking, "If Lincoln was in Washington DC on July 2, 1863, was his left foot there also?" Or, "Were all of Lincoln's children younger than him?" What we have here is a curious new form of literature, a sort of high-tech Zen Buddhist koan that jars our understanding into sudden self-awareness: questions no sane human being would ever have thought of asking.

There is an ironic but highly valuable quality to AI in all its forms. The effort to simulate or surpass human intelligence is uncovering subtleties and paradoxes about the human mind we might never have imagined. By way of heroic failures, AI is teaching us how truly strange real intelligence is. There is an intuitively immediate all-at-onceness to superficially simple everyday projects like making breakfast or going shopping that seems to have nothing to do with the formal step-by-step procedures that go into programming a computer. One field of AI, however, has made remarkable progress in elucidating the ineffability of intelligent activities like this. Often, by quizzing specialists closely about their work, computer programmers can tease out procedures, assumptions, values that can then be formally specified. The result is an Expert System, one of the few practical applications of AI. Edward Feigenbaum sees such systems as the gateway to the next era of machine intelligence; he calls it "knowledge processing," as opposed to mere *data* processing. Whatever he may mean by "knowledge," it surely represents a more complex approach to thinking than once prevailed in the field.

Expert systems are ingenious, but they remain narrowly specialized in ways that clearly leave something essential about the human mind unexplained. While individual expert programs may perform impressively in neatly defined areas like medical diagnosis, selecting stocks, or prospecting for oil and metals, no one system can be designed to do what any other system can do. Yet it is precisely such global integration that characterizes human intelligence. This is indeed what makes judgment possible: the capacity to step outside the decision and see it from a different perspective. As helpful as Expert Systems may be in many areas, in matters where judgment and personal responsibility matter (like the practice of medicine) nobody would want to rely on the machines for more than preliminary guesswork. After all, how many software firms would be willing to run the risk of medical malpractice suits if their diagnostic programs glitched?

MEANWHILE,
BACK AT THE CARNIVAL...
■

On the other hand, if AI scientists have pulled back on their claims, the computer industry continues to tout its wares as flamboyantly as ever. With the Cold War and the arms race generating less budgetary support, Information-the-Science may now be less compromisingly connected with Information-the-Weapon; but it still remains embarrassingly beholden to Information-the-Commodity. So the merchandising of hardware and software remains as much of a carnival act as ever, with endless new attractions along the midway, all of them being brazenly oversold. While the price of such basic items as memory chips and hard disks continues to fall, new fascinations like desktop publishing, multimedia, and interactivity serve to keep the consumers consuming. New hardware and software constantly push toward the purchase of bigger, faster equipment and more complex programs, none of which is nearly as necessary to have, as cheap to buy, or as friendly to use as the advertising pretends. What P. T. Barnum earned by convincing everybody in the nation that they just *had* to buy a ticket to see Jumbo the elephant amounts to peanuts compared to the billions that Bill Gates of Microsoft has taken in from sales of Windows, a big, expensive, and (in its early versions) clunky imitation of the Macintosh graphical user interface. What made so many people rush to buy Windows? Gates made it seem like the only relief in sight from the cumbersome DOS program he had foisted upon his customers in the first place.

And what, overwhelmingly, do the hardware and the software get used for outside their day-to-day business applications? The computer industry remains embarrassingly dependent upon much that is simply tawdry. Games and amusements continue to be the mainstay of the technology in the mass market. As of the early 1990s American parents were paying more for video games (over $5 billion) than for tickets to the movies. Manufacturers are hoping to increase that figure tenfold by the end of the decade by including 3-D, virtual reality, adult versions of "Star Trek" and "Yoshi's Cookies"—probably spiked with a heavy dose of pornware, or "erototronics," as it is called in *Future Sex,* a magazine that specializes in computer-mediated titillation. "Adult" bulletin boards have proven to be one of the growth areas of the technology. Advertising "A Hundred Lines of Hot Modem Fun At Your Fingertips! With Both Straight and Gay Sections," the language and imagery have grown potent enough to raise issues of censorship. Responding to police raids in some cities, system operators have addressed the question of X-rated material at conferences with some urgency. "More and more boards are including the X-rated material for a simple reason—their subscribers want it."[5] Most of these amusements are benign, if silly; some are not. In Austria kids can now purchase neo-Naziware videogames called *Aryan Test* and *KZ Manager* which allow players to run death camps and gas inferior races.[6]

Even the business community gets suckered into wasting precious resources on expensive computer digressions like chasing fonts through desktop publishing programs and cranking out 256-color graphics-laden fast-step CD-Rom "presentations" that are more sizzle than substance. One study I have come across estimates the amount of time spent fussing with in-house newsletters, especially trying out this and that font, may cost American industry tens of millions of dollars in lost time.

The electronic bulletin boards, in which some see adumbrations of a new democratic forum, are also frequently taken up with trivial or less-than-idealistic pursuits: dating services, jokes, ticket sales, soap opera summaries, investing, and, more and more often, shopping. In France, it is estimated that more than half of what passes through the national Minitel computer-telephone network is sexual banter. The Internet has set aside an entire branch of the system (Alt.Sex) for pornographic chat and pictures. Perhaps this is inevitable with a technology that shades off so abruptly into entertainment, but it is nonetheless disappointing—as if the mighty railroad train, once the leading-edge invention of civilization, had been dependent on selling cut-down versions of itself to be used as roller coasters in amusement parks. Admittedly, an objection like this is a matter of taste and should not be pressed too seriously. But I have often wondered how cognitive scientists and idealistic hackers must feel, knowing that the technology some among them regard as the salvation of democracy and the next step in evolution is being squandered on so many unbecoming uses.

THE END OF THE WAR MACHINE?

■

Another issue that was central to the first edition: the power of the computer to concentrate ever-greater decision-making power in the wrong few hands. Of the problems I discuss under that heading in Chapter 10, one has decidedly and surprisingly improved—though not for technological reasons. What I refer to as "the War Machine," the computerized control of thermonuclear weaponry, has receded as a threat to our freedom and survival in recent years. Though the Russian government that has taken over from the former Soviet leadership still possesses more than thirty thousand nuclear weapons (ten thousand of them capable of reaching targets in the United States), the complex of international political changes we refer to as "the end of the cold war" has made the forty-year balance of terror seem far less terrifying. The worst danger to which I addressed myself in dealing with the military uses of high tech—that of all-out Soviet-American nuclear war initiated by computer error or by the hair-trigger response of forces kept on instant alert—has all but disappeared. Much that I say about that grim possibility might have been removed from this edition. But I have decided to let the section stand, with minor corrections, for an important reason. I present it as Exhibit A in the indictment I serve against the cult of information. The underlying concern I voice in dealing with nuclear weapons is not really tied to the particular facts and figures of the arms race at a given point in history. Rather, it has to do with the overweening confidence of computer scientists in their systems—and with our willingness as a society to believe what those scientists tell us about the absolute reliability of their programs.

At the same time, we should bear in mind that much of that military technology still exists and is as error-prone as ever. In one respect, we may even be worse off than before. As nuclear weapons proliferate around the world, the chance of regional conflicts achieving nuclear proportions increases. We now have more nuclear powers than ever before, many of them living side by side in deep distrust, their armed forces on round-the-clock alert, their undertrained technicians nervously fingering the red button. As Daniel Ellsberg warns us, "Worldwide, although the risk of nuclear war between NATO and the former Warsaw Pact powers has virtually vanished, the chance that some nuclear weapons will kill humans somewhere may be higher than before."[7]

Another study by Scott Sagan reminds us that computerized weapons systems must still remain a cause for serious concern precisely because the cold war has ended.

> The collapse of the Soviet Union has subjected its nuclear command and control system to unprecedented and unanticipated tensions.... Intercontinental-range strategic nuclear weapons are likely to be deployed in Russia, Kazakhstan, and Ukraine for many years to come, and the safety of these weapons will likely be strained by emerging political, ethnic, and civil-military conflicts in the region.

Sagan observes that many of the new nuclear powers that have been created out of the fragments of the old Soviet Union "may not be able to afford even a modicum of mechanical safety devices and modern warning sensors and will therefore be more prone to accidents and false warnings."[8]

As things now stand, our military leaders can have no clear idea who controls the world's remaining thermonuclear weapons systems; all accountability is being lost in the progressively fragmenting international community. Nor can anybody say with certainty what programs those weapons now obey, or how competent their new and anonymous keepers may be in dealing with this delicate and deadly technology. The "War Machine" is far from being a historical curiosity.

THE ADVENT OF THE MONEY MACHINE
■

Even as the threat of thermonuclear Armageddon lessens, in another area of our lives, almost by way of negative compensation, things have grown more menacing. To the other categories of computer abuse I list in Chapter 10 of this book (the Surveillance Machine, the Polling Machine, the War Machine) I would now add "the Money Machine." As in the worlds of law enforcement, political campaigning, and the military, so now in the world of high finance the computer has fallen into the wrong hands and is being used in ways that have radically altered international economic affairs. Programmed trading, a form of Expert System that has been steadily under development since the 1960s by some of the best mathematical brains in the nation, has at last become a disruptive and all but dictatorial force in world finance—to such a degree that patterns of investment and speculation generated by computers have become an independent factor determining the shape of the market.

Electronic cash management and funds transfers using the speed of computers and global telecommunications networks date well back into the 1960s; but the first indication the public received that the technological magic that made same-day funds possible might be a mixed blessing came in May 1984 when, following little more than rumors in the press, Continental Illinois Bank of Chicago, the seventh-largest bank in the United States, was reported to be insolvent. Foreign banks, mainly Japanese, responding to rumors about Continental's dubious financial health, had suddenly withdrawn billions of dollars in one-day overnight deposits. A massive run on the bank had begun in the international banking community. Continental, it was feared, was carrying far too many bad loans and was not financially stable. The reports turned out to be true; the bank had made many big, bad investments, mainly in oil companies. Poor judgment in the banking world is nothing new; what was new about the story were the scale of the misjudgment and the way in which such immense mismanagement could be kept out of sight. As the story unfolded, it became clear that Continental had been covering up its true condition by using its state-of-the-art instant-communications capacity to execute the sort of rapid electronic transfers of short term funds that computers and global telecommunications make possible. The transfers amounted to as much as $8 billion in overnight funds and $35 billion in one-week deposits. Now Continental had fallen victim to its own sleight-of-hand methods; the same electronic network it had been using to stay afloat had turned against it to produce a bank failure so huge that the federal government had no choice but to bail Continental out at the public expense.[9]

A year after the collapse of Continental Illinois, a major brokerage house, E. F. Hutton, was indicted by the Justice Department in a multimillion-dollar computer scam. Hutton was caught fast-shuffling funds between scores of banks throughout the United States in such a way that the company could write checks against deposits that did not exist except as computer records flashing across the electronic network—a form of high-tech check kiting.

Front page sensations like these were the public's first significant experience of the destabilizing potential that computers had assumed in the financial markets. Over the next year, commentators raised questions about another new computer-driven business practice: programmed trading. Might it be introducing too much speed and speculation into the markets? Not everybody saw much to worry about; there was certainly nothing illegal about the practice. *Time* magazine quoted optimistic insiders who even believed the new high-speed technology represented the "threshold of a golden age of capitalism." Other observers were more skeptical; they saw in the growing use of neural networked systems ominous possibilities for new forms of financial manipulation that would be dominated by a handful of institutional investors and programmed traders equipped with the best expert investment systems money can buy.[10]

The skeptics turned out to be right. In October 1987, programmed decisions to buy and sell by large institutional investors triggered the worst collapse in the history of the New York Stock Exchange.

In effect, too many of the programs that had been cleverly devised by the "rocket scientists" (as the hackers of the financial world are called) at major brokerage firms were doing the same thing at the same time. What each of the institutional investors was seeking to do was to protect itself by choosing the safest selection of risk-reducing options and futures: "portfolio insurance," as it is termed. But the net result was a cascading series of self-fulfilling prophecies operating as a feedback loop. The market went haywire.

After the crash, the Securities and Exchange Commission imposed "circuit-breakers" to head off any future disaster of this kind. But these are of limited value in a financial marketplace that has become round-the-clock and international; damping the panic in one stock exchange will only divert it elsewhere.

The simple fact is that, thanks to the computer, information about money has now become as valuable as money itself. And those who can process the most information the fastest are in the best position to profit—often in ways that escape any effective legal control. The computerized hand can move faster than the regulatory eye. As a result, the instability produced by high-speed computerized operations has become endemic. It has in fact been institutionalized in the signature financial instrument of the nineties: the "derivative," by far the most exotic and elusive entity ever to appear in the world of money.

Derivatives are new categories of financial "products" that could only achieve the prominence they enjoy where lightning-fast transfers are possible. They allow a variety of speculative maneuvers keyed to minute fluctuations in the price action of markets that deal in interest rates, foreign currency, stock indices, collateralized mortgages, and commodities. One observer calls derivatives "a concept out of *Alice in Wonderland*.... In this strange and eerie electronic world, Japanese pension funds can buy American bonds backed not by gold or corporate assets, but by stacks of car loans made by Detroit."[11]

Interest rate swaps are among the most popular derivatives; these allow speculators to "surf the yield curve" between the day-to-day (or even hour-to-hour) differences in long-term and short-term obligations—for example, the spread between fixed and variable mortgage interest rates. Traders can make contracts on future interest rates, then trade the contracts separately from the money to which the rates were originally attached. Major banks are among the big players in these tricky games. Since the accounting practices associated with derivatives are terra incognita even to regulators, nobody knows for certain how much money is tied up in this new market, but the figure is certainly in the hundreds of billions. The credit exposure of the banks on sums like this is enough to worry *Barron's* magazine, which asks in a major editorial report if the explosive popularity of derivatives might not lead to a "meltdown" on the global market greater than the panic of '87.[12]

Those who are complacent about the risks rely heavily on the sort of "dynamic hedging" that only programmed investment can provide. This is among the chief services provided by the "quants," the computer experts who account for the ascendancy of derivatives in the markets. Creating an optimum portfolio made up of such complex abstractions requires the ability to assimilate huge amounts of information with maximum speed. So too, the split-second trading in currencies by speculators that has played havoc with monetary policy around the world is uniquely a computer phenomenon. In 1993 the French government, after expending billions in an effort to shore up the franc, was forced to capitulate and devalue its currency. The traders it was up against not only had the capital to get their way but the computer power to take instant advantage of currency fluctuations and to move funds at the push of a button.

> The new masters of the universe [*Barron's* reports in its survey] are as likely to have degrees in engineering or computer science. In their high tech world of probability curves and elaborate securities pricing models incorporating lots of Greek letters, there's little room for the once-venerated qualities of trading intuition and social polish....These days [the nerds] even have their own trade group—the International Association of Financial Engineers. Imagine that.

As the financier Felix Rohatyn sees it, "twenty-six-year-olds with computers are creating financial hydrogen bombs."[13]

But risk is not the only liability to these computer games; an opportunistic preoccupation with quick and massive profit-taking may pose a greater problem, especially as banks grow more and more involved with derivatives and other speculative financial products. For the high rollers in the marketplace, the temptation to make overnight billions by shuffling electronic values has become a major distraction. Most worrisomely, banks have been seduced into diverting their capital away from what Joel Kurtzman calls "the real-economy...where products are made, trade is conducted, research is carried out, and services rendered. The real-economy is where factory workers toil, doctors tend the sick, and teachers teach, and where roads, bridges, harbors, airports, and railway systems are built."

But in the real-economy, profits can take a long while reporting in. These days smart guys don't waste their time in the real-economy; they vandalize it and move on across the buzzing networks. Inevitably, restless and globally footloose capital drifts toward the international electronic casino where the returns come at the speed of light. Writes Kurtzman:

> Over the years, especially during the 1980s, real-economy companies have been hit by wave after wave of corporate takeovers, with the stock market conspiring in those takeovers by camouflaging rather than revealing true value. These companies have also been handed a big bill from the firms that sell their stocks for the thrill of participating in financial markets that are rigged against real-economy companies.

So Kurtzman asks of the high-flying "megabyte marketplace" that now devours the true wealth of nations: "When the economic unit is the globe, where do people fit in?"[14]

Like the other examples I offer of computer power "in the wrong hands," the money machine raises issues about the social value of the computer that make for neo-Luddite pessimism. The question of balance once again is central. List the pros and the cons of the technology and give them their proper weight. Granted, it is now possible for concerned citizens with PCs and Macs to log into electronic conferences on their local bulletin board, to debate, to gripe, to complain and petition. On the other hand we have the money machine, which makes possible the electronic highjacking of the world's financial markets by a small number of privileged traders who play the game for paper billions. As a result, the capital resources that we need to generate paychecks, useful products, research and development, and helpful services are diverted from long-term investment to short-term speculation. What citizenly use of this technology can counterbalance a shift of power on this scale?

One comes back to the basic economic fact of the matter: computer technology, both the hardware and the software, is a commodity on sale to those who can afford it—and the most powerful machines continue to be in the wrong hands.

EDUTAINMENT
FROM APPLE II TO METROID II
■

A particular interest in the 1986 edition of *The Cult of Information* was the role of the computer in education, a lively topic of discussion and promotion at that time. The computer industry continues to cultivate the field, but I would judge that a great deal of the shine that once surrounded the vision of the electronic classroom has rubbed off—at least among the educators. Even though there are more computers than ever in our schools (since the early 1980s, the number of personal computers in U.S. schools has risen from fifty thousand to 2.4 million), their place in the curriculum remains highly uncertain. Certainly the predictions that were being made a few decades ago that public education would be revolutionized by the advent of the electronic classroom have fallen flat. In 1969, for example, the National Education Association confidently predicted (in a report titled "The Teacher and His Staff") that by 1994 every student in the United States would be equipped with "computer-information bank consoles" and international video phones.

Computers are only the most recent wave of educational technology; since the 1950s educators have been through two generations of hype about all the good things they can expect from various kinds of "teaching machines." They have learned to be skeptical. As two close students of educational technology observe, "We thought that mere acquisition was sufficient to begin using these new technological delights, but have learned that there were no quick and easy roads to success. . . . We have learned that educational technology is a problem-solving process, not a product." [15]

More to the point, an increasing number of educators have begun to recognize that classroom technology is emphatically *not* neutral but carries with it significant (if subliminal) cultural, ethical, and epistemological presuppositions. The computer is inherently a Cartesian device embedded in the assumptions of a single intellectual style within a single culture of the modern world. The very metaphors that surround it bespeak a conception of the mind as logical machinery; the constant references to the "productivity" that the computer promises endorse the values of the marketplace and the western ethos of progress. In a critique that draws upon Jacques Ellul, Martin Heidegger, and Jürgen Habermas, the educator C. A. Bowers concludes that "the designers of educational software, in not being more aware of the phenomenological traditions of thought, have simply ignored the epistemological problem of how to represent the cultural foundations of a person's tacit knowledge, which is highly contextual, through a medium that decontextualizes knowledge."[16]

There is a built-in conservatism to American public education that is deeply rooted in the professional self-interest of teachers and the entrenched localism of our country's sixteen thousand school districts. Teachers have not been quick to learn computer skills, and even less quick to redesign the chalk-and-talk curriculum in favor of confused and untested schemes—even when they come attached to free equipment like the many Apple II computers that were donated to American schools in the 1980s. None of the more radical proposals for computer-based educational reform, like Seymour Papert's ambitious LOGO program I critique in Chapter 4, has found a solid, aggressive, and growing constituency. Instead we continue to have what one study calls "a national hodgepodge" of ideas and prescriptions.[17]

In large part the high-tech standoffishness of classroom teachers can be justifiably traced to a false start. In the early 1980s, "computer literacy" by and large meant teaching pupils to program in some simple language like BASIC. That orientation betrayed astonishing shortsightedness on the part of experts who should have known better. I noted in the first edition of this book that the availability of well-developed application programs made programming courses a waste of time; that is even more the case now. As sophisticated software has flowed onto the market, there is little need for the sort of low-level amateur programming that can be taught on cheap equipment in limited time. Like everybody else, schools can now buy whole off-the-shelf packages for classroom use. The fact that many computer enthusiasts did not see this coming hardly inspires confidence.

Most of the packages, however, have turned out to be more hype and puffery than well-conceived instructional material. One estimate has it that of the ten thousand programs in the pedagogical market-place as of the early 1990s, perhaps two hundred are of some value.[18] Among these, basic word processing—a valuable but hardly exhilarating use of the technology—dominates the interest of edu-cators. But even here, where we have a clear, practical application of computer skills, teachers report that they can spend more time teaching pupils how to find their way around the word processing program than they spend actually using the computer to improve expression and thought. This is hardly surprising; every computer program has its "learning curve." The simple fact is, when it comes to writing, learning how to use a computer takes more time than learning how to use a pencil. The same could be said about graphics and science programs in comparison to learning how to use a paintbrush, crayons, and most lab equipment. When it comes to the three Rs, only 'rithmetic clearly benefits from computerization. Plac-ing a complex machine between the student and reading and 'riting puts more distance between intention and result.[19]

Whatever the sources of curricular indecision and lethargy may be, the conservatism of American educators has been powerfully supplemented by a new factor: fiscal limitations. When computers first began to penetrate the classroom, the assumption was that an Apple II or an IBM PC, plus some basic software and a low-cost dot-matrix printer, represented a long-term capital investment. But machines like the aging Apple II, which still makes up some 50 percent of the installed base of school computers, are moving steadily toward obsolescence, despite the continued production of software designed for them. Teachers may be resourceful in making the most of the old machines, but both they and their students are constantly made aware that there is later and better merchandise on the market. Many of the kids are aware of that fact from the games they use at home or at the video arcade. And the latest, most eye-popping programs that have entered the educational market require hard disks and much memory, as well as CD-ROM drives. Though the cost of everything electronic continues to decline, the purchase of add-ons as costly as CD-ROM players and sound cards in any great quantity is no easy expenditure for financially strapped school systems. Even when there are ways of networking such facilities, the installation and maintenance of networks can be a heavy expense—especially in schools where the wear and tear on fragile equipment can take a fierce toll. All the money has to come from other parts of the curriculum. As long as "edutainment," as the industry calls its latest mélange of multimedia tricks, requires as much computer power as it does, it will lie beyond the reach of many schools.

This may be the greatest obstacle computer enthusiasts now confront in touting their wares. If the data merchants have their way, the main thrust of edutaining technology will be toward ever-more-expensive gimmickry with ever-less quality control. But they are pushing a costly substitute for books and blackboards, one that many school districts, plagued by a backlog of social issues, simply cannot afford.

That factor has shown up dramatically in an unusually comprehensive and conscientious survey of computers in our schools that was sponsored in the early 1990s by *Macworld* magazine.[20] The findings were sobering. Charles Piller, who headed the study, concluded that we are rapidly creating a "technological underclass in America's public schools." While the survey did find schools where computers were being used imaginatively as an integrated part of a high-level curriculum, it found many more schools where the machines were limited to drill-and-practice sessions, and far too many where computers were simply going unused. This led to an important insight: *Mere statistics, like computer-to-student ratios, tell us nothing about the real on-site value of the technology.* Many computers that get tallied in superficial studies turn out to be broken relics stacked away in closets and storerooms. This is poignantly true of schools in minority neighborhoods. "Poor schools," the *Macworld* study observes, "tend to use computers so rigidly and ineptly as to repel students. Poor schools create refugees from technology." In a follow-up article for *The New York Times*, Piller concluded, "Instead of becoming instruments of reform, computers are reinforcing a two-tier system of education for the rich and poor."[21]

Moreover, even if the will and the skill were there to use the machines well, in many school districts the funds educators divert to computers will have to come out of urgently necessary programs like vaccinations or school lunches or campus security. There are schools where controlling the handguns on campus counts for more than teaching computer literacy. We are reminded that our nation's schools are woven into a dense political and sociological fabric that has everything to do with morale, teachability, opportunity, safety, and survival.

Social and financial problems of this magnitude would compromise effective educational use of computer technology even if what that technology offered included intellectually reputable choices. But it is not at all the case that academic quality can be guaranteed. We will turn to the mental and psychological impact of computerized instruction in Chapter 9, when we consider the effects upon literacy. Suffice it to say here that as the CD disks fill up with spectacular effects, the reading habits encouraged by interactive materials—at least the versions I have seen—run the risk of overloading and further fragmenting the attention span (already so badly battered) that is basic to intelligence. There is an unresolved tension between computer literacy (still a catchphrase in search of a meaning) and plain old print literacy that will not be resolved as long as the data merchants promote their wares for shortsighted profiteering motives.

Computers raise another issue in the classroom. By far the strongest argument for going high tech in the schools has been the promise of employment; computer literacy supposedly represents the royal road to a good job. But, by a cruel irony, in the greater global economy that surrounds our schools, the main effect of automation and cybernation is to deskill, disempower, and disemploy people from the assembly line up through middle management. Computers have come to play a central role in downsizing companies and in the creation of a part-time, temporary, low-paid, nonbenefited workforce. The brutal economic fact of life in today's marketplace is that we could generate more good jobs by outlawing computers than by multiplying them. Once again the basic truth about public education is clear: our schools do not exist in a vacuum. They are surrounded by and permeated by social and economic forces that pose more problems in the lives of our children than any machine will ever solve—unless videogames are intended to be the circus that will keep otherwise restless citizens preoccupied in the New World Order.

THE IDEAL OF
THE ON-LINE COMMONWEALTH

■

Does it *have* to be like this? Does this remarkable technology *have* to be swamped by silly commercial novelties and abusive social power? Of course not. There is no law that says information technology *must* fall victim to mindless consumption and technocratic manipulation. There are any number of principled, politically concerned hackers who are struggling to salvage the computer for better uses. Bulletin boards across the country are being employed as worldwide citizens' information and discussion facilities. Many see the expanding Internet (whose promise we will discuss more fully in Chapter 9) as the beginning of a democratic renaissance. Combined with full and free public access to government archives, the Internet may one day largely supplant newspapers and television news, with their many limitations and biases, as a customized news service. Some look forward to new forms of electronic publication that will replace print-on-the-page with new image and sound capabilities; purely electronic magazines already exist, and some authors have begun to "publish" their works over networks, requesting a voluntary fee from their readers.

Though there will always be debate about the best technology to select, the Clinton-Gore administration, with its commitment to a public "data highway," would seem to be setting the course for a national information infrastructure. If information is what our embattled democracy needs, people—at least those who can afford the bill—should soon have no great difficulty filling the need in the "wired world" that some predict. In fact, navigating the surplus may be the great problem. There are difficulties and expenses involved in making use of the opportunity, but these need not be insurmountable. With enough skill, anyone owning a cheap second-hand computer and a modem can access many networking services. It is now possible to exchange mail, news, and expertise across the globe at a cost that may be as low as a local phone call or a subscription to a daily newspaper.

And there are other good possibilities. Chapter 9 suggests how the nation's libraries might become the vital center that would provide maximum democratic access to the burgeoning electronic plenty within an ethic of public service. The libraries are, I suggest, our best hope of turning the sprawling potentiality of information technology into a true public utility.

For all the reservations I may express about computers and their uses, my heart goes out to the heroic spirits who recognize what power we have here to do the right thing—and who struggle to keep that power under democratic control. They are the conscience of the technology. We will also review their efforts in Chapter 9.

Nor is the promise of computer technology limited to the political arena. At the Media Lab at the Massachusetts Institute of Technology—the Bauhaus of high tech—new artistic and expressive possibilities are being brilliantly explored. The more optimistic assessments of the electronic wonders there being created look forward to a "technological populism" and a new "computer-enhanced individuality" in which everything will be cheaply digitalized and wholly customizable.[22]

What I have seen and sampled among the new genres that Stewart Brand calls a "techno-feast of goodies" can be dazzling in the extreme. As one might predict, among all the goodies, an author would be most curious about the promise of the "electronic book." Will it inherit the future the way the printed book displaced the handwritten manuscript? The E-book is being promoted as a push-button cornucopia of spectacular multimedia effects: hypertext interactively linked at every point to film, animation, graphics, music, voice, all miniaturized to the size of a Sony Walkman, and possibly made available as a domestic production facility. Every home its own MGM.

As in the case of desktop publishing, I find it hard to imagine that the technology needed to produce the most impressive electronic results will ever be affordable by ordinary users like myself, or that the skills will be within our reach. The benefits of the E-book will most likely come to us by way of buying them ready-made—as we do the printed word. Will they be affordable? There are special problems here that are far from solution. Some are painfully ironic. It turns out that even those who would seem to have the capital and the cunning to exploit these astonishing possibilities may find the road into virtual reality blocked by one of the most traditional barriers imaginable. It is called "copyright," and it entails paying for the privilege to use a created material.

The producers of E-books are entrepreneurs operating in a free, competitive market out to make all the profit they can. But they are learning that producing an E-book means entering a jungle of property rights held by those who are just as eager to turn a profit. In the cultural marketplace, everything—words, images, music, lyrics, logos, voices, photos, film footage—is property owned by somebody; entrepreneurs now routinely buy up and hoard every last seemingly worthless shred of created material. And a fully packed CD-ROM disk needs a lot of that material: hundreds of megabytes of it.

High tech comes surrounded by an aura of big bucks; precisely for that reason, everybody wants a piece of the multimedia pie, and nobody is willing to sell cheap. Software Toolworks of Novato, California, producer of the highly successful Grolier Multimedia Encyclopedia, is one of the largest CD-ROM software companies in the world. In the early 1990s, it set about producing *The Twentieth Century Video Almanac*, a five-disk interactive compendium of film, music, and graphics. The project required a feature-film-sized production team in which the writer was a minor player. Legal skill proved to be far more crucial. Why? Because rounding up all the permissions involved took as much time as the technical work; the bargaining was fierce, the prices demanded were high. Everybody who so much as appeared in the background of a picture or film clip expected to be paid. Permissions availability became the main editorial factor determining what got included; the "art" had to be worked in around the copyrights. The fees demanded might have been prohibitively high, but Software Toolworks was able to argue that its market for this CD-ROM would be quite limited, perhaps under one hundred thousand sales (at some $200 for the five disk set). But what happens if the E-book medium booms, as Software Toolworks and all its competitors hope that it will? The price of everything can only go up—and so too the cost to the buyer.[23]

Interestingly, in print publishing, standards of fair use and a scale of reasonable permission fees for graphics and illustrations have been worked out over generations; nobody expects to make a killing off somebody else's book (except perhaps for the song-lyric vendors, who are notorious bandits). But the E-book has no such tradition to draw upon. Its association is with the sky's-the-limit motion picture marketplace where all concerned expect to get rich quick. In the new, uncharted world of the E-book, where permissions wrangling and litigation are apt to go on endlessly, the CD-ROM may become the first cultural genre invented wholly for the financial benefit of lawyers.

Whenever I find myself having doubts whether increasingly powerful media like these will ever be brought under the creative control of mature aesthetic minds, I try to remind myself that once upon a time the printing press, the camera, the piano, the orchestra, and motion pictures were innovations with no cultural track record. But one thing I know for certain: the minds that use these powers well will still have to master the art of thinking. Though the medium may be zero-cost infinite bandwidth networks, the media users will have to exercise the same mental muscles as the artists of Lascaux and draw upon the same creative sources. If there is anything particularly pernicious in the lore of high tech it is the facile assumption that just maybe the machines will do the thinking (and the feeling, and the judging, and the creating) for us, and do it better. The irony behind this technology is the tendency it encourages in some of its most talented and enthusiastic developers to cheapen—or even try to replace—the mind that created the technology in the first place.

AND FINALLY . . .
A FEW WORDS FOR THE REST OF US
■

Despite the problems I mention here, I fully accept that information technology is here to stay—at least for as long as the world industrial economy survives. (No guarantees about that, to be sure.) It has the permanence of a mature technology.

What is a mature technology?

One that finally generates as many problems as it solves.

As we have learned from every earlier wave of invention, machines are jinnis that get out of control. They reshape the world in unforeseen ways. The railroad and the automobile "solved" the problem of rapid transportation—only to finish by depleting our store of nonrenewable fossil fuels, fouling the air, and destroying the integrity of cities. Modern medicine "solved" the problem posed by numerous infectious diseases, only to finish by giving us the population explosion, ever-more-resistant strains of bacteria, and the ethical dilemma of protracted senility.

The computer "solved" the problem of fast, cheap data processing in a business culture drowning in red tape and paperwork, only to finish by destroying the rights of privacy, concentrating the political and commercial control of information in ever fewer hands, mesmerizing our children with bad art and pernicious nonsense, and menacing us with "computer errors" vast enough to paralyze whole societies. A clever few find ways to work around these vices and maximize the advantages of each new technology; the computer-proficient can sound quite smug about their command of databases and on-line resources. Many earn well from new, more sophisticated media. But the sum total of good and bad gets visited on the rest of us—and especially on the generations to come, who are simply born into the technology's inevitable downside.

The rest of us: These days one comes across that plaintive phrase more and more often in computer literature. It refers to those who are not hackers or computer experts of any kind—and who have no wish to be. "The rest of us" are a lot of us: people without the time, talent, inclination, or money to "get into" this or any other technology, like the 40 percent of Apple computer users who reportedly cannot find their system folder, or the millions of PC users who have no interest in working out a half-dozen different Config.Sys. files to custom boot their computer. A widely reported 1993 market survey by the Dell Computer Corporation concluded that there is a growing population of this kind, more than enough in the adult population to make bestsellers out of books with titles like *DOS for Dummies,* or *The Complete Idiot's Guide to Windows:*[24] documentation that mercifully talks down to the real-life users of these complex, often bizarrely engineered machines. The survey called them "technophobes"—meaning people who would just as soon trade in their computer for an old-fangled typewriter. Seasoned hackers who delight in building a better Macintosh desktop or debating the virtues of the latest Windows graphics cards might do well to pay more attention to this population. Among them we find many of the true computer professionals of our society: the clerks and secretaries and self-employed home-office technoclunkers who earn their living sitting at computers all day and who are more worried about the pains in their wrists than which conference on The WELL to log on to when they get home. I suspect the future of the technology has a great deal more to do with the needs and values of this public than with the high-flying aficionados at the local Macintosh Users' Group.

I work with many of these people in my teaching job: the office workers who suffer with each new program they must learn, who struggle with each new software upgrade that needs to be endlessly fine-tuned before they can get on with their jobs, who groan with each baffling piece of hardware that gets visited upon them like a curse. Many still cannot handle basic DOS commands or decode the obscure little icons that their friendly Macintosh insists are so much better than words on the screen. Sometimes they come to me in exasperation asking questions: why can't they run this new graphics program the department just purchased? Answer: you have to buy another monitor with a more expensive video card. (Video card?) Or they wonder, when they try to install the new Mac-something desktop publishing program, why their monitor keeps flashing the message "Disk Full." Answer: your disk is *full*; you have to buy a bigger one. Or they ask why the Windows program they just loaded runs at a snail's pace and keeps locking up and losing the last few hours' work. Answer: you have to buy a lot more memory and a faster chip. Or they ask for a dozen kinds of help I cannot begin to provide, though I suspect the answer is usually that they have to buy something they don't have that will be obsolete next year at this time when they notice all the same problems coming back at them.

I once attended an educational computer conference that featured an elaborate interactive genetics program developed to run on a supercharged NeXt workstation—equipment costing far more than most schools in our system can afford. It was deucedly clever but far from being purely "intuitive," as its designer kept insisting. The faculty member I was sharing with during the demonstration wasn't getting very much out of the exercise; she was having far too much trouble keeping her mouse on the table so she could get the little arrow in the right box. She kept hitting the wrong button and then could not find her way back. The exasperated demonstrator came over to tell her, "Look, it's *easy*. Just do this." Click-click-click. Like most hackers, he was proud to the point of arrogance that he qualified, that he knew how, that he *belonged* to the brave new wired world. And indeed he was very fast on the click. My colleague, lacking the requisite hand-eye dexterity, finally gave up and asked me to take over. "I never could work one of those things," she confessed in a guilty whisper, as if she ought to be ashamed of herself. I returned the confession. "I'm pretty klutzy with a mouse too." And I proceeded to make all the same mistakes.

"The rest of us" keep hearing about the spectacular benefits of desktop publishing, multimedia, interactivity; but whenever we thumb our way through the documentation, we realize that we are way out of our technological depth. And whenever we look at the price tag, we know we are out of our financial league.

There is the problem, right before our eyes. The machines may not be smarter than we are, but we may not be proficient enough or moneyed enough to hold our own with those who own and exploit the machines. The cult of information is theirs, not ours. They use it, and they use it against us. What "the rest of us" are offered as "access" to the information society is hardly enough to make us real citizens of the information age: it may be little more than a diversion. True, we can now use our modems to send E-mail to the new on-line White House, but there is no law that says anybody has to read what we send. And if there were, would it matter? We may soon have programs that make it possible to defeat the purpose of rapid, personal communications. A teaching colleague of mine, swamped by the E-Mail he receives from the students in one college course—much of which he finds repetitious, garbled, or witless—has developed a program that scans what he receives for keywords and generates boilerplate responses.

"The rest of us" get games to play and programs that will balance our checkbooks and catalogue our recipes. Maybe eventually we will get 3-D subscription virtual sex. We can rent CompuServe or log onto the local electronic bulletin board to check the running file of light-bulb jokes or to flame away on an issue or two. But even if we can buy the technology, we don't own it—not in any substantial way that gives us power. I, for example, am grateful that high tech has provided me with a great substitute for my old Smith-Corona on which to write my neo-Luddite lament. Perhaps one day I will become proficient enough to find my way through a MUD (a Multi-User Dungeon) on the Internet. But all the while I keystroke away, I suspect that the data-surfers at the IRS and the FBI and TRW are gliding through every secret I ever thought I had, and that the hot young quants at Morgan Stanley are using their rather more powerful machines to vandalize the banking systems of six nations. While the rest of us cling to the margins, the power and the profit of the technology gravitate elsewhere. The solution is once again becoming the problem.

But then the history of technology has always been a faltering search for Promethean power and utopian perfection. Every mature technology brings a minimal immediate gain followed by enormous long-term liabilities. The computer is the latest entry in that history, still bright with promise for its enthusiasts but surely destined to join the lengthening file of modern technological treachery that Aldous Huxley began compiling in his prophetic *Brave New World*. By now we should know what the Luddites of old learned before us: every tool ever invented is a mixed blessing. How things will balance out is a matter of vigilance, moral courage, and the distribution of power.

Whenever I begin to despair over such matters, I conjure up a few consoling images: Charlie Chaplin sliding woefully down the gullet of the assembly line, Laurel and Hardy fleeing for their lives before a runaway trolley car. There is a certain healthy amusement to be enjoyed in the irony of seeing our species victimized by the machines we invent to liberate ourselves—*provided*, that is, we heed the great lesson that underlies the human comedy. Namely, that there will never be a machine that leaves us wiser or better or freer than our own naked mind can make us—nor any that helps us work out our salvation with diligence.

Selected Bibliography

Boden, Margaret. *Artificial Intelligence in Psychology*. Cambridge, Mass.: MIT Press, 1989.

———*The Creative Mind: Myths and Mechanisms*. New York: Basic Books, 1991.

Bowers, C. A. *The Cultural Dimensions of Educational Computing: Understanding the Non-Neutrality of Technology*. New York: Teachers College Press, Columbia University, 1988.

Brand, Stewart. *The Media Lab: Inventing the Future at MIT*. New York: Viking, 1987.

Buschman, John, ed. *Critical Approaches to Information Technology in Librarianship*. Westport, Conn.: Greenwood Press, 1993.

Carroll, Paul. *Big Blues: The Unmaking of IBM*. New York: Crown Publishers, 1993.

De Klerk, Ann, and Peter V. Deekle, eds. "The Future of the Book in an Electronic Age." *Liberal Education* 79, no. 1 (Winter 1993).

Dreyfus, Hubert, and Stuart Dreyfus. *Mind over Machine: The Power of Human Intuition and Expertise in the Era of the Computer*. New York: Free Press, 1988.

Dreyfus, Hubert. *What Computers Still Can't Do*. Cambridge, Mass.: MIT Press, 1993.

Dublin, Max. *Futurehype: The Tyranny of Prophecy*. New York: Dutton, 1991.

Forester, Tom, ed. *Computers in the Human Context: Information Technology, Productivity, and People*. Cambridge, Mass.: MIT Press, 1989.

Forester, Tom. *Silicon Samurai: How Japan Conquered the World's IT Industry*. Cambridge, Mass.: Blackwell Publishers, 1993.

Kosko, Bart. *Fuzzy Thinking: The New Science of Fuzzy Logic*. New York: Hyperion, 1993.

Kurtzman, Joel. *The Death of Money: How the Electronic Economy Has Destabilized the World's Markets and Created Financial Chaos*. New York: Simon & Schuster, 1993.

Kurzweil, Raymond, ed. *The Age of Intelligent Machines*. Cambridge, Mass.: MIT Press, 1992.

Levy, Steven. *Artificial Life.* New York: Random House, 1992.

Mander, Jerry. *In the Absence of the Sacred: The Failure of Technology and the Survival of the Indian Nations.* San Francisco: Sierra Club Books, 1992.

Mann, Thomas. *Library Research Models: A Guide to Classification, Cataloging, and Computers.* New York: Oxford University Press, 1993.

Minsky, Marvin. *The Society of Mind.* New York: Simon & Schuster, 1985.

Moravec, Hans. *Mind Children: The Future of Robot and Human Intelligence.* Cambridge, Mass.: Harvard University Press, 1988.

Papert, Seymour. *The Children's Machine.* New York: Basic Books, 1993.

Piller, Charles. *The Fail-Safe Society: Community Defiance and the End of American Technological Optimism.* Berkeley: University of California Press, 1991.

Piller, Charles, et al. "America's Shame: The Creation of the Technological Underclass in America's Public Schools." *Macworld* (Special Issue on Personal Computers in Education), September 1992.

Postman, Neil. *Technopoly: The Surrender of Culture to Technology.* New York: Vintage Books, 1993.

Sagan, Scott. *The Limits of Safety: Organizations, Accidents, and Nuclear Weapons.* Princeton N.J.: Princeton University Press, 1993.

Searle, John. *The Rediscovery of the Mind.* Cambridge, Mass.: MIT Press, 1992.

Sheff, David. *Game Over: How Nintendo Zapped an American Industry, Captured Your Dollars and Enslaved Your Children.* New York: Random House, 1993.

Solomonides, Tony, and Les Levidow, eds. *Compulsive Technology: Computers as Culture.* London: Free Association Books, 1985.

Warren, Jim, et al., eds. *Computers, Freedom and Privacy.* Los Alamitos, Calif.: IEEE Computer Society Press, 1991.

THE CULT OF INFORMATION
■

"INFORMATION, PLEASE"

■

INFORMATION OLD-STYLE

■

When I was growing up in the years just before World War II, information was nothing to get excited about. As an intellectual category, it held a humble and marginal status. Few people would have conceived of it as the subject of a "theory" or a "science"; it was not associated with an advanced technology that lent it glamour as well as extravagant financial value. Probably the most common public use of the word was as part of the phrase "Information, please." That was how you asked the operator for telephone numbers before we had 411 to dial. There was also, through the 1930s and 1940s, a popular radio program by that name which challenged listeners to stump a panel of experts by sending in unlikely questions about assorted trivia. Who was the shortest president of the United States? What grand opera contains the longest duet? What mammal reproduces by laying eggs?

That was the way most people thought about information in those days: disjointed matters of fact that came in discrete little bundles. Sometimes what was in the bundles was surprising, sometimes amusing, sometimes helpful. Most often it took the form of a number, name, date, place, event, or measurement that answered a specific question beginning with who, what, when, where, how much. Such matters got talked about in ordinary words; they did not require esoteric mathematical formulations or a special technical vocabulary. Occasionally information might be urgently important —like knowing where to press to stop the bleeding—but it was not regarded as something for which there was an insatiable public need. Certainly nobody would have credited it with the status it has acquired in our day—that of a billion-dollar industrial commodity that we should want to see produced in limitless quantities.

Of course, everybody knew there were certain businesses and professions which needed to keep lots of files filled with information. There were the accountants, the lawyers, the engineers. The standard white collar occupations—banking, insurance, brokerage houses, real estate—were characterized by rooms filled with olive-drab filing cabinets and patrolled by busy platoons of file clerks. Above all, there was the government, which, as census taker, tax collector, law enforcer, had always been the record keeper par excellence since the earliest days of civilization. Steadily, since the beginning of the nineteenth century, the governments of the industrially advanced societies had found themselves being drawn into ever more administrative responsibilities, until the task of minding official data threatened to become an end in itself. Duties like supervising the economy, keeping track of the work force, handing out the dole, allocating jobs, revenues, resources, were taking up more and more of the attention of political leadership in the urban industrial nations. For some early social scientists like Max Weber, this expanding paper reality of social statistics represented one of the worst vices of modern society: the bureaucratization of life, the conversion of experience into numerical abstractions.

By and large, the data processing responsibility of all these professions, public and private, was more bemoaned than celebrated. It was seen as a dispiriting necessity that could be left to low-status, usually poorly skilled office help. The familiar image of the office worker that we find in the stories of Dickens and Gogol is that of pale, pinch-faced scribes shuffling through overflowing ledgers, soulless statisticians and actuarials totaling up endless columns of figures, undernourished office clerks digging through dusty files to find an elusive memo. These were the people at the bottom of the bureaucratic ant heap. Herman Melville caught something of the general perception of these unfortunates in his famous tale of "Bartleby the Scrivener," the neat and efficient clerk whose relentlessly dispiriting toil finally turns him into a zombie.

The image of data keepers got no brighter even when their occupation passed beyond the pen and pencil stage and finally entered the machine age. It was in order to save time and office space for the government and the white collar industries that business machines came into existence during the early years of this century. The key punch, the comptometer, the collator, the addressograph—all these were information processors. But nobody would have seen them as anything more than ingenious sorting and counting contraptions, of about as much intellectual interest as the air brake or the dry cell battery. Their inventors are hardly remembered; the companies that manufactured them were of no great weight in our industrial economy; those who operated them remained low-level clerical help. For the most part, the data minders of the economy were "office girls" who might have been trained in high school or at business college and who toiled at their monotonous jobs without hope of promotion. If anything, the work they did was still usually seen by more humanistic sensibilities as a sorry example of the ongoing massification of modern life.

In Elmer Rice's bitter Broadway satire *The Adding Machine* (1923), the protagonist is an office clerk aptly named Mr. Zero. He is a pathetic nonentity, a "poor, spineless, brainless boob" who is lost in a wasteland of filing cabinets. At the end of the play, he is offered a "superb, super-hyper-adding machine"; it is the most spectacular business machine that can be imagined. Even so, the play finishes by identifying Mr. Zero as a form of life lower and less useful than a serf. He is "a slave to a contraption of steel and iron," and the work he does is portrayed as the epitome of dehumanization. At the hands of Mr. Zero and his kind, people are reduced to statistical phantoms; yet those who perform the deed possess neither power nor status. They are themselves mere ciphers in the system.

In my youth, I had a taste of this dingy subservience. In the early 1950s, I worked as a file clerk for a major insurance company whose windowless basement was a honeycombed cavern of coffin-black filing cases and bound records shelved to the ceiling. Along with a score of lads fresh out of high school, I ran interoffice mailers and bulging sheaves of memos around the building from department to department. We were treated like so many slaveys. From time to time our supervisor, trying to boost our flagging morale, would remind us that we were the life's blood of the company. Without us, even the top executives could not make a move. But we knew we were the lowest of the low. The work was a fatiguing bore, and we got paid the flat minimum wage. None of us stuck with the job longer than we had to.

ENTER UNIVAC

■

The best known relic of Mr. Zero's era, the paleolithic period of the early business machines, was the Hollerith punchcard, which dates back to the 1890s. Eventually, it would become an emblem of human alienation in an increasingly bureaucratized world. Somewhere in the early 1960s, its familiar injunction would be elaborated into a popular appeal for human understanding: "I am a human being. Do not fold, spindle, or mutilate."

But by the time that plea was voiced, the punchcard was all but obsolete, replaced by far superior means of tracking data. At the hands of innovative firms like Sperry-Rand, Control Data, and Digital Equipment Corporation (IBM was actually quite laggardly in the field until the early 1960s), the business machine was undergoing an unexpected and rapid evolution. Spurred along by military necessity during World War II and afterward by the needs of the Census Bureau, it was maturing in the direction of becoming an electrical filing device that assigned a numerical address to the data it held and could then perform a variety of rapid calculations and transformations with those data. And that, in its most rudimentary form, is a computer: a device that remembers what it counts, counts what it remembers, and retrieves whatever it has filed away at the touch of a button. The woeful young women who once tended the cumbersome key punch in the back office would surely have been amazed to know that someday there would be "information scientists" who regarded their clanking and clacking machines as the distant ancestors of a form of mechanized intelligence possibly superior to the human mind.

The word *computer* entered the public vocabulary in the 1950s, when the most advanced models of the device were still room-sized mechanical dinosaurs that burned enough electricity to present a serious cooling problem. The first computer to enjoy a significant reputation was UNIVAC, the brainchild of John Mauchly and J. P. Eckery, with important contributions from the famous mathematician John von Neumann.[1] UNIVAC was the first stored-program computer; it was based on military research done at the University of Pennsylvania during the war. Its later development was helped along by contracts from the National Bureau of Standards and Prudential Insurance; finally it was bought by Remington Rand in the 1950s for a variety of data services. But UNIVAC's public debut was little more than a media gimmick. The machine was loaned to CBS television to make polling predictions in the 1952 elections. This number-crunching behemoth (it contained 5,000 vacuum tubes, but used a new, compact magnetic tape system rather than punchcards to store data) was programmed to analyze voting statistics for CBS in key districts and to compare them with early returns on election night. By doing so, UNIVAC gave a projection that quickly calculated which candidate would most likely win.

There is an amusing anecdote about UNIVAC's introduction to the American public that evening. At CBS election headquarters, the esoteric machine, which the anxious electronic engineers were coddling like a spoiled child, was regarded as a mere sideshow attraction. So when UNIVAC, drawing upon a mere 5–7 percent of the popular vote, began projecting a landslide for Dwight Eisenhower, the CBS experts refused to report its prediction. The worried technicians then agreed to adjust the machine to keep it in line with the network pundits. Still UNIVAC insisted on an Eisenhower sweep, even in the solid Democratic South. Finally, when its predictions proved accurate, the experts conceded, publicly confessing that UNIVAC had indeed outguessed them and that the machine's apparent inconsistencies that night were due to human interference. UNIVAC had predicted an electoral vote for Eisenhower of 438; he finished with 442, within 1 percent of UNIVAC's startling prediction. This was an impressive display of what an advanced data processor could do, so impressive that for a short period the brand name UNIVAC bid fair to displace the generic name *computer*.

White collar work was one of the last occupations to enter the machine age. Well after the mines, the factories, the farms had been mechanized, office workers were still scribbling away with pen and pencil, hand-filing their papers in cabinets and loose-leaf binders. Even the typewriter (which appeared in the 1880s and did so much to bring a new generation of women workers into the offices) was a low-level manual tool, the technological equivalent of the long-defunct hand loom. Until well into the twentieth century, one looks in vain in magazines for advertisements that feature any sort of data processing equipment, let alone for books and articles celebrating their inventors and manufacturers. Compare this with the situation today, when the slickest, most futuristic ads in print and on television are those touting computers for the office, and you have a striking measure of how information has risen in status. The technology of the humble data keepers has finally outmatched the rolling mills, the dynamos, the railroads.

"Today," a leading telecommunications firm anounces in an imposing full-page advertisement, "information is the most valuable commodity in business. *Any* business." In times past, one would have thought of information as more of a lubricant that helped get commodities produced, or perhaps the upshot of a service like a doctor's diagnosis or a lawyer's legal opinion. And its value would not be constant (let alone universally or invariably supreme) but would vary with its accuracy and applications. But these days information is freely called product, resource, capital, currency. There is no limit to how high the rhetoric may be aimed. In a 1984 TV spot commercial, Frank Herbert, author of *Dune,* a work which at once invokes the vistas of science fiction, intones a small hymn to technological progress for Pacific Telephone's Infosystems. "The real revolution of the Information Age," he announces, "will not be one of hardware, but of the human spirit. It will be the chance to be more than human." Seemingly, a promise of godlike possibilities at hand. The product he is pitching is simply another electronic office system, one of several on the market. Yet, as the extravagant language suggests, the transition to the computer has come to be seen as more than a matter of new machines replacing old. The new machines have the look of something like an evolutionary leap forward in the history of industrialism. They are a new species of technology, one which has seemed from its first appearance to be flirting with the mysteries of the mind itself.

CYBERNETICS AND THE SECRET OF LIFE

■

In my own life, there was a book that did more than UNIVAC to revise my understanding of information and the machinery that manipulated it. In 1950 the mathematician Norbert Wiener wrote a pioneering and widely read study called *The Human Use of Human Beings*, a popularized version of his classic 1948 work *Cybernetics*.[2] For the general reading public, this engaging and provocative little book landmarked the appearance and high promise of "cybernation," the word Wiener had coined for the new automative technology in which he could discern the lineaments of a second industrial revolution. In the pages of his study, the computer was still an exotic device without a fixed name or clear image; he quaintly refers to it as "an ultra-rapid computing machine." But even in its then primitive state, that machine figured importantly in what was for Wiener one of the key aspects of cybernation: "feedback," the ability of a machine to use the results of its own performance as self-regulating information and so to adjust itself as part of an ongoing process.

Wiener saw feedback as far more than a clever mechanical trick; he regarded it as an essential characteristic of mind and of life. All living things practice some form of feedback as they adapt to their environment; here then was a new generation of machines reaching out toward the status of a sentient animal, and so promising to take over kinds of work that only human intelligence had so far been able to master. And not only work, but certain kinds of play as well. Wiener was much impressed by the research then under way to build chess-playing machines; this served as further evidence that machines would soon be able to process data in ways that approach the complexity of human intelligence. "To live effectively," he concluded, "is to live with adequate information. Thus, communication and control belong to the essence of man's inner life, even as they belong to his life in society."

Wiener was claiming nothing less than that, in perfecting feedback and the means of rapid data manipulation, the science of cybernetics was gaining a deeper understanding of life itself as being, at its core, the processing of information. "It is my thesis," he wrote, "that the physical functioning of the living individual and the operation of some of the new communications machines are precisely parallel in their analogous attempts to control entropy through feedback."

Some five years after Wiener's book was published, a new field of study based on his thesis announced its presence in the universities, an intellectual hybrid of philosophy, linguistics, mathematics, and electrical engineering. It was called artificial intelligence, or AI. The key assumption of AI was clear from the outset; in the words of two of the discipline's founding fathers, Alan Newell and Herbert Simon, "the programmed computer and human problem solver are both species belonging to the genus 'Information Processing System.'"[3]

A few years further along (1958), and Newell and Simon were pitching their hopes sky high:

> There are now in the world machines that think, that learn and create. Moreover, their ability to do these things is going to increase rapidly until—in the visible future—the range of problems they can handle will be co-extensive with the range to which the human mind has been applied.[4]

At the time they made the prediction, computers were still struggling to play a creditable game of checkers. But Simon was certain "that within ten years a digital computer will be the world's chess champion."[5]

Wiener himself may or may not have agreed with the glowing predictions that flowed from the new study of artificial intelligence, but he surely did not endorse its optimism. On the contrary, he regarded information technology as a threat to short-term social stability, and possibly as a permanent disaster. Having invented cybernetics, he intended to function as its conscience. *The Human Use of Human Beings,* as the phrase itself suggests, was written to raise public discussion of the new technology to a higher level of ethical awareness. Automated machines, Wiener observed, would take over not only assembly line routine, but office routine as well. Cybernetic machinery "plays no favorites between manual labor and white collar labor." If left wholly in the control of short-sighted, profit-maximizing industrialists, it might well "produce an unemployment situation, in comparison with which . . . even the depression of the thirties will seem a pleasant joke."

Two years after Wiener issued that warning, the first cybernetic anti-utopia was written. In *Player Piano*, Kurt Vonnegut, Jr., who had been working in the public relations department of General Electric, one of the companies most aggressively interested in automation, imagines a world of intelligent machines where there is "production with almost no manpower." Even the barbers have been displaced by haircutting machines. The result is a technocratic despotism wholly controlled by information technicians and corporate managers. The book raises the issue whether technology should be allowed to do all that it can do, especially when its powers extend to the crafts and skills which give purpose to people's lives. The machines are slaves, Vonnegut's rebellious engineer-hero insists. True, they make life easier in many ways; but they also compete with people. And "anybody that competes with slaves becomes a slave." As Vonnegut observes, "Norbert Wiener, a mathematician, said all that way back in the nineteen-forties."

MESSAGES WITHOUT MEANINGS
∎

In the same year Wiener produced his study *Cybernetics,* Claude Shannon of Bell Laboratories published his ground-breaking paper, "A Mathematical Theory of Communication," which established the discipline of information theory, the science of messages. Shannon's work is universally honored as one of the major intellectual achievements of the century. It is also the work most responsible for revolutionizing the way scientists and technicians have come to wield the word *information* in our time. In the past, the word has always denoted a sensible statement that conveyed a recognizable, verbal meaning, usually what we would call a fact. But now, Shannon gave the word a special technical definition that divorced it from its common-sense usage. In his theory, information is no longer connected with the semantic content of statements. Rather, information comes to be a purely quantitative measure of communicative exchanges, especially as these take place through some mechanical channel which requires that message to be encoded and then decoded, say, into electronic impulses. Most people would have assumed that information had to do with what happened in the understanding of a speaker and a listener in the course of a conversation. Shannon, working out of Bell Labs, was much more interested in what might be happening in the telephone wire that ran between speaker and listener. In his paper, the fundamental concepts of information theory—noise, redundancy, entropy—are rounded up into a systematic mathematical presentation. Here, too, the "bit," the binary digit basic to all data processing, first appears to take its place as the quantum of information, a neatly measurable unit by which the transmitting capacity of all communications technology can be evaluated.

One can see how useful such a calculus of communications traffic is for electrical engineers dealing with the problem of channeling signals over phone wires or from space satellites, and wanting to do so with the greatest possible economy and clarity. But from the outset, Shannon was beset by the understandable confusion that arose between his restricted use of "information" and the conventional meaning of the word. From his point of view, even gibberish might be "information" if somebody cared to transmit it. After all, a message translated into a secret code would appear to be gibberish to anyone who did not know the code; but it would be well worth sending by anyone who did. The early information scientists easily fell into thinking this way about messages and their transmissions; many of them had served as cryptographers during the war. Still this was an odd and jarring way to employ the word, and Shannon had to admit as much. Once, when he was explaining his work to a group of prominent scientists who challenged his eccentric definition, he replied, "I think perhaps the word 'information' is causing more trouble . . . than it is worth, except that it is difficult to find another word that is anywhere near right. It should be kept solidly in mind that [information] is only a measure of the difficulty in transmitting the sequences produced by some information source."[6]

For a time, Shannon considered dropping the word and using another—like communications theory. With a name like that, the new field would have had more distance from the need for meaningful content which we associate with information. For example, a disease can be "communicated"—a transmission of great consequence but without intelligent content. At one point, John von Neumann suggested—not very helpfully—that Shannon use the word *entropy*. But information became the word, a choice which Fritz

Machlup has called "infelicitous, misleading, and disserviceable"—the beginning of the term's history as "an all-purpose weasel-word."[7]

What we have here is an example of something that has happened many times before in the history of science. A word that has a long-standing, common-sense meaning is lifted from the public vocabulary and then skewed toward a new, perhaps highly esoteric definition by the scientists. The result can be a great deal of unfortunate confusion, even among the scientists themselves, who may then forget what the word meant before they appropriated it. The way physicists use the words *motion, time, gravity, simultaneity* has only a tenuous connection with commonplace, everyday experience. The word *order* in thermodynamics has a specialized application that at certain points diverges markedly from its normal meaning. Perhaps the most notorious example of such confusion involves the word *intelligence* as it has been reshaped by the psychologists. Among the IQ testers, "intelligence" is whatever certain highly eccentric academic tests measure. The result is a neat, numerical score: high scores mean high intelligence, low scores mean low intelligence. But neither the tests nor the scores may have any relationship to what we regard as real intelligence (or its absence) as we judge things in the midst of life.

In much the same way, in its new technical sense, *information* has come to denote whatever can be coded for transmission through a channel that connects a source with a receiver, regardless of semantic content. For Shannon's purposes, all the following are "information":

$E = mc^2$

Jesus saves.

Thou shalt not kill.

I think, therefore I am.

Phillies 8, Dodgers 5

'Twas brillig and the slithy toves did gyre and gimble in the wabe.

And indeed, these are no more or less meaningful than any string of haphazard bits (x!9#44jGH?566MRK) I might be willing to pay to have telexed across the continent.

As the mathematician Warren Weaver once put it, explaining "the strange way in which, in this theory, the word 'information' is used. . . . It is surprising but true that, from the present viewpoint, two messages, one heavily loaded with meaning and the other pure nonsense, can be equivalent as regards information."[8]

One might expect that anyone reading through the list of items above would immediately note that each stands on a markedly different intellectual level. One statement is a moral injunction; one is a mathematical formulation; one is a minor point of fact; one is a theological teaching; and the last is deliberate (though charming) nonsense. But once they have all been transformed into electrical bits, and once the technicians have got us into the habit of labeling them all information, these vital differences—which it would, for example, be rather important to draw out for children as part of their education—cannot help but be obscured.

To be sure, Shannon's work is highly technical and therefore largely inaccessible to the general public; nevertheless, its influence has been enormous. As information theory has come to be widely applied in our high tech economy, it has had a twofold impact upon our popular culture.

First of all, once "information" had been divorced from its conventional meaning, the word was up for grabs. Following the lead of the information theorists, scientists and technicians felt licensed to make ever broader and looser use of the word. It could soon be applied to any transmitted signal that could be metaphorically construed as a "message"—for example, the firing of a nerve impulse. To use the term so liberally is to lay aside all concern for the quality or character of what is being communicated. The result has been a progressive blurring of intellectual distinctions. Just as it is irrelevant to a physicist (from the viewpoint of the purely physical phenomenon) whether we are measuring the fall of a stone or the fall of a human body, so, for the information theorist, it does not matter whether we are transmitting a fact, a judgment, a shallow cliché, a deep teaching, a sublime truth, or a nasty obscenity. All are "information." The word comes to have vast generality, but at a price; the *meaning* of things communicated comes to be leveled, and so too the value.

The effect is similar to that which the mathematical theory of games had upon people's thinking in the 1950s and 1960s. From the viewpoint of games theorists, chess, poker, business investments, arguments between parents and children, collective bargaining, thermonuclear war came to be seen as "games"—in the sense that certain general strategies could be applied to all of them. This was a valuable insight into many forms of competition and negotiation, but it was gained at great cost. Around the theory of games, a literature and discourse of military strategy grew up whose authors felt licensed to discuss the annihilation of the human race as casually as one might discuss a hand of cards. For, after all, these were simply different kinds of "games." On balance, the result of this intellectual sleight-of-hand was a lamentable bamboozling of the public, who came to see arguments made in this esoteric terminology (all decked out with many numbers) as intimidatingly authoritative.

Secondly, information theory *worked*. In its own field of application, it provided the electrical engineers with a powerful tool that contributed significantly to rapid innovation. With UNIVAC, the original vacuum tube computer had reached the limit of its development, and still the machines were too big and slow to carry out truly sophisticated programs. In the course of the 1950s and 1960s, however, these limitations were overcome by the development of the transistor and integrated circuit. These highly miniaturized conductors allowed the computer to be compacted and its processing functions to be vastly accelerated. At the same time, thanks again to Shannon's work, the computer was finding its way into the world's burgeoning telecommunications network so that it could extend its power beyond local, on-site use. This permitted computers to communicate with one another over great distances, and eventually, with the deployment of space satellites, to remain instantaneously in touch around the world. While the computer was shrinking physically to desk-top size, it was taking on a new, disembodied, electronic "size" that dwarfed all previous technology in the scope of its power. In our own day, these two developments—miniaturization and telecommunications outreach—have allowed even the most modest personal computer to link into information networks that span the planet, giving them, in the view of some enthusiasts, the dimensions of a global brain.

Achievements of this astonishing order were bound to shift our understanding of information away from people (as sources or receivers) toward the exciting new techniques of communication. This is because the main concern of those who use information theory is with apparatus, not content. For that matter, the theory does not even require a human source or receiver on either side of the apparatus. The source might just as well be a ballistic missile registering its trajectory on radar; the receiver might just as well be a computer programmed to trigger a retaliatory strike. Such a situation fulfills all the mathematical requirements of the theory.

Thanks to the high success of information theory, we live in a time when the technology of human communications has advanced at blinding speed; but what people have to say to one another by way of that technology shows no comparable development. Still, in the presence of so ingenious a technology, it is easy to conclude that because we have the ability to transmit more electronic bits more rapidly to more people than ever before, we are making real cultural progress—and that the essence of that progress is information technology.

THE BIOCOMPUTER
■

Between them, Wiener and Shannon radically reconceptualized the meaning of information, lending the term a new mathematical precision without which the computer might never have developed much beyond the power of UNIVAC. But their professional work was too esoteric to find an audience outside the world of the logicians and technicians. For the general public, the intriguing image which Wiener had raised in *The Human Use of Human Beings*— that of information as the basis of life—found its most dramatic support from another, unexpected quarter: biology—or rather, the *new* biology, where the most highly publicized scientific revolution since Darwin was taking place.

In 1952, microbiologists James Watson and Francis Crick announced that they had solved the master problem of modern biology. They had broken the "genetic code" hidden deep within the molecular structure of DNA. The very use of the word *code* in this context was significant. For one thing, it immediately seemed to link the discoveries of the biologists to those of the new information theorists, whose work had much to do with the "encoding" of information. The word also carried with it the thrill of an espionage story and, in fact, harked back to the original use made of the computer in England: to break the German secret code during World War II. No sooner had Watson and Crick published their breakthrough than the DNA molecule came to be universally seen as something like a tiny cybernetic apparatus that stored and processed microscopic bits of chemically encoded data. Supposedly, these coded messages controlled discrete physical processes in the replication of living things. Soon, the entire code of the double helix would be unscrambled and its message might be read off bit by bit like the memory store of a computer. As John Pfeiffer of MIT described the function of DNA in a 1960 television documentary on CBS, "The program's patterns of chemical bases may be compared to patterns of holes or magnetic spots on paper tapes fed into electronic computers."[9] The DNA "program" has not turned out to be quite that simple, but in the first flush of discovery, it seemed that Wiener's proposition had been confirmed: cybernetics and biology had found a common ground.

Since its inception, the new biology has been so tightly entwined with the language and imagery of information science that it is almost impossible to imagine the field developing at all without the aid of the computer paradigm. One biologist identifies "the theoretical tool" that unlocked the chemistry of life as

> the new sciences associated with the development of computers. Theories of "control," "feedback," and "information transfer" were collated in 1948 by the American engineer and mathematician Norbert Wiener under the name of "cybernetics." . . . Biochemists seized on these new concepts in order to probe the ways in which the cell controlled and regulated its own metabolism.

The job of the cyberneticist, he explains,

> is the study of *information transfer:* the converting of information from one form to another—the human voice into radio waves and back into sound once more, or a complex

mathematical equation into a set of punched holes on a tape, to be fed into a computer and then into a set of traces on reels of magnetic tape in the computer's "memory store." . . . To him, protein synthesis is just such another case. The mechanism for ensuring the exact replication of a protein chain by a new cell is that of transferring the *information* about the protein structure from the parent to the daughter cell.[10]

One is left to wonder: could the revolution in biology have occurred if the model of the computer had not been conveniently at hand waiting to be adopted? This would not be the first time a technological metaphor served to launch a scientific breakthrough. In the seventeenth century, at the very beginning of modern science, astronomers and physicists appropriated the model of the clock to explain the mechanics of the solar system and soon taught their society to see the entire universe as a clockwork instrument.

However much the new biology may have borrowed from the preexisting cybernetic model, it repaid the debt manyfold by lending information a mystique it could not have acquired in any other way. In effect, it became the secret of life. From a data-computing mechanism as tiny as the DNA molecule, all the subtle complexity of life on earth had evolved. As John Pfeiffer confidently put it, "This is automation at the molecular level." Here was an astonishing demonstration of how much could be pieced together out of mere particles of data. It was as if God Himself, formerly the great watchmaker in the sky, had been updated into the cosmic computer programmer. Within another decade, by the early 1960s, it became commonplace for people to speak not only of their genes but of their minds and private psyches as being "programmed." If it was not yet the case, as Wiener had predicted, that cybernetic machines would become more like people, certainly people were coming to see themselves more and more as a kind of machine: a biocomputer.

Ironically, as the new biology has grown a bit older, it has changed in ways that no longer make the simple cybernetic model seem quite so persuasive. In the early days, the genetic code looked as if it would be a lot easier to crack than has turned out to be the case. Initially, it was assumed that the message of the genes might be read off as so many fixed, linear sequences of nucleotide bases, much like the digital bit-string in a computer. More recently, as problems of developmental regulation have gained prominence in the field, genes have become a lot trickier to interpret. The mysterious process of "transposition" has begun to draw attention. The work of Barbara McClintock, among others, suggests that genes may actually pick themselves up and move about in the genome, almost purposefully changing their meaning as they alter their position in response to some larger context.[11] So far the biologists have no model to use for that context, but neither computers nor cybernated systems would seem to serve. Maybe the context is something like an "idea" about the whole organism and its relationship to the environment. If this is so, then the cybernetic model that did so much to launch the new biology might be totally misleading. For there are no computer programs that behave this way. If they did, it would amount to saying that they had a mind of their own—and that way lies science fiction, not serviceable technology. Yet, for lack of a better choice, the data processing image lingers on, rendering biology in the late twentieth century more mechanistic than physics.

Every historical period has its godword. There was an Age of Faith, an Age of Reason, an Age of Discovery. Our time has been nominated to be the Age of Information. If the name takes, the fortuitous connection between cybernation and the new biology will have to be credited with lending information much of the vogue it has come to enjoy. Perhaps there is another reason for the increasing popularity and generality of the word, one that tells us something important about an era that is willing to accept such a seemingly characterless designation. Unlike "faith" or "reason" or "discovery," information is touched with a comfortably secure, noncommittal connotation. There is neither drama nor high purpose to it. It is bland to the core and, for that very reason, nicely invulnerable. Information smacks of safe neutrality; it is the simple, helpful heaping up of unassailable facts. In that innocent guise, it is the perfect starting point for a technocratic political agenda that wants as little exposure for its objectives as possible. After all, what can anyone say against information?

But in contemporary America, even a godword does not enter the popular consciousness in a decisive way until it can somehow be bought and sold in the marketplace. Only then can it be coveted as a possession, paid for, taken home, and owned. More importantly, only then does it qualify to receive the attention of the advertisers who have the power to turn it from an interest into a want, from a want into a need. In the course of the 1950s, information had come to be identified with the secret of life. By the 1970s, it had achieved an even more exalted status. It had become a commodity—and indeed, as we have seen, "the most valuable commodity in business. *Any* business."

THE DATA
MERCHANTS

■

HIGH TECH AND THE CONSERVATIVE
OPPORTUNISTS

■

The mass merchandising of information is one of the later chapters in the big economic story of our time. For the better part of the past generation, the American economy has been steadily shifting its center of gravity both financially and demographically. The movement is out of the old urban centers of the Northeast/Midwest and into the Sunbelt, out of the smokestack industries and into that complex of sophisticated new electronic/aerospace technologies called high tech. This historic transition has been visibly under way at least since the mid-1960s, say, since the building of the Cape Canaveral launch site in Florida and the Johnson Space Center in Houston. But it was not thrust significantly upon the public awareness until the early 1980s, when two best-selling books—*Megatrends* by John Naisbitt and *The Third Wave* by Alvin Toffler—packaged it for popular consumption and labeled it as the rise of the "information economy," the advent of the Information Age.[1]

Books like these belong to that immensely popular category of contemporary literature called futurology, an ungainly hybrid of potted social science, Sunday supplement journalism, and soothsaying. They feature breezy scenarios of Things To Come pitched at about the intellectual level of advertising copy. Sensational snippets and zany catchphrases fill every page with breathtaking amazements; glittering predictions whiz by on all sides. Reading Naisbitt and Toffler is like a fast jog down a World's Fair midway. We might almost believe, from their simplistic formulation of the information economy, that we will soon be living on a diet of floppy disks and walking streets paved with microchips. Seemingly, there are no longer any fields to till, any ores to mine, any heavy industrial goods to manufacture; at most these continuing necessities of life are mentioned in passing and then lost in the sizzle of pure electronic energy somehow meeting all human needs painlessly and instantaneously.

Thus, Naisbitt, charting the "megatrend" from "industrial society to information society," describes the new economic order as one in which

> we now mass-produce information the way we used to mass-produce cars. In the information society, we have systematized the production of knowledge and amplified our brain-power. To use an industrial metaphor, we now mass-produce knowledge and this knowledge is the driving force of our economy.

In the space of three sentences, one notes that "information" has become synonymous with "knowledge," as if there were no significant distinction between the two, and we finish with the idea that *knowledge* is being "mass-produced." But since knowledge (like "brainpower," if this means something like intelligence) is the creation of individual minds and has a great deal to do with the quality of thought, what relationship—even of a metaphorical kind—does this bear to the assembly-line construction of a car from interchangeable parts? Depth, originality, excellence, which have always been factors in the evaluation of knowledge, have somewhere been lost in the fast, futurological shuffle. As we will see, this is a liability that dogs every effort to inflate the cultural value of information.

Naisbitt, however, is not one to loiter over fine distinctions. Rather, he hastens forward to call for "a knowledge theory of value to replace Marx's obsolete labor theory of value" because "in an information society, value is increased by knowledge." This leads him to the conclusion that knowledge (or is it information?) is destined to be the principal product (or is it service?) of our economic life in the near future. With approval he quotes an expert who observes, "We are working ourselves out of the manufacturing business into the thinking business."

It is difficult to see that writing like this (and the passage is typical) has any meaning at all, so deep are the confusions that underlie it. An industrial economy is fundamentally a manufacturing economy; high tech itself requires manufacturing. The technology is constituted of machines; the machines exist to produce hard goods, ultimately the food, clothing, shelter, and transport our flesh and blood demands. A high tech economy remains a manufacturing economy if the factories have been automated and the number of service occupations multiplies. Even when industrial capital is exported to foreign places (Taiwan, Hong Kong, South Korea), manufacturing has still not been eliminated from the economy, but only internationalized under the same ownership. It may then be interesting to ask why such relocation is happening and who decided to make it happen. We might then discover that the movement is taking place at the hands of multinational firms in search of a cheap, non-organized work force and subsidies from needy, cooperative governments. It may also be important to ask with respect to such developments what their effect is upon our own economy. Is there, for example, the need to maintain some healthy balance between the production of goods and services, and can market forces alone be trusted to strike that balance?

These are not issues that much concern the futurologists. Answering them would take the discussion into many tangled and unpleasant areas of controversy regarding investment choices, the costs and conditions of labor at home and abroad, the social control of capital. They prefer frothier subjects: life styles, new commodities, consumer fashions. Mainly, they dwell upon the goods, services, careers, and amusements that will be available in the Information Age to affluent professionals and upper-middle-class families. They write to showcase the good times to come for those who can afford the benefits.

But if Naisbitt, Toffler, and company are meager of substance, they nevertheless brim with the sort of noncontroversial trendiness that easily catches on among business types and public officials in search of attractively packaged convenience food for thought. Thus, the Office of Technology Assessment has been quick to pick up the theme, somberly announcing in a major declaration that "the United States has become an information society dependent on the creative use and communication of information for its economic and social well-being." The National Committee on Excellence in Education agrees in another key public document, hastening to recommend that all students be put through at least a half year of study in computer science.[2] For obvious reasons, AT&T endorses Naisbitt-Toffler economics in its advertising, extravagantly announcing that "Like it or not, information has finally surpassed material goods as our basic resource." It is, indeed, "a new form of capital, one that is arguably more critical to the future of the American economy than money capital."

More significantly, a growing contingent of politicians has homed in upon the glowing prognostications of futurologists—though often merely at the buzz word level. Since the early eighties, presidential candidates like Gary Hart, Jerry Brown, and Jack Kemp have sought to find the solution to America's economic ills in high tech. Noting that candidates like Walter Mondale and Michael Dukakis who have gambled on the support of a traditional blue collar and ethnic constituency have suffered badly, they have angled their campaigns to gain a growing new constituency: Sunbelt voters and young, highly educated, but job-worried professionals across the country who are high tech-dependent. Bill Clinton and Al Gore in particular took the lesson to heart in fashioning a new, energized image for the Democratic party based upon a retooled defense establishment and a revamping of our national information infrastructure. Gore, a principal congressional sponsor of the so-called information superhighway, which would link universities, "digital libraries," and workstations everywhere, has made that project the Clinton administration's main commitment to the future of a radically restructured high tech industry. More strikingly, elements of the radical right have also sought to stake out the high tech frontier. Crusading Sunbelt conservatives like Georgia Congressman Newt Gingrich have been surprisingly quick to appropriate the glamour of the Information Age for their own purposes. Their goal has been to design a flashy, updated style of conservatism that borrows heavily upon the futurologists to create a sense of forward-looking confidence. "The most powerful force changing our society is the information revolution," Gingrich announced in a 1984 book (*Window of Opportunity*) which bore the endorsements of former President Reagan, Jack Kemp, and Alvin Toffler. "It is as powerful as the word 'revolution' suggests."[3] Gingrich's text offers a rapid tour of the high tech frontier: computers, aerospace, telecommunications. Even the words of Carl Sagan are pressed into service to validate the importance of "man's leap beyond the planet," which Gingrich, chairman of the Congressional Space Caucus, sees as a prime business opportunity. Indeed, once the space shuttle has been fitted out to accommodate tourists, we will have "populism in space."

Along with Jack Kemp and other congressional right wingers, Gingrich has organized the Conservative Opportunity Society as a major political voice of the Information Age.[4] COS defines itself as "high tech, futurist, populist, and conservative." It is "anti-tax, anti-welfare state, and anti-communist." Its intention is to retire the cautious, often dour image that has for so long characterized conservatism. Instead, the Conservative Opportunists mean to provide a sharp, upbeat contrast to what Gingrich sees as the "gloom and despair" of the liberals, with their concern for the environmental limits of growth. COS opts for a "bright optimistic future" that is briskly in step with technological progress. In the troubled 1960s, Gingrich observes, "our hippies overshadowed our astronauts and the anti-technological bias of the Left overshadowed the possibilities of the computer age." There was "an epidemic of technological abhorrence" abroad in the land, which led to "the negative mindset of the welfare state bureaucrats." It also produced widespread immorality, sexual license, and a general decline of patriotic and traditional values: "a life without God." COS means to reverse all that. It hopes that by way of massive supply-side tax concessions, it can offer the high tech entrepreneurs the incentives necessary for a new era of growth. Growth, the Conservative Opportunists insist, is the panacea for all the nation's economic ills: unemployment, inflation, trade imbalances. There are even some daring members of the movement who are prepared to cast the old fiscal conservatism to the winds as a drab remnant of the past. The economist Paul C. Roberts, once an aide to Jack Kemp, insists that even the sort of unprecedented deficits accumulated under the Reagan administration must be seen as "transitional or temporary" and should be cheerfully met by all the borrowing the Treasury Department needs to do.[5] In the sunny heavens of high tech, deficits are only passing clouds. Sooner or later, the information economy will outgrow its debts, no matter how large.

If COS makes good in its aggressive bid to take over the Republican party, the result will be a strange brew of old-time religion, social Darwinist ethics, anticommunist chauvinism, and Flash Gordon technology. Such a potent right wing alliance of the Sunbelt and the space age was shrewdly foreseen by the conservative analyst Kevin Phillips as far back as 1968. He called it "the emerging Republican majority" and recognized Ronald Reagan as one of its most promising leaders.[6] Several years later, in 1982, the equally conservative futurologist Herman Kahn would be boosting that majority as the secret of "the coming boom" of the Reagan presidency.[7] He depicted it as a coalition of social, economic, and defense conservatives grounded in the money and ethos of the Sunbelt. All that alliance needed, so Kahn argued, if it was to become the right wing equivalent to the Roosevelt New Deal, was "an ideology of progress" to offset the no-growth economic philosophy that became a popular talking point during the 1970s. And this he felt it had discovered in the futuristic dynamism of the information economy, the way forward to "a world of opportunities, glamour, options."

SUNBELT POLITICS AND
THE WARFARE STATE
■

As the futurologists and their political disciples present it, the rise of the information economy in America is a matter of manifest industrial destiny, a change so vast and inevitable that it might almost be a natural process beyond human control. It is hardly that. The conversion to high tech has been the result of deliberate choices on the part of our political and corporate leadership. To begin with, it was intimately linked to the steady militarization of our economic life since the beginning of World War II, without which very little of our aerospace and electronic technology would exist at all. The high tech industries remain significantly tied to the Pentagon budget. That has long been obvious with respect to NASA and nuclear power, but the nation's most important computer development investments were also funded and controlled from military sources. Most importantly, these have included the Defense Department's

Information Processing Techniques Office and the twelve-company consortium, the Microelectronics and Computer Technology Corporation at Austin, Texas, which was launched under the chairmanship of a member of the National Security Council and CIA.[8] Had the Cold War not abated, this tie with the military establishment would have become even more binding. The United States might have embarked upon the crushingly extravagant Strategic Defense Initiative (the "Star Wars" missile defense system), which acquired determined political and corporate support during the Reagan administration.

It is revealing that members of COS like Gingrich and Kemp are careful to make a special appeal for vastly expanded military spending as part of their program, regardless of the deficits that may result. However strongly the Conservative Opportunists may insist upon crash dieting the federal government to reduce its bulk and cost, the Pentagon is always exempted from the prescription. This is especially understandable on the part of Sunbelt conservatives; the come-lately prosperity of states like Gingrich's Georgia is vastly dependent on the largesse of the military. Through the eighties, Sunbelt states received the lion's share of the Defense Department's contracts, more than twice the share they were awarded in the mid-1950s. California alone came in for more than two and a half times as much defense spending as any other state, an increasingly fragile military-industrial dependency Californians have lived to regret. Meanwhile, over the last thirty years, the Midwestern "rust bowl" has seen its share of military contracts dwindle; the only way many firms in that part of the country were able to enjoy a portion of the defense budget was by subcontracting for Sunbelt companies.[9] The more conservative mood of America during the 1970s and 1980s surely had much to do with the increased wealth and voting power of the Sunbelt, the traditional stronghold of retirement communities, evangelical churches, and generally nativist values. But, in turn, this rightward political tilt resulted in large measure from steady Western and Southern diversion of military money over the past generation. The information economy would seem to arrive not only with a military bias but with built-in conservative demographics.

It is thanks to the financial leverage provided by this firm commitment to the warfare state that the corporate community was able to engineer the wrenching break with America's industrial past we now find ourselves in. In large part, the advent of the information economy means that our major corporations are rapidly retiring two generations of old capital or moving it abroad. As they do so, with the rich support of military contracts, they are liberating themselves from the nation's most highly unionized labor so that investment may be transferred into more profitable fields. High tech is not only glamorous; it pays off handsomely, especially if those who are collecting the profits are excused from paying the social costs that result from running down old industrial centers and disemploying their work force in favor of relocating in the mainly "right to work" (nonunion) Sunbelt states. Such costs of the transition are most often "externalized" by the high tech firms, meaning they are swept out of sight and ignored. But they remain a liability of the total economy that must be paid for eventually. For example, some two thirds of the "new jobs" created in our economy in the late 1970s and 1980s and so loudly trumpeted by the Carter and Reagan administrations are low-skilled, part-time service employment. When once highly trained factory workers are squeezed into work of this kind—say, as janitors, security guards, or fast-food servers—they have taken an economic drubbing. With them, whole sectors of the economy decline to a lower standard of living and diminished expectations. The labor movement sees this erosion of middle-class industrial jobs as the beginning of a permanent "two-tier society," with fewer and fewer high-paying jobs in the highly skilled nonunionized upper tier.[10]

For that matter, even those who find work in high tech may be hired on at drab, poorly paid, nonunionized positions. It is becoming notorious that the new microchip plants, as dazzling as their work may sound to the world beyond the factory walls, come close to being sweatshop operations for the low skilled, mainly female work force they employ. High tech is, in fact, already an example of the two-tier society, with practically no mobility across the great divide. At the top are the entrepreneurs, inventors, and engineers, who live and move in the industry's fast lane. At the bottom are the production workers, for whom, in the words of Everett Rogers and Judith Larsen, "Silicon valley means low-wage, deadend jobs, unskilled, tedious work, and exposure to some of the most dangerous occupational health hazards in all of American industry. It is a dark side to the sparkling laboratories that neither barbecues, balloons, nor paid sabbaticals can hide."[11]

For those who own the information economy, some of the most valued information in the business is the know-how of professional union busters, who have found one of their best markets in high tech. The industry remains almost wholly without labor organization in the United States. Even so, in the constant drive to cut costs, assembly-line high tech has proven to be highly exportable; it is easily relocated to Asia or Latin America, where the work force is usually younger and more female, meaning cheaper and more docile.[12] Further adding to the insecurity of those who work in the information economy is the prominence of risky and speculative investments within the high tech industries, where, since the beginning of the 1980s, we have seen whole markets—like that for video games, home computers, cellular telephones—rapidly cycle through from boom to bust.

What those who celebrate the information economy have overlooked is the fact that high tech, if it is to be an authentic long-term contribution to the wealth of the nation as a whole, must be gracefully grafted upon the existing industrial system, using its skills, labor, resources, and manufacturing centers. It cannot abruptly supersede that system and hope to stand alone. Yet that is what futurologists like Naisbitt suggest when they describe "the information economy" as something that stands in stark contrast to "the industrial economy" and must now replace it—not only with a new technology, but with a murky new "knowledge theory of value." Such a historical scheme is nonsensical. Information technology is an outgrowth of the existing industrial system, which has always been dependent on the "knowledge" that undergirds invention, management, and marketing. Like the electrical, automotive, or chemical technologies that came before it, high tech arises as another stage in the ongoing industrial process. These technologies do not displace one another; they overlap, compound, and must be coordinated. In high tech America, even computer enthusiasts remain more dependent for their survival on the fieldworkers who pick the crops and the construction workers who build the buildings than they do on computer programmers or investment counselors working with spreadsheets.

High tech is embedded in the texture of industrial history; it needs to be planned into existence. Otherwise—left to the whims and impulses of the marketplace as the Conservative Opportunists would prefer—it will become the same sort of jolting, humanly wasteful leap from one economic stage to another that produced the worst hardships of the first industrial revolution. No humane society would choose a second industrial revolution that repeated the same mistakes.

But inevitably, as the nation's economic resources are catapulted into high tech, the output of that investment has to be sold. Some of these products—the missiles, space shuttles, laser weapons—will always be restricted mainly to military buyers. The computer industry, on the other hand, while heavily dependent on military contracting, has also had access to a good-sized civilian market, at least for its more expensive equipment, in business and public administration. The question arises: can the latest generation of micro- and mini-computers be merchandised on a larger scale as mass consumption items? Can the general public be persuaded to see information as a necessity of modern life in the same way it has come to see the refrigerator, the automobile, the television as necessities? The computer makers are wagering billions that it can. Their gamble has paid handsomely and lost disastrously with each turn of the business cycle. Yet, it is primarily from their advertising and merchandising efforts that information has come to acquire a cultlike following in our society.

MEGAHYPE

■

Through the early 1980s, I found myself working on a science fiction novel dealing with computers and computer scientists.[13] As part of the exercise, I consulted several experts in the field with a view to sizing up the state of the art and its probable near future. Since information technology is fast moving, I felt I needed a baseline for the novel so that I might have some fairly reliable idea of what computers might (and might not) be able to do when the book got into print and for the next four or five years thereafter—the better to know where fact left off and fantasy began.

After talking to several experts and enthusiasts—some academic, some in industry—I realized I had a problem. When it came to the power of computers, nearly everybody I met was prone to vastly optimistic exaggeration. Machine translation . . . conversation in ordinary language . . . total mastery of chess . . . face and voice recognition . . . creative writing . . . legal decision making—there was nothing these machines could not do, or would not soon be able to do. How "soon," I would ask. The answer was never too clear. Possibly by next year, almost certainly in another two or three, for absolute sure by the end of the decade. In any case *sooner* than you might think. At one discussion I attended, one of the world's foremost authorities in artificial intelligence asserted his firm conviction that a computer capable of surpassing human intelligence in all fields was certain to be built . . . within the next five to five hundred years. For, *in principle* (this phrase comes to be repeated on all sides like a liturgical response), nothing is impossible.

It soon became clear to me what the source of this optimism was and why I was having such trouble pinning down realistic predictions about the future of computers. All these people—the academicians as well as the industrial experts—were part of the information economy. They worked in firms tied to that economy, or consulted for them, or were linked to academic programs financed in some degree by those firms or by their military customers. From the viewpoint of these funding sources, it was important to be upbeat and bullish about computers, for this was their merchandise. The experts easily adopted that viewpoint, because the health of the computer industry was the life's blood of their profession. Not only that, but the media, which frequently come by for interviews, are always in the market for amazing predictions; the journalists want authoritative reports that corroborate the futurologists. In turn, reports of that kind feed back into industry projections of future growth, helping to sell stock and attract venture capital.

In short, the experts were *selling.* They were in the habit of extrapolating astonishing "megatrends" for the press, the public, the funding agencies. It was only when I applied persistent skeptical pressure—say, with respect to machine translation, or the ability of computers to "read" and "summarize" a book, a story, a lecture— that I might finally evince an honest admission of how deucedly difficult such problems really were and how far off a solution might be.

But in the marketplace such pressure is absent, and so optimism is free to soar until it reaches the sky-blue zenith—at which altitude it is indistinguishable from conventional advertising hype. If one were to believe the public relations copy of the computer industry, electronic data processing has become the heartbeat of the economy. Without it, our lives would come to a standstill. That may very nearly be true over a wide range of the business world. When the computers are down, the banks do not function, investments cannot be made, the planes do not leave the ground nor can their tickets be sold, the newspapers cannot be printed, inventories cannot be checked, bills cannot be sent or paid, more and more assembly lines must stand idle. Very likely the nation could not be defended from instant annihilation by its enemies.

Is it wise to commit the society so massively to a technology that is so vulnerable to widespread breakdown, error, sabotage, and criminal tampering? The computer makers and computer scientists have no doubt that it is. And having won the commanding heights of the economy, they are moving rapidly to find other frontiers for investment. The current effort is to graft the microcomputer on to as many aspects of daily life as possible, so that our homes, workplaces, and schools will soon be no less dependent on the flow of electronic information. Without a steady supply, the children will not be able to learn, checkbooks will go unbalanced, appointments will not be scheduled, taxes will not be paid . . . possibly dinner will not reach the table.

The office work force is currently one of the major targets of the data merchants. As word processor and electronic file case, the computer has an obvious place in the white collar world. With that much initial leverage among the paperwork occupations, the computer industry has raised the prospect of the fully automated office where paper itself will become obsolete. On the video surface of the "intelligent desk," we are told, there will soon be floating simulations of memos and reports. All company records will be on-line, data bases for every purpose will be instantly accessible through vastly integrated, all-in-one organizing-accounting-managing programs. Word-processed documents will be distributed far and wide from terminal to terminal and simultaneously filed with abundant cross-indexing. Electronic mail will be the rule. Speech recognition equipment will take over dictation; everything will function by voice command; even the computer keyboard will be obsolete. When it is necessary to hold a meeting, it will be done by teleconferencing among colleagues and contacts at all points in the building or around the world.

The fully computerized office will do for white collar work what the automated assembly line has done in the factories: it will "save" labor by eliminating it, starting with the file clerks and secretaries, but soon reaching to the junior executives and the sales force. Possibly these casualties of progress will find work at Burger King down the street, where the cash registers come equipped with pictures, not numbers, or as the janitors who clean up whatever there is left to clean up at the end of the day—at least until these jobs are turned over to robots. There may soon be no one left in the high-rise ziggurats of our cities but a small elite of top-level decision makers surrounded by electronic apparatus. They will be in touch around the globe with others of their kind, the only decently paid work force left in the information economy, manipulating spreadsheets, crafting takeover bids, transferring funds from bank to bank at the speed of light, arranging "power lunches." As time goes by, there will be less and less for them to do, for even decision making can be programmed. As one team of management scientists has observed,

> There is no reason why we cannot program computers actually to take decisions and, by means of generating the appropriate piece of paper or other output, to implement their decisions by initiating action. There is no intrinsic difference between a business decision and the decisions which are involved in a production process control system—an area regarded as perfectly legitimate for computerization.[14]

At that point, even the corporate leadership will not have to report to the office. Most of what needs to be done by way of human intervention will be done out of the home. One forms an eerie vision of the high industrial future: a vista of glass towers standing empty in depopulated business districts where only machines are on the job networking with other machines.

As for the home, the futurologists have a computerized scenario for it as well. It will become an "information center" organized around a computer that is linked by its busy modem to a worldwide array of data bases. The new electronic family will read its mail and the news of the hour off a video screen; it will bank, shop, invest, learn, and play at its interactive terminal. Nobody need ever leave the house, which will become school and workplace by virtue of the earth-girdling information networks that serve it. The Japanese are already aggressively selling automated computer-designed houses. A number of integrated home automation systems have also appeared at the more affluent fringes of the American marketplace. They have catchy names: Homeminder, Tomorrowhouse, Smart House. If one has the proper wiring to accommodate the master panel, the house can be set on automatic to heat, cool, and ventilate itself without human intervention; no need to finger the thermostat or open the window. The home will be continuously monitored by all necessary security and emergency services. As one walks from room to room at night, one will not even have to flip the light switches on or off; the energy-efficient computer will sense and respond to every move. Speaking appliances will intone advice and warnings about their own proper use. Alvin Toffler looks forward to a house of the future so electronically responsive that, should it detect a leaking toilet, it will automatically consult with all the other home computers on the street to find the name of a good plumber—and schedule the repair. He calls this living in an "intelligent environment."[15]

Even friendship and personal warmth will be electronically mediated: the home terminal will be linked with numerous computer bulletin boards that will supply conversation, advice, gossip, humor, dating services—all the social commerce for which people once had to go in search of human beings in clubs, cafés, pubs, parks, and bars. Toffler predicts the coming of "electronic expanded families," a sort of computerized commune that might span the continents. Another enthusiast, Myron Krueger, expects to see the computer mature into an "intimate technology" that can be programmed for "electronic sex." For example:

> A sequence of ministrations ordinarily requiring two hands could be carried out automatically, allowing the lover to lavish attention elsewhere, just as one can set up rhythms on an electronic organ. Indeed, it is just possible that sexual concerts may arouse the masses of the future. . . . It is possible to postulate circumstances that would lead to such a development and lead many people to accept it.[16]

An article in the magazine *The Futurist* takes these possibilities several speculative steps forward to what one would hope was intended as the ultimate absurdity. But the prediction is not offered in that spirit; it is dead serious.

The ultimate house may be a structure whose computer brain, equipped with sensors and linked through telecommunications networks to computer data banks and the brains of other houses, has developed an awareness of its own existence, and an intimate knowledge of its inhabitants. . . . This development will greatly add to our ability to "believe in" the computer as a conscious entity. Once your house can talk to you, you may never feel alone again.[17]

As far-fetched, and perhaps as unsettling, as this image of conscious and attentive microprocessors may seem, Steven Jobs of Apple Computer expects something like this well before the end of the century. He speaks of it as a shift from the computer as servant to the computer as "guide or agent."

It's going to do more in terms of anticipating what we want and doing it for us, noticing connections and patterns in what we do, asking us if this is some sort of generic thing we'd like to do regularly, so that we're going to have . . . the concept of triggers. We're going to be able to ask our computers to monitor things for us, and when certain conditions happen, are triggered, the computers will take certain actions and inform us after the fact.[18]

. . . let us hope apologetically, when they make the inevitable big mistake.

At times, one cannot decide whether to weep or laugh at what the Information Age supposedly has in store for us. Pamela McCorduck hopes to see the home of the future equipped with a "geriatric robot" that will solve "the problems of aging."

The geriatric robot is wonderful. It isn't hanging about in the hopes of inheriting your money—nor of course will it slip you a little something to speed the inevitable. . . . It's there because it's yours. It doesn't just bathe you and feed you and wheel you out into the sun when you crave fresh air and a change of scene, though of course it does all those things. The very best thing about the geriatric robot is that it *listens*. "Tell me again," it says, "about how wonderful/dreadful your children are to you. Tell me again that fascinating tale of the

coup of '63. . . ." And it means it. It never gets tired of hearing those stories, just as you never get tired of telling them. It
knows your favorites, and those are its favorites, too.[19]

It might almost be a Samuel Beckett play . . .

HACKERS AND HUCKSTERS
■

As far-fetched as this futuristic brainstorming may be, it reveals what
the data merchants think the public wants. If they are right, they
leave us with a dismal picture of our cultural state. One shudders to
believe there can really be an audience that takes fatuous and infan-
tile applications of the computer like these seriously. How many
people can there be who need to have their every least activity mediated—and presumably validated—by a machine? Ironically, the
worst casualty of such megahype may be the computer itself. It is a
remarkable invention that deserves our admiration over a wide range
of uses. But at the hands of its enthusiasts, this ingenious machine is
reduced to a trivial plaything, the carrier of silly, sybaritic values.

There is a point, however, at which the public relations hoopla
surrounding the computer shades off into a twilight zone where
potted metaphysics and science fiction freely mingle. Here, the hackers and the hucksters become convenient allies in the task of lending
the cult of information a much more intimidating character. We
begin to hear heady predictions by knowledgeable people of computers that will one day be smarter than people. How smart? One
computer scientist at the University of California blithely tosses off
the remark: "I think there'll be an all-knowing machine someday.
That's what we're about."[20]

Behind this line of thought there lies a long, steady process of
anthropomorphizing the computer as a surrogate human intelligence. As long as the computer was simply a number cruncher, it
was rarely seen as much more than a super adding machine. It took
its first important step toward mindlikeness soon after World War
II, when the word *memory* was adopted for its storage capacity. No
one had ever used that word in reference to the old Hollerith busi-

ness machines. Their means of holding and processing data was too obvious and cumbersome; they were clearly doing nothing more than fast-shuffling punchcards which had to be fed in and taken out by people.

But with the invention of stored program machines like UNIVAC and more sophisticated magnetic core systems, it became far less apparent to the public how computers retained data. Where was all the information being hidden away in these increasingly more compact machines? The engineers spoke of the computer has having a "memory," an attribute of mind. The machines "remembered" things, vastly more things than people did, and—mysteriously— were able to produce total recall at the push of a button. On the other hand, when it came to human brains, it seemed obvious that, as Robert Jastrow of NASA observed, "The amount of information and wiring that can be crammed into a cranium of fixed size is limited."[21]

Now, there is no evidence that human brains are anywhere near exhausting whatever limit they may have; nor do we have any reason to believe that cerebral volume has any relationship whatever to the function of thought, even to that of remembering. Is it possible that what we loosely refer to as "forgetting" in the human brain is exactly that form of storage and processing which makes information most usable for significant thinking? Might it be the case that the retention of too much data—more than a single mind can judiciously deal with—compromises the quality of thought? In print or in person, I have surely come across a great many people who lose their intellectual way in a forest of facts. "Data, data everywhere, but not a thought to think."[22] On the other hand, a rather decent amount of important culture has been created over the millennia by societies that, perhaps with good reason, placed little value on the collection of raw data. These are not views one would expect the data merchants to entertain. Instead, they fall back on the authority of the computer scientists, who make it possible for companies like Sony to advertise a computerized tape deck that is "so ingenious it actually compensates for the shortcomings of your memory."

Once the faculty of memory was metaphorically conceded to the machines, their mindlikeness was free to soar to superhuman heights. For if thinking is essentially data processing, as the cyberneticians insisted, then the mind that holds the most data is potentially the superior mind, especially in the complex modern world, where there is far too much information reporting in for human brains to handle.

> The human mind [observes the Stanford University cognitive scientist Avron Barr] not only is limited in its storage and processing capacity, but it also has known bugs; it is easily misled, stubborn and even blind to the truth. . . . Intelligent systems, built for computer and communications technology, will someday know more than any individual human being about what is going on in complex enterprises involving millions of people.[23]

The futurologists have been quick to pick up on this theme: modern social complexity leads to computer supremacy. "An information bomb is exploding in our midst," Alvin Toffler announces. "People and organizations continually crave more information and the entire system begins to pulsate with higher and higher flows of data." We have already reached the point where "no one can keep the many complexities in mind while trying to think through a solution to the problem." But salvation is at hand.

> Because it can remember and interrelate large numbers of causal forces, the computer can help us cope with such problems [i.e., crime, housing, urban decay] at a deeper than customary level. It can sift vast masses of data to find subtle patterns. . . . It can even suggest imaginative solutions to certain problems by identifying novel or hitherto unnoticed relationships among people and resources.[24]

In a passage like this, one notes how the computer has been personified into a mental agency apparently working on its own initiative. Its power to store data has mysteriously matured into the power to find "subtle patterns" in society and to suggest "imaginative solutions" to political dilemmas.

A remarkable machine indeed. Does it exist? Will it ever? The author does not say. Why should a pop sociologist hold himself responsible to a higher standard of credibility than the scientists and technicians who are in charge of the technology? Computer scientists I. J. Good and Christopher Evans have blithely predicted the invention of an ultra-intelligent machine (UIM) somewhere in the 1990s which will be far smarter than any human intelligence and quite capable of taking over all major political decisions, including matters of war and peace.[25] Good, writing in the early seventies, was even then looking forward to a time when the UIMs will go into business on their own and produce "an intelligence explosion."

> The UIM will enable us to solve any practically soluble problem and we shall perhaps achieve world peace, the elixir of life, the piecemeal conversion of people into UIPs (ultra-intelligent people), or the conversion of the world's population into a *single* UIP.

In a book titled *Machines Who Think*, Pamela McCorduck, an expert in artificial intelligence, goes that prospect one further. She predicts that the UIM will "convert the entire universe into an expanded thinking entity."

In what spirit do computer enthusiasts offer up wild prognostications like these? It is hard to say. Sometimes, as in the case of Good's remarks, there is a marked pathos behind the exuberance. In such an ultimate extension of "user friendliness," the computer has been cast in the wishful role of a benign angelic protector that will relieve us of adult responsibilities that have become too burdensome. On the other hand, some computer scientists appear to relish the tough-minded bravado that comes of debunking what they take to be human delusions of grandeur. Marvin Minsky of MIT is in that category. Over the years, he has cut a colorful public figure in the media by impishly sniping at whatever anyone nominates as a special, possibly rather complicated quality of the human mind: common sense, judgment, intuition, creativity. Or, for example, emotions. Nothing very remarkable there, Minsky tells us: "I think we'll be able to program emotions into a machine once we can do thoughts.... I'm sure that once ... we've decided which emotions we want in a machine, that it won't be hard to do."[26] Working from such a minimal conception of human personality, Minsky has no difficulty concluding: "I think what we have learned is that we are probably computers." Such facile remarks are not without their influence. Sherry Turkle, who has made a study of children in highly computerized schools (including one much influenced by the work of Minsky's MIT artificial intelligence laboratory), found students who readily characterized themselves as "feeling computers, emotional machines."[27]

Whatever the intention behind these speculations, we see reflected in them a well-developed motif in Western technological history. The machines we have invented might be said to fall into two major categories: *strong machines* and *smart machines*. Strong machines (the steam engine, dynamo, airplane) have had their share of public appreciation; but smart machines have elicited a very different response, a sense of self-effacing awe that has more than a touch of the pathological about it. The original smart machines were various kinds of clocks, governors, and player piano–type animations. We may no longer be that much impressed by the quaint old counting and timekeeping instruments we see in museums, but for some centuries of our past, clocks and clockwork devices exerted a strange charm over Western thought. The clock was, after all, a machine that seemed to be able to enumerate and regulate; it appeared to possess a sense of intelligent, mathematically precise order that had long been regarded as a peculiarly human gift. The clock's connection with mathematics—even if it was nothing more than regular counting—was especially fascinating to the scientists since it echoed their own taste for exact, objective measurement. Clockwork mechanisms, like music boxes and various wind-up toys, could be "programmed" (as we would say today) to mimic intelligent activities: even to play musical instruments, to write with pen on paper, to play games.

In contrast to strong machines, whose status has always been that of beasts of burden (hence we measure their strength as "horsepower"), smart machines have normally been treated with far more respect. They have a seductive appeal to the scientific imagination, which has freely borrowed them as models of the universe at large, often reshaping our experience of the world to make it fit that model. And in this there can be the real danger that we fall prey to a technological idolatry, allowing an invention of our own hands to become the image that dominates our understanding of ourselves and all nature around us.

The computer is the latest episode in this scientific infatuation with mechanistic metaphors borrowed from smart machines. Once again, as in the age of Newton, the scientists need to be reminded that the organisms (human beings) which came before mechanisms are far more remarkable pieces of work than the tools they may occasionally invent when they are not spending their time singing songs, making jokes, telling tales, or worshiping God.

SILICON AND NATURAL SELECTION
■

In the early 1920s, Karl Capek wrote a play called *R.U.R.* in which the concept (and the word) *robot* first appeared. The robot was a sentient clockwork mechanism, a machine with a human face. More than an abstract model of intelligence, it could be imagined as having a life of its own. For example, in Capek's play, the robots turn into restless metallic Marxists; they rebel against their human exploiters and take over. This image of the humanoid machine has given rise to a line of thought that is now well represented among the computer enthusiasts as the ultimate expression of mechanistic supremacy. The computer has received an evolutionary interpretation which marks it out for a spectacular destiny. It may survive its maker and become the dominant species of "life" on earth.

This is a fresh note in the Western world's technological history. The theme has emerged in any number of science fiction tales; but as of the early 1960s, there were computer scientists who had begun to take some of their own metaphors seriously and literally. If the computer is a "brain" possessing "intelligence," might it not be likened to a biological "species"? And if that species is passing through "generations" in its development, then might it not be said to be "evolving"?

Of course, many machines—refrigerators, automobiles, vacuum cleaners—also undergo progressive improvement as they pass from model to model. We do not ordinarily speak of this as evolution. But when we come to the computer, its status as a smart machine places it in a special category. It is not simply accumulating improvements; it is becoming more sentient, more mentally competent, more autonomous.

John Pfeiffer of MIT was among the first to entertain the proposition that the computer's development deserved to be thought of as evolution in the strict, literal sense of the word. In his book *The*

Thinking Machine (1962) he argued that the computer was, uniquely, a technology whose limits could not be specified. This gave it a certain unpredictability, almost a willful freedom over against its human maker. "From this standpoint, the machine is always ahead of him, and will be ahead of him for an indefinite future." Especially under pressure of "the information explosion which already threatens to overwhelm us," human beings will have to allow the computer's unrestrained development to continue. This will make "the evolution of computers . . . a significant part of human evolution."[28]

Thinking along similar lines a decade later (1972), John Kemeny of Dartmouth, inventor of the BASIC programming language, was prepared to forecast a "symbiotic evolution" on the part of the human and computer "species."[29] With the human race facing the threat of extinction on many fronts, he saw such a "significant evolutionary change" as our best hope for making appropriate use of the "information-rich world" we had created around us.

These were benign predictions that still imagined a humanly beneficial coevolution on the part of human beings and computers. But some artificial intelligence experts are not at all convinced that the computer's evolution need be synchronized with that of the obviously deficient human brain. "The amount of intelligence we humans have is arbitrary," Marvin Minsky observes. "It's just the amount we have at this point in evolution. There are people who think that evolution has stopped and that there can never be anything smarter than us." Minsky disagrees; that would be like saying "that a person can't build a house any higher than he can reach."[30]

These evolutionary speculations tie in neatly with the idea that social complexity necessitates computer dominance. In effect, the conditions of modern life become a selective force that favors a new species, one better adapted to the scale and pace of the industrial future. Dr. Gordon Pask has called the new entity "micro man":

> The rapid proliferation of computation, communication, and control devices is coming to form what we call the "information environment." We believe, however, that the change is not merely quantitative. Underlying it are much deeper qualitative changes in the relationship between machines and human beings. These changes . . . are leading to the evolution of a new species, a species we have dubbed "micro man."[31]

Is micro man human or mechanical? Pask believes the question is beside the point. "The distinction between human thought and machine thought is becoming untenable. We envisage a revolutionary expansion of mind, be it individual, social, or wrought in material-other-than-brain-stuff."

It is important to underscore the assumptions that inspire these visions of human obsolescence. If thinking is simply a matter of information processing, then indeed there is no significant distinction to be made between the way human beings think and machines think, except to recognize that machines are better at the task. And if processing information is the commanding need of the time, then the machines obviously have to be granted a selective advantage. But what sort of "selection" are we discussing here? Not natural, but cultural selection surely. The "information environment" is, after all, a thing of our own making. It should, therefore, be within our power to change it to serve our own values. It is a grim vision of life that assumes we must timidly become the victims of the culture we have created.

How far can that fatalistic scenario be pushed? Robert Jastrow foresees the computer as the advent of an "intelligence beyond man's." It is "the child of man's brain rather than his loins" and "will become his salvation in a world of crushing complexity." But that alliance of human and machine will be unstable. The computer will continue its runaway evolution. Whereas

> human evolution is a nearly finished chapter in the history of life . . . We can expect that a new species will arise out of man, surpassing his achievements as he has surpassed those of his predecessor, *Homo erectus*. . . . The new kind of intelligent life is more likely to be made of silicon.[32]

At this high level of speculative fever, we are no longer discussing the mere cleverness of machines; the moral resolve and biological fitness of our own species are being weighed in the scales of evolutionary survival . . . and found wanting.

There is a fascinatingly convoluted interplay of ideas at work here. At first, the biologists borrowed from cybernetics to explain genetics as an information transfer mechanism. Here, we see the computer scientists borrowing from biology to suggest the evolutionary nature of data processing technology. Culture is like that; it often grows by metaphorical elaboration, one field of thought borrowing from another for suggestive images. But at a certain point, metaphorical elaboration becomes plain bad thinking. That point is where the metaphors stop being suggestive and are taken literally.

Nevertheless, slipshod thinking like this, voiced by experts in the field, has become mixed into the folklore of computers. It permeates the technology with a haunting sense of human inadequacy and existential failure. On the surface, the futurologists and the data merchants offer effervescent promises of convenience, affluence, fun and games; but their breezy optimism is laid over dark speculations about human obsolescence. That despairing motif comes with the machines and cannot help but shape our response to the new technology, even in its most trivial applications. Have we created something like a mind, one that is better suited to the alienating conditions of modern society, better able to cope with the pressure, the anxiety, the moral tension? If that were so, it might be taken as a damning judgment upon the inhumanity of the social order we have created for ourselves. But some computer scientists clearly regard it, instead, as an indictment of human nature itself; we possess a mind which is not fit to survive. That conclusion might be left floating at a high speculative level awaiting the outcome of the next thousand or million years of evolutionary selection. But in the meantime it can be given significant political substance. It can lead to the self-serving argument that more power should be entrusted to the machines the computer scientists have invented and control.

TECHNOPHILIA
■

To some degree, the ideas we have reviewed here, zany and extravagant as they may be, are part of a tradition that is as old as industrial society. They may be seen as extreme expressions of technophilia, our love affair with the machines in our lives. This is not the first time people have projected their hope for happiness and their image of perfection upon the latest magic gadget to come along. The steam engine, the electric dynamo, the automobile, the airplane—each in its time held a similar position as the reigning emblem of progress.

Such technological infatuations come and go as each new wave of invention and investment makes a place for itself in our dynamic industrial economy. A century and a half ago, a Victorian futurologist filed this bit of doggerel with the *Illustrated London News:*

> Lay down your rails, ye nations near and far—
> Yoke your full trains to Steam's triumphal car.
> Link town to town; unite in iron bands
> The long-estranged and oft-embattled lands.
> Peace, mild-eyed seraph—Knowledge, light divine,
> Shall send their messengers by every line. . . .
> Blessings on Science, and her handmaid Steam!
> They make Utopia only half a dream.

What was the object of his utopian aspirations? The railway. With the benefit of hindsight, it is easy to see how naive and overwrought such expectations can be. Still, for the most part, we might be willing to bear with the salvational longings that entwine themselves around new technology. I think, however, the current fascination with the computer and its principal product, information, deserves a more critical response. This is because the computer does so ingeniously mimic human intelligence that it may significantly shake our confidence in the uses of the mind. And it is the mind that must think about all things, including the computer.

In our popular culture today, the discussion of computers and information is awash with commercially motivated exaggerations and the opportunistic mystifications of the computer science establishment. The hucksters and the hackers have polluted our understanding of information technology with loose metaphors, facile comparisons, and a good deal of out-and-out obfuscation. There are billions of dollars in profit and a windfall of social power to account for why they should wish to do this. Already there may be a large public that believes it not only cannot make judgments about computers, but has no *right* to do so because computers are superior to its own intelligence—a position of absolute deference which human beings have never assumed with respect to any technology of the past.

As it penetrates more deeply into the fabric of our daily life, enjoying at every step along the way the exuberant celebration of its enthusiasts and promoters, the computer holds the possibility of shaping our thought, or rather our very conception of thought itself, in far-reaching ways. This is all the more likely to happen within the near future because of the massive scale on which the computer is entering the schools at all levels and there forming an entire generation of students.

THE HIDDEN
CURRICULUM

■

THE CHIMERA OF COMPUTER
LITERACY

■

In an effort to prime the pump for future sales of its product, the computer industry has at various times sought to make its wares available to universities and entire school systems at cut rate or free of charge. In California, which might be expected to set the national standard for high tech education and where over 80 percent of the schools had computers, Apple Computer placed one of its machines as a free gift in every school in the state. This amounts to some 10,000 computers valued (as a tax write-off for Apple) at $20 million. Atari, IBM, and Hewlett-Packard were quick to make similar offers, spurring Apple to propose placing a free computer in every school in the United States—something approaching 100,000 machines. The U.S. Congress, however, refused to grant Apple's requested tax credit of $64 million for the donation.[1]

As the market for home computers remains uncertain, the effort to place microcomputers in the schoolrooms of the nation has become more intense. But even without the benefit of such corporate favors, the number of computers in the country's schools, according to a survey in the *Journal of Educational Computing Research,* has risen from 50,000 in 1980 to 2,400,000 in the early nineties. Supposedly, the number of school computers will continue to grow, reaching a one-for-one pupil–computer ratio by the mid-1990s: a computer on every desk. America is not alone in this effort; with strong government backing, the British, French, and Japanese are also pressing to computerize their classrooms. In Japan 70 percent of the high schools were scheduled by the Ministry of Education to have computers before the end of the eighties; the French have launched an official campaign under the banner "100,000 Computers in Our Schools" targeted on 1995. The British, with the benefit of generous government subsidies, lead the pack with nearly 100 percent of the schools microcomputerized.[2]

In the United States, the machines are by no means evenly distributed. As we noted in the Introduction, they tend to accumulate in the richer school districts. Writing in *The New York Times* (August 7, 1992) Charles Piller and Liza Weiman charge that computers may be reinforcing "a two-tier system of education for the rich and poor." Seeking to offset such imbalances, a majority of the California legislature called for the spending of some $30 million per year through the late 1980s to make certain that every student in the state, rich or poor, spends at least one hour each week in front of a video display terminal. Congress has debated (and tabled) several bills aimed at closing the computer "equity gap" between school districts; one proposal has called for budgeting up to $700 million a year to do the job of spreading computer literacy evenly across the nation.[3] The National Committee on Industrial Innovation—a citizens' group organized by former California Governor Jerry Brown—took a slightly different tack. It called for the establishment of one demonstration school in each state devoted to fully computerized instruction, a recommendation which would cost some half a billion dollars.[4]

These are ambitious and costly plans. By way of keeping matters in perspective, Jerry Brown has observed that none of the programs under discussion would cost as much as a single Trident submarine. True enough; but it is also the case that these educational millions are being budgeted for machinery at a time when the average teacher in America has a starting salary that is barely above the official poverty level. Against that background, what all the proposals highlight, with their belated call for rational planning, is that the computer has made a wastefully ragged and disruptive entry into the school systems of the nation. For the most part, the schools (or mainly trend-conscious administrators and anxious parents, less so teachers) have responded with the promptness and the gullibility of well-trained consumers to the commercial pressure of the computer industry. The instant folklore which has been scripted by the data merchants holds that children have a "natural affinity" for computers which "can be a powerful tool for teaching the information skills needed for life in an information society." [5] Indeed, so great is the instinctive love and skill that children bring to the computer that their troglodytic parents and teachers, like a species on the brink of extinction, may be in no position even to understand the passion that stirs in their offspring, let alone offer instruction. "Today's moms and dads must feel much like European parents felt in the nineteenth century when their children were emigrating to the New World," writes educator Barbara Deane. "Here we stand, not only waving our children off into a brave new world that we can scarcely imagine, but expected somehow to provide them with guidance in the use of computers—giving them maps, so to speak, of a land we do not know." Similarly the creator of a British computer literacy program tells us that "in the future, our children will be thinking in ways that we can't even envision at the moment. The computer is providing them with an intellectual tool that they can drive and control to achieve mental feats which we would probably consider absurd—if we knew what they were likely to be!" [6]

In the 1960s there was much talk of a generation gap; but that was understood to be a moral and political discrepancy. In the Information Age, the gap is purely technological, a matter of programming talents and keyboard virtuosity. "Kids and computers click," possibly in a way that leaves their parents no option but to stand aside and watch with amazement—but only after they have gone shopping and bought the equipment.

Undeniably, some kids click with computers. The emphasis, however, belongs on *some*—as in the phrase, *some* kids click with violins, or *some* kids click with paintbrushes. But there are no millions being spent to bring violins or paintbrushes into the schools. Initially, there was a simple justification for favoring computers over violins in the budgetary priorities of the schools. It was embodied in the catchphrase *computer literacy*—a seemingly undeniable necessity in the Information Age. Lacking that skill, children would grow up to be unemployable. In Britain, Apple has been crusading to computerize the schools with the slogan "Our kids can't wait."

But what is computer literacy? The original meaning of the phrase had to do with teaching programming—mainly in BASIC, the simplest and most widely used of the high-level computer languages. But by the late 1970s, doubts had arisen. For one thing, many computer scientists had come to regard BASIC as a limited and retrograde choice among the many languages available. But more importantly, why teach programming at all when there is so much preprogrammed software coming on the market? For most purposes, the software does the job better than a rough, amateur program. There seemed to be no general need for the skill, outside of preparation for a career specifically in programming, which requires much more training than schools can provide. True, it somewhat demystifies computers to learn a little basic programming—if it is taught correctly. (The same can be said of learning how to take apart a car, or a stereo, or a refrigerator—all skills that help one penetrate the secrets of modern technology.) But is it worthwhile to give children any hands-on training at all in the use of a machine that changes so much from year to year? Did it pay to learn word processing by way of WordStar when superior programs, like Macwrite or Word-Perfect, were on the way? The fact is, each new generation of computers requires fewer special skills, requiring less "literacy" of users, in much the same way that advances in automotive engineering have made driving a car easier.

As programming slipped out of the curriculum, computer literacy became more and more of an educational chimera. Teachers were often left with no better employment for their computers than to use them as electronic flashcards or for low-grade drill and practice at basic subjects—no great advance upon the less than enthralling computer-aided instruction materials and teaching machines of the 1960s. Some states (California, New York, Virginia, Minnesota) have spent generously to train their teachers in various computer skills, but that does no good when there is no clear idea as to whether the schools are to teach *about* computers, or *through* computers, or *by way of* computers.

Another problem: generally, teachers have found very little in the way of programmed instruction that integrates with existing curricula and their own experienced teaching methods. Should they, therefore, retool to fit the demands of the machine? Would that be "cost effective"? Even if they are willing to do so, which software are they to choose? There is a strong consensus among educators that most of what the market has to offer is poor, usually no better than crudely adapted video games with some immediate visual appeal but little intellectual substance. One survey cited in *The Education Digest* in 1992 estimates that only some 200 of the 10,000 educational software programs on sale were of any value.[7] Here the federal government has moved to help clear a path for the computers to enter the classroom. The Department of Education has awarded Harvard University a $7.7 million grant to establish an Educational Technology Center, whose purpose is to test and develop superior software. One dilemma with which the center is apt to confront the schools: good software is expensive to use. Students may quickly exhaust the benefits of low-grade software; a few minutes apiece on the machine, and they may have finished the drill or solved the problem posed by a trivial game. On the other hand, software that is challenging, absorbing, and highly interactive—and there is at least a smattering of that around—is machine-time intensive. Each student has to be given a decent chance to work out the problems. At best, the materials can be used in small groups. In any case, there have to be more machines. It might almost be expected that the computer industry would have to have a vested interest in high-quality software, if only as a means of selling more of its hardware.

A SOLUTION IN SEARCH OF PROBLEMS
■

Joseph Weizenbaum of MIT once described the computer as "a solution in search of problems." There could be no better example of this than the way elementary and high schools are dealing with the machine. As things now stand, there is an atmosphere of urgent concern nationally and locally about *somehow* putting this magnificent solution to work in the schools—if only the right problem could be identified. The concern is understood to be something we owe our children but which also relates to national prestige and power. There is much talk about "catching up" or "staying ahead," about training the prospectively jobless and selecting the gifted for rapid advancement. But when it comes down to actual classroom assignments, is the computer to be a *subject* or a *vehicle* of instruction? If it is a vehicle, what materials is it to carry? How much of the curriculum should it be allowed to take over? Is the curriculum to adapt to the computer, or the computer to the curriculum?

Obviously, these questions should be answered before purchases and retraining programs are budgeted. But once the computers arrive, either paid for or free of charge, it is difficult not to do *something* with them. So the teachers scramble to improvise educationally defensible uses. Perhaps sometimes they succeed.

Hovering over the cloudy concept of computer literacy there is the standard futurological assumption that the machine will someday connect the students with a wealth of data and make them citizens in good standing of the Information Age. As a matter of fact, few if any schools are teaching students how to access and search data bases. Wisely so; teaching that complex skill would surely be premature (and highly expensive) at any point before college. Meanwhile, the only information the children are receiving from the computer is that contained in software designed to teach, or help teach, the existing curriculum. In this respect, the machine has less information to offer than a textbook or workbook. Its data processing is necessarily being limited to the job of supplementing the text or other classroom materials: illustrating, animating, testing, and drilling. Some computer enthusiasts regard this as a low-grade use of the computer; "a waste of time, energy, and money," comments Robert Scarola. Such software "reinforces the idea of computers as routinizing machines."[8]

Those who believe the computer does these supplementary things well argue that it offers the student attractively animated displays and simulations to work with, plus self-paced, individualized instruction. Above all, it is instantaneously interactive. This means that instead of having to wait for a paper or workbook to be graded, and so losing momentum, students see their responses evaluated and corrected before their very eyes as soon as they give them. Often the machine gives them some cute electronic strokes for good work. It pipes a cheery little tune, beeps, flashes, shows a smiley face, or conjures up a little froggy figure to perform a victory dance.

As a matter of personal taste, I must say that I find the pictorial animations and most of the graphics that computers bring into the classroom to be aesthetically degraded, even ugly. The pictures may move, but they are nonetheless an eyesore. Computer art at the level of the most expensive animated and three-dimensional graphics software can be authentically creative. But nothing remotely like this is apt to make an appearance in the schools. For one thing, the equipment is fabulously expensive, since it takes a great deal of heavy-duty mathematical processing to compose a fine-grain color picture. (The computer graphics generator marketed by Lucasfilm's Industrial Light and Magic division costs over $125,000.) For another, only trained professionals can use these machines properly. The animations that one finds in most affordable educational software may be clever by ordinary machine standards; it probably takes thousands of lines of code to program all the choppy, pixel-blockish gyrations. Hackers take satisfaction in that, but theirs is hardly a reliable artistic standard. Much of what they praise is just wretched to look at; it does not even come up to a mediocre Walt Disney level of cartooning. Have computer enthusiasts ever honestly pondered what long-term visual exposure to such junk art does to children's taste? Even worse, some teachers try to make use of the computer's low-grade graphic abilities to teach "art," lowering the subject to the level of the machine. One exception here may be the remarkably flexible Apple Macpaint program, which does a striking job of simulating the capacities of pencil and brush. But even so, why is this preferable to training the hand in the use of a real pencil and brush directly on paper?

In any case, animation (such as it is) and interactiveness are unquestionably the computer's most worthwhile educational features. Where drill and problem solving are concerned, it is always best to have a quick comeback. But this could, of course, be provided by the teacher—if there were enough teachers. The computer makers are banking on the assumption that there will never be. Their hope is that, given the choice between hiring people and buying machines, the public will not prove willing to pay the price of humanly individualized instruction and humanly interactive classrooms. Indeed, they are helping things turn out that way by spreading the word that: (1) teachers hate drill and exercise and would prefer to be freed for other, more creative purposes; and (2) teachers are very bad at drill because they become impatient and bossy, whereas (3) the computer is "the most patient of teachers."

If, on the other hand, you ask unemployed teachers if they are unwilling to be hired to handle drill and exercise, you are apt to get another viewpoint. They may even tell you they believe they can do the job with care, flexibility, and imagination out of their professional concern for children. What computers may be freeing most teachers for is joblessness. And that is a pity. Because even at the low-level task of drill, it helps to have a human intelligence at work, offering an encouraging smile here, a jibe there, a wink and a nod, perhaps catching the blush or stammer that reveals the nature of a student's problem. Isn't all this utterly obvious? Why, then, does it drop out of sight as soon as computers are under discussion? I had teachers who were quite adept at handling classroom exercises with patience and sensitive watchfulness; I could not have been alone in that experience. In any case, what does it do to the students' morale to be told that the drill they need in order to learn is a great bore, or possibly an obstacle to the teacher's "productivity"?

Not long ago, the hottest item on the computer industry's educational agenda was the "intelligent machine tutor," under development by IBM, Xerox, and Apple, among others. Hewlett-Packard has donated some $50 million to various universities to work up some combination of artificial intelligence and laser disk video graphics that might function as a "computer tutor" capable of teaching abstract concepts and engaging in spoken conversation. For computer scientists, it is no doubt exciting to ask: "Can we invent a machine that does what a teacher does?" But there is another question one might ask: "Why should we want to invent a machine to do that in the first place?" There was never any difficulty in answering that question where the machine was intended to take over work that was dirty, dangerous, or back-breaking. Teaching is hardly any of these. Indeed, it would seem to be one of those "human uses of human beings" to which people might expect to turn when the robots have "saved" their labor on the assembly lines.

There is no way around the fact that the computer makers have a vested interest in the technological unemployment of willing and available teachers. They are selling a labor-saving machine in an economy where that labor is abundant and could be had for a decent wage. Whenever the little stick-figure froggy does its dance, there is a would-be teacher somewhere who does without a paycheck.

Other than functioning as a mechanical teacher's aid—or teacher's replacement—does the computer offer anything distinctive as an educational device, something all its own that a teacher could not do as well? There are educators who believe it does. (In the next chapter, we will review one of the most impressive proposals of this kind: the Logo program of Seymour Papert.) Here, we will note that the best interactive, problem solving software—games like the much-praised *Rocky's Boots* (created by Warren Robinnet and available from The Learning Company)—can bring unique features into the classroom. These are mostly playful, animated exercises in symbolic logic. The animations are as dreadful as any, but the concept behind the games is sophisticated and could not be executed with the same challenging quality except on an interactive computer. Software of this caliber is special; it is also potentially very expensive to use since it is machine-time intensive for each child. The better the software, the more hardware a school may have to buy to give all the students a chance.

Is the teaching of symbolic logic justified? Well, why not? It is intellectually substantial as a subject in its own right. Some would argue that it has a more general benefit: it can help train the mind to think clearly. That is a somewhat antiquated and dubious assumption. It is grounded in the creaky old idea of faculty psychology, which holds that there are certain mental muscles, like logicality, which should be developed for their general utility in life. For centuries Latin was doggedly taught in the schools on the same mistaken premise that it contributed to orderly habits of thought. Like the Latin masters of old, computer scientists understandably feel the same way about their favorite subjects: mathematics and logic.

Probably symbolic logic teaches nothing more than symbolic logic; but some students are good at it, enjoy it, and deserve to have the experience along with whatever else they are offered in the classroom. It can do no harm; whether it justifies the cost of the technology is another matter. But of one thing educators can be certain, and on this point they owe their students absolute candor. Clever educational software like *Rocky's Boots* will make no greater contribution to the students' employability than will rudimentary courses in outmoded forms of programming. In the job market students will face when they leave school, the choice high tech careers will require many years of more professional and specialized education. Even so, those careers will be for the high-achieving few. For the many, the five most available jobs in the information economy will be employment as janitors, nurse's aides, sales clerks, cashiers, and waiters.[9]

One might almost conclude from this fact that what the young most need to defend their interests in life is an education which will equip them to ask hard, critical questions about that uninviting prospect. Why is the world like that? Who made it that way? How else might it be? There are subjects that, when properly taught, help people answer those questions. They are called social science, history, philosophy. And all of these are grounded in the sort of plain, old-fashioned *literacy* that gives inquiring minds access to books, to ideas, to ethical insights, and social vision.

THE COMPUTERIZED CAMPUS
■

The computer has entered the world of higher education a great deal more smoothly and decisively than it has made its way into the elementary and secondary schools. Universities, after all, have more internal control over their choices than do bureaucratically congested school systems. This is also the province of learned men and women, scholars and experts who are supposedly prepared to make discriminating judgments that rise above the whims of the marketplace. Yet the campuses have also been targeted for a massive merchandising campaign by the computer makers, and the effort seems to be sweeping all before it.

Many leading universities purchased their first computer in the mid- to late 1960s, one of the IBM hulking giants. It became *the* campus computer, a proud and expensive possession that was frequently displayed as a sign of status. It was usually parked in an air-conditioned computer center and used mainly for administrative data processing. In short order, school records became computer printouts; grades and scheduling were done with punchcards. The better endowed schools, especially those with strong science departments, quickly moved to acquire a few more of these big mainframes for their technicians; these were used as widely as possible on time-sharing arrangements that were often the arena of intense competition and bickering on the part of the faculty.

By the early 1970s, the universities began to set up multiterminal computer labs, where students as well as faculty might be permitted to lay their hands on the technology. Once again, prestigious departments would push to have their own, autonomous labs for their majors as a sign of status. About this time, optional courses in computer programming began to appear, mainly for students in the sciences, engineering, and business. The society was by then becoming highly computerized in all its major sectors; but there were few educators who thought computer literacy, in any interpretation of the term, had an urgent place in higher education. Significantly, things changed in the universities when the market changed. In the 1980s, with the advent of the microcomputer, a readily salable item, the computer industry went after academia with one of the most intense mass marketing efforts in business history. The goal has been nothing less than to place computers in the hands of every teacher and student. With the help of grants, donations, and stupendous discounts ranging up to 80 percent, the companies have succeeded in striking a number of what they hope will be bellwether deals with schools large and small. The campuses have not displayed much sales resistance to these blandishments.

Though there are only 3,400 degree-granting institutions in the United States, higher education is one of the richest markets in the information economy. It includes schools like the University of Texas, which owns more computers (18,500 Apple Macintoshes) than any other non-government operation in the world. Through the decade of the 1980s American universities are estimated to have spent some $8 billion dollars on computers. A big school like the three-campus University of Michigan (45,000 students) can budget as much as $50 million a year; but even a small school that sets out to achieve the goal of being fully wired can be a prodigious consumer of computer technology. For example, Carnegie-Mellon University with only 5,500 students has spent as much as $15 million in a single year on the new technology.[10]

Nor is it only the immediate demand they generate that makes the universities so attractive to the data merchants. The schools are the gateway to a student market populated by prospectively high-earning professionals and white collar workers, the ideal computer buyers of the future. When it comes to campaigning for computer literacy, the universities are a far richer prize than the high schools. Even schools as influential as Harvard, Yale, and the University of California at Berkeley have seriously considered imposing such a requirement. Still more welcome than a literacy requirement would be a *property* requirement: namely, that owning a computer should be a condition of admission. This is happening, mainly at engineering schools but also at the three United States service academies. Though the machines may be well-discounted, this is surely a remarkable innovation. Has there ever been another instance of the universities making ownership of a piece of equipment mandatory for the pursuit of learning? One school, Dallas Baptist, which is among those that require every entering student to buy a computer, has gone so far as to reshape its curriculum to emphasize the computer; it insists that at least three assignments per term in each freshman course should require the use of a computer.[11]

The prospect of the fully networked university has made computer makers eager to strike ever more advantageous deals with the schools. Companies have resorted to all sorts of inducements, including generous giveaway programs. IBM has been part of $50–$70 million programs at both MIT and Brown. Since the mid-1980s, AT&T, the largest donor, has donated over $285 million in computer labs and equipment to some 60 universities.[12] In addition to offering faculty members discounted or even free computers, some companies have negotiated joint research and development projects that purchase and merchandise courseware developed by professors. The universities are a rich source for instructional innovation and the rewards can be handsome; the most widely marketed educational program, now used in hundreds of schools, is a chemistry course developed at the University of Illinois.

There is no question but that information technology will expand steadily at the universities, most obviously in technical and scientific fields. If only as word processors (the use that predominates among students) the computer has staked out a permanent place in every university department. But even the arts and humanities have a greater stake in the computer. Some of the most ambitious projects for full-text computer access, like the Center for Electronic Texts in the Humanities at Princeton and Rutgers, the E-Text Center at the University of Virginia, or the Center for Scholarly Technology at the University of Southern California, are campus-based. Since the initial euphoria that greeted the computer on campus in the early-1980s, however, some educators have grown cautious about the more extravagant pedagogical claims made for the new technology. In a major national forum in 1989, many teachers cited the troubling issues that arise from unlimited, often unmanageable information access; teaching in a "blizzard of information" raises as many problems as it solves. Some urgently called for a greater emphasis upon the distinction between raw data and knowledge, judgment, and intellectual integration.[13]

Despite these reservations, EDUCOM, the consortium of some

600 universities and 110 corporations that has become the principal lobbying agent on the campuses for new technology, continues to make ambitious predictions about the electronic campus of tomorrow. With each new computer development, EDUCOM spells out a scenario of dazzling possibilities. For example, EDUCOM tells us that when interactive multimedia finally reach the campus in full force, students will be able to find everything they need for a customized, self-paced education in one neat software package. Lecture courses will vanish; modem-to-modem tutorials with the instructor will take the place of class attendance. Instead of being "the sage on the stage," professors will become "the guide at the side" of the magic box.[14]

As if these predictions were not attractive enough, EUIT, EDUCOM's Educational Uses of Information Technology unit, has found a new enticement: cost cutting. Techniques like distance video instruction and interactive programs promise to reach more students with fewer teachers. Computerized instruction may become for the campus what automation has become for the assembly line: the royal road to down-sizing. This is a strong card to play in an era of budgetary restraint; it may even overcome the reservations some might have about the initial cost of the more expensive technology now on the market. The hardware necessary to run "Columbus," IBM's multimedia extravaganza on the life of the great explorer, is priced at $10,000 per system. Costly, but not if one considers how many teaching assistants and lecturers it will cut from the payroll.[15]

Cost cutting is the preferred managerial style of the 1990s. In that respect EDUCOM is in brisk step with the times. But as sophisticated as methods of down-sizing may be, the overall process is a bleak symptom of the nation's economic decline. And quite as much so on the campuses as in manufacturing and the white collar workplace. What EDUCOM's bright prospectus leaves out of account are the ambitions that bring many students to school in the first place. If the computer is used to slash salaries and eliminate teaching positions, what is a college degree going to be worth to those whose goal it is to become educators? There comes a point in the computer enthusiast's image of our cultural destiny that leaves creativity and imagination only one outlet: programming software, designing hardware. The fact that lecturing is an intellectual talent with its own distinct virtues, that the classroom encounter between teacher and student can be a rewarding experience in its own right, even the possibility that there are indispensably valuable things that can be done with the blackboard and the pencil elude the technician's worldview. A great deal that programmers see fit to eliminate in favor of their own narrow skills may be precisely that "human use of human beings" that was supposedly the greatest promise the computer had to offer.

If all works out as the computer makers would have it, there may one day be fully networked campuses where all the students and all the teachers do indeed have micros, and then perhaps they will rarely have to meet at all. They will simply exchange assignments and grades electronically. Networks may even outgrow the campuses that created them—as at the University of Houston, where teachers and students can link up from their own homes. Then, professors can not only grade their students electronically, but network with them at all hours of the day and night, and perhaps watch on line while assignments are processed across the video screen, making helpful suggestions along the way. (Of course, this sort of round-the-clock, unpredictably intrusive fraternization would be possible now by way of telephone. Which is why, in my experience, professors go to great lengths to keep their phone numbers private. I am not certain why the computer terminal, always on and demanding attention, is supposed to make unrestricted teacher-student interaction more enticing.) The ultimate goal of networking on the grandest scale is to become a "wired city" that expands into the surrounding community. Together with Bell Telephone and Warner Communications, which holds the local cable television franchise, Carnegie-Mellon University is planning to do just that in the Pittsburgh area.

One would be hard-pressed to find another time when a single industry was able to intrude its interests so aggressively upon the schools of the nation—and to find such enthusiastic receptivity (or timid surrender) on the part of educators. This is all the more remarkable when one considers that probably no two teachers or computer scientists could come up with the same definition of "computer literacy"—the goal that launched the campaign. As for the general intellectual benefits of that skill, of these there is no evidence to be found beyond the claims of the computer industry's self-promotional literature, filled with vague futuristic allusions to life in the Information Age. Yet if the computer makers succeed in their hard sell, we may soon be graduating students who believe (with their teachers' encouragement) that thinking is indeed a matter of information processing, and therefore without a computer no thinking can be done at all.

"The great university of the future will be that with a great computer system," Richard Cyert, president of Carnegie-Mellon, has announced.[16] A dramatic statement of conviction. Doubtless many educators wish their schools had the resources his university has been able to muster in laying claim to such greatness, even though it remains obscure how quantities of computational power translate into quality of learning. There is no question but that computers have a valuable role to play as computing devices in the technical fields, as electronic record keeping systems, or as word processors. Taken together, this is a sizable contribution for any single invention to make in the daily lives of students and teachers. But the computer enthusiasts have promised that the new technology will do more than merely replace the slide rule, the typewriter, and the filing cabinet. Its benefits supposedly reach to intellectual values at the highest level, nothing less than the radical transformation of educational methods and goals. The computer, after all, is the bountiful bringer of information, which is widely understood by educators themselves to be the substance of thought. Even Dr. Ernest Boyer, president of the Carnegie Foundation for the Advancement of Teaching, who has raised many keen criticisms on the waste and misuse of computers in the schools, agrees that "in the long run, electronic teachers may provide exchanges of information, ideas, and experiences more effectively (certainly differently) than the traditional classroom or the teacher. The promise of the new technology is to enrich the study of literature, science, mathematics, and the arts through words, pictures, and auditory messages."[17]

How disappointing it is, then, to see so much of this glowing promise come down to mere promotional gimmickry. There is, for example, the image of the fully networked campus which currently stands as the ultimate goal of computerization in the universities. Without leaving their dorms, students will be able to access the library card catalog; they will be able to log on to a student bulletin board to exchange advice, gossip, make dates, find a ride, buy used books. They will be able to submit assignments electronically to their instructors.

Yes, these things and a dozen more *can* be computerized. But why *should* they be? They all get done now by the most obvious and economical means: students walk to the library, the student union, the bookstore, to a nearby coffeehouse or cafe, where they meet other human beings. They talk, they listen, they make arrangements. Outside of disabled students (for whom computers can be a boon), who ever found these ordinary perambulatory activities so burdensome as to be worth the cost of an expensive technology to eliminate them? Indeed, it has always been my thought that an intellectually vital campus is one designed in its architecture, grounds, and general spirit to make such daily human intercourse graceful and attractively frequent—rather than one that spends millions to spare its students the exercise of leaving their dorms.

When enthusiasts come up with artificial uses like these for the computer, they are really doing nothing more than teaching another lesson in technological dependence, a vice already ingrained in our culture. For obvious commercial reasons, they are intruding a machine into places where it was never needed. Similarly, the prospect of having students submit assignments by some form of electronic mail is simply endorsing the sort of pseudo problem (like "static cling" or "wax buildup") that exists only because the hucksters invented it in the first place to sell a product. I have come across computer advertising that seems determined to make me forget that the red pencil—underscoring, circling, working along the margins and between the lines of the page (things no computer can do)—is one of the most practical teaching tools ever invented. Every experienced teacher knows this; but the ads are out to embarrass me into agreeing that, as a full-fledged member of the Information Age, I should be dealing exclusively with floppy disks, light pens, and video screens.

I will admit that, to a degree, one's criteria of educational greatness may involve matters of personal taste. Some people relish the image of schools where ranks of solitary students in private cubicles sit in motionless attendance upon computer terminals, their repertory of activities scaled down to a fixed stare and the repetitive stroking of a keyboard. I find this picture barely acceptable even where it may be justified episodically for a computer-specific exercise: some drill, computation, or graphics work. The image becomes no more appealing when I am told that working with computers is a marvelous occasion for socializing: the students cluster around the machines, taking their cues from its directives, debating the fine points of this or that response to its queries. As an educational ethos, both these situations strike me as simply another form of technological desiccation in our lives, appearing in the one place we might most want to save from its blight.

My own taste runs to another image: that of teachers and students in one another's face-to-face company, perhaps pondering a book, a work of art, even a crude scrawl on the blackboard. At the very least, that image reminds us of how marvelously simple, even primitive, education is. It is the unmediated encounter of two minds, one needing to learn, the other wanting to teach. The biological spontaneity of that encounter is a given fact of life; ideally, it should be kept close to the flesh and blood, as uncluttered and supple as possible. Too much apparatus, like too much bureaucracy, only inhibits the natural flow. Free human dialogue, wandering wherever the agility of the mind allows, lies at the heart of education. If teachers do not have the time, the incentive, or the wit to provide that, if students are too demoralized, bored, or distracted to muster the attention their teachers need of them, then *that* is the educational problem which has to be solved—and solved from inside the experience of the teachers and the students. Defaulting to the computer is not a solution; it is surrender.

But there are other issues that transcend taste, questions of educational theory, social policy, and professional ethics. It is simply wrong for any priorities about our schools to be set by those with commercial interests at stake. That vice has plagued public schools in the past; it may be more advanced now than ever, as the schools invest in glamorous machines without any clear idea of their use. They are doing so because they have absorbed mindless clichés about "information," its intellectual value and vocational urgency, that are little better than advertising copy. This has led them to overlook the degree to which educational problems are political and philosophical issues that will not yield to a technological fix.

To mention only the most obvious of the issues on which the ethics of the teaching profession require candor:

- Disruptive or alienated students in the schools may reflect an anxiety, even a desperation that stems from their disadvantaged social condition or from the compulsory nature of the school system itself; no matter how equitably the computers are spread through the classrooms, these students are not apt to find the will to learn.
- Students who are being sold on computer literacy as an

easy response to their job hunger are simply being deceived; what they are learning in a few computer lab experiences will not make them one iota more employable.

- Teachers who are falling back on flashy software as a convenient classroom entertainment are wasting their students' time and demeaning their own profession.

One senses how distorted the discussion of education has become in the Information Age when educators begin to draw not only upon the products but upon the language and imagery of the industrial marketplace. "Productivity" is the word Dr. Arthur S. Melmed of the Department of Education uses to define "the central problem of education. The key to productivity improvement in every other economic sector has been through technological innovation. Applications of modern information and communication technologies that are properly developed and appropriately used may soon offer education policy makers . . . a unique opportunity for productivity management."

Along the same lines, Richard Cyert of Carnegie-Mellon predicts that his school's computer network "will have the same role in student learning that the development of the assembly line in the 1920s had for the production of automobiles. The assembly line enabled large-scale manufacturing to develop. Likewise, the network personal computer system will enable students to increase significantly the amount of learning they do in the university."[18]

Computers, as the experts continually remind us, are nothing more than their programs make them. But as the sentiments above should make clear, the programs may have a program hidden within them, an agenda of values that counts for more than all the interactive virtues and graphic tricks of the technology. The essence of the machine is its software, but the essence of the software is its philosophy.

POWER AND DEPENDENCY
■

Anyone who has watched children almost hypnotically absorbed by the dazzling display of a video game cannot help but recognize the computer's peculiar power to spellbind its users. Fortunately, the most excessive form of this electronic enchantment seems to have lost its hold on the adolescent imagination; the video arcades are fast declining in popularity. But what we have seen there at its extreme is a capacity to fascinate that has been connected with the computer since the earliest stored-program machines arrived in the universities. It reaches back to the first generation of young hackers at a few select computer labs, like that at MIT. Hackers have always been a freakish minority, highly gifted minds for whom the intricacies of the computer can become an obsession, if not an addiction; yet they play a crucial role in the history of the technology. They were the first to give themselves fully to the strange interplay between the human mind and its clever mechanical counterfeit. That interplay deserves the careful attention of educators because it carries within it a hidden curriculum that arrives in the classroom with the computer.

Among the hackers, one of the main attractions of the machine was the enthralling sense of power it gave its user, or rather its master. For one did not simply use a computer, one had to take intellectual control of it. This was a complex machine, an "embodiment of mind," as Warren McCulloch once described it, and it could easily elude effective application. Yet, even when it did so, its misbehavior arose from some rigorously consistent extension of its programming that demanded understanding. It was not like an automobile, which would malfunction simply because a part wore out; its problems were not merely physical. They could only be corrected by tracking the bug through the dense logic of the machine's program. But if the hacker mastered that logic, he could bend the computer to his will. ("His" is historically correct here; notably, nearly all the early hackers, like most hackers since, were male, many of them living in "bachelor mode.") As one computer genius reported to Steven Levy, who has written the best history of the early hackers, there was a day when he came to the "sudden realization" that "the computer wasn't so smart at all. It was just some dumb beast, following orders, doing what you told it to in exactly the order you determined. You could control it. You could be God." [19]

But the satisfaction of becoming the machine's God, of lowering it to the status of a "dumb beast," is not available to everyone; only to those who can outsmart the smart machine. First it has to be respected as an uncanny sort of mind, one that can perform many mental tricks better than its user. The relationship of the human being to the machine is, thus, an ambivalent one, a complex mixture of sensed inferiority and the need to dominate, of dependence and mastery. "Like Aladdin's lamp, you could get it to do your bidding." That is how Levy describes a certain exhilarating moment of truth in the early hackers' encounter with the computer. But like Aladdin's lamp, the machine holds a genie more powerful than the human being who temporarily commands its obedience.

The word *power* is freely sprinkled through the literature of computers. The computer is a "powerful tool"; it is fueled by "powerful theories" and "powerful ideas." "Computers are not good or bad," Sherry Turkle concludes in her study of the psychology of young computer users. "They are powerful."[20] As we have seen, computer scientists have been willing to exaggerate that power to superhuman, even godlike dimensions. Perhaps it will soon be "an intelligence beyond man's." These heady speculations on the part of respected authorities are not simply whimsical diversions; they are images and aspirations that weave themselves into the folklore of the computer and become embedded in the priorities that guide its development. They are intimately involved in the sense of power that surrounds the machine, even as it is playfully presented to children at the basic level of computer literacy.

This can be a deeply illuminating educational moment for children—if it comes to them in the right way. It is their introduction to the form of power that most distinguishes their species: the power of the mind. At some point, they must learn that the phantom cunning and resourcefulness of the mind provides a greater biological advantage than size and strength, that intelligence counts for more than the brute force of muscle or of engines that replace muscle. In ancient Greece, children learned the value of cunning from the exploits of Odysseus, the man "of many devices." American Indian children learned cleverness from the mythic figure of Coyote the Trickster. All folklore features these masters of guile, who teach that a good trick may outdo the strongest sinews in the risky adventures of life.

In the modern West, the survival power of the mind has come to be concentrated in the "many devices" of our technology, and now most importantly in a smart machine which is the culmination of that technology. Whatever simple, gamelike computer exercises children may learn, they are also learning that the computer possesses what adults regard as the highest kind of power, a power that is similar to what human beings do when they lay plans, store up information, solve problems: something mindlike.

Because of this mindlikeness, the little box with the video screen on top, which doesn't look anything like a person, has come to be surrounded by all sorts of personifications. One "talks" to the computer. It "understands"—or doesn't understand. It "asks" and "answers" questions. It "remembers" things. It says "please" and "thank you." Above all, it "teaches" and "corrects" because it "knows" things and knows them better. If computer literacy takes hold in our schools, students may not be learning these mindlike qualities from another human being, but most often from a machine. Even if they are also learning from a teacher, the teacher will not be a "powerful" device. No one—certainly no computer scientist—has ever described a teacher's mind as "a powerful tool." Why not? Because teachers cannot know as much as the box. The box can hold lots more information. Even if the little computer in the classroom is limited in its capacity, the children know there are other, bigger computers that are running the world they live in. They can be seen in the bank, the store, the doctor's office. And when all the computers are put together, they have a power no teacher can have. They never make mistakes. That is the power which adults respect and would have children aspire to: the power of always being right, quickly and absolutely. But this is a power that can only come through the machine. As one children's book puts it: "Computers never make mistakes. If there is a mistake, it is made by the people who are using the computer or because the computer is broken."[21] The mixture of loose, anthropomorphic metaphors, interactive software, and commercial imagery that accompany the computer into the classroom brings with it a clear, if subliminal, lesson. It is the lesson the computer's inventors and dominant users have ingrained in the technology: a conception of thinking, of order, of intellectual priorities. It goes something like this:

Here is a form of power. It is a power of the mind. It is the greatest power of the mind—the power to process limitless information with absolute correctness. We live in an Information Age that needs that power. Getting a job, being successful, means acquiring that power. The machine has it; you don't. As time goes on, the machine will have more and more of it. It will deserve that power because it fits better with the world than human brains. The only human brains that can be trusted are those that use the machine to help them think.

This lesson can be transmitted in an unthreatening, even inviting way. That is the style of all computer instruction. Start simple. Make it fun. Build confidence. Ideally, the machine should be "user friendly"—a curiously condescending phrase which suggests that the machine is being kind enough to simplify and slow down for less talented users who need to be babied along. Most encouraging of all, the machine will share its power with its users. It can be domesticated and brought into one's home as a mental servant. All one needs to do is adjust to the machine's way of thinking. Becoming computer literate, comments Paul Kalaghan, dean of computer science at Northeastern University, "is a chance to spend your life working with devices smarter than you are, and yet have control over them. It's like carrying a six-gun on the old frontier." [22]

A PRIVATE UNIVERSE

■

To those who gain access to its power, the computer offers a tempting reward. As one hacker puts it: "You can create your own universe, and you can do whatever you want within that. You don't have to deal with people." [23] Once again, this is an attraction that can be seen at its extreme in video game addicts. But it is there even in the current fascination of financiers and business people with spreadsheet manipulations. On the computer, one can create a self-contained fantasy world of exact logic, predictable parameters, selected data points. At some point, where one's talent to work the machine has developed sufficiently, that world laps over into one of the computer's most impressive technical capacities: simulation. For engineers and scientists (possibly even behavioral scientists) this can be an invaluable resource. It offers the chance to investigate imaginary scenarios, running through one "what if" after another. But the graphic precision and commanding clarity with which a simulation unfolds on the video screen may lead to a serious confusion, especially for children. The model—a neat, predictable private universe—may begin to look like a better "reality."

Simulation, one must remember, applies *only* to models. The computer, on cue, manipulates a set of hypothetical assumptions about reality, not reality itself. It may do this to study the long-range or extreme implications of those assumptions, or perhaps to play off assumptions against one another. In all that it does in this mode, the computer can never be "wrong." Its simulations will always be coherent and logically consistent. Of course, what it is doing may have no relationship whatever to the world outside its program. Yet, because it offers a manageable little "reality" of its own, it may tempt its user's attention away from the messy, frustrating angularities of imperfect daily life. This is especially apt to be the case where hypothetical "facts" take the place of data for the sake of the simulation.

Here, for example, is "a system for teaching research design through computer simulation" as one of the major educational software companies presents it in its instructional material. The system is called Exper Sim (for experimental simulation), a program available as part of Control Data Corporation's much publicized PLATO courseware. Exper Sim is a way of teaching "scientific method" by simulations that overcome the "time limitations" of the classroom. As Control Data explains the program, it enables "students to run experiments on a computer which has been programmed to generate appropriate data. The computer serves as a replacement for actual data collection, saving time and obviating the need for costly lab space, equipment, and supervision."

One notes at once how, in the name of economy and efficiency, the student's experience is being restricted to the computer, which, supposedly, contains all the data needed. In the experiment, the student receives a list of variables from the instructor, formulates a hypothesis, and "considers what data he would like to collect to test that hypothesis." The experiment is then fed into the computer, which provides him with "raw" information of the sort he would have collected had he actually performed the experiment. After analyzing these data, the student plans another experiment aimed at refining his research strategy and expanding his conclusions.

What one sees here is the very real possibility that the student and the computer will become a closed system which reaches "conclusions" based on nothing but simulations. The machine has become a "replacement for actual data collection." But how is this possible? Computers process information; they do not "collect" or "generate" it.

This confusion shows up more dramatically in the use of computers to redo classic experiments for educational purposes. One such example is Mendel's famous breeding experiments, which underlie the laws of genetic inheritance.[24] A simulation can be run which rapidly displays the predicted outcome of the theory over many generations. Obviously, this saves a great deal of time. But it also goes a long way toward falsifying real science. Because this is *not* an experiment; it is the *simulation* of an experiment, and thus a severe reduction of reality. The experiment, after all, already edits reality for purposes of focus and control; the simulation now edits the experiment by eliminating the real scientific work involved: the careful arrangement of apparatus, the manipulation of materials, the false starts and pitfalls, the watchful, often boring waiting, the painstaking discriminations among results. But even worse, it neatly eliminates the risk, which is the whole point of experimentation. True experiments must stand the chance of failing to prove their hypothesis. In the simulation, however, everything always comes out right, because Mendel's theory and all his judgments have been programmed in. Yet, scientists who have troubled to repeat Mendel's work have always had to struggle with the fact that real, living sweet peas (or fruit flies) never fall obediently into discrete categories. They present blurred, fuzzy, intermediate, and borderline cases, which require difficult judgments on which different observers disagree. Perhaps, as some scientists suspect, even Mendel allowed his theory to shape his data: an important aspect of science for students to learn. How truly scientific are simulations that make reality more "theoretically" neat than it ever proves to be?[25]

Simulations are a step away from the disorderly reality around us into the tidy fictions of the computer. Where the computer's often dramatic graphic powers and magisterial calculations are combined with its highly touted mastery of information, this can create the impression that students are in touch with a superior, self-sufficient reality inside the machine, a reality which they have the power to control. They need go no further. Were it not for the inordinate praise and soaring hype that surround the computer, this might not be a serious danger. Children, and the public generally, would recognize that the "universe" which we can create on a computer screen is a small, highly edited simulation of reality. Moreover, it is a universe created by a small, highly edited simulation of *ourselves*. Only one narrow band of our experience is represented in the computer: logical reason. Sensual contact, intuition, inarticulated common-sense judgments, aesthetic taste have been largely, if not wholly, left out. We do not bring the full resources of the self to the computer.

We live in a world where electronic images and simulations are already crowding the larger, more intractable facts of life out of people's awareness. In our pursuit of order in an unruly world, we resort to spreadsheet projections, war games, economic forecasting, global modeling, electoral polling—the many computer abstractions that are supposed to help us manage a chaotic reality. From the time children begin playfully to pick their way through its make-believe logical landscape, the computer promises the power to understand, control, and always be right. But that power weakens toward illusion whenever we forget that what it commands is a figment of logical structures, hypothetical assumptions, and selected data—all of our own making and choosing. That illusion deepens toward pathos whenever we forget how limited a part of our own human nature went into the creation of that figment.

Of course, teachers can correct all along the line for these confusions on the part of students. But will there still be teachers in the electronic classroom? Will there be enough of them with sufficient authority in the eyes of their students? Will they, themselves products of the Information Age, still know any other reality than the computer's reality? Above all, will they believe they have the right to correct a machine which, they have been told, is rapidly evolving toward "an intelligence beyond man's"?

THE PROGRAM WITHIN THE PROGRAM

■

THE CASE OF LOGO

The computer has entered the schools on a wave of commercial opportunism. As one might expect, this has led to a great deal of often wasteful trial and error on the part of educators. The computer industry, promising the moon, has been willing to endorse any use of its product, no matter how frivolous or misconceived. Teachers have been left to pick their way through the claims as best they can. Some may hit upon beneficial applications, but there has been no overarching pedagogical philosophy to guide their improvisations.

In the midst of the confusion, there has been one notable exception. Seymour Papert, cofounder of artificial intelligence studies at MIT, is among the few computer scientists who has sought to develop a consistent educational philosophy for the use of the computer. That philosophy is deeply grounded in the complex learning theories of the Swiss psychologist Jean Piaget, with whom Papert studied for several years. The result of this merger between Piagetan psychology and artificial intelligence is the programming language Logo, which Papert has sought to elaborate into a comprehensive curriculum. More than a few clever pieces of software or a single course of study, Logo is offered as part of a radically new vision of education, the most systematic effort thus far to think through the role of the computer in the schools. At least in the view of Marvin Minsky, Papert's partner at the MIT artificial intelligence laboratory, this ranks him as "the greatest of all living educationalists."

Papert has been at work on Logo and its applications since the mid-1960s. Along the way, he has spun off the widely used educational program called Turtle Graphics and written the book *Mindstorms* (1980). He was also briefly drawn into an instructive adventure in computer politics. In the early 1980s, the French government was inspired by politician and journalist Jean-Jacques Servan-Schreiber to set up a major computer research facility, the Centre Mondial Informatique et Ressources Humaines in Paris. Servan-Schreiber's special interest was in helping Third World countries to "jump into the new information society." At his invitation, Papert wrote the key paper formulating the center's program. Along with Nicholas Negroponte of MIT, he became its codirector. Papert's vision for the center was an idealistic plan for the use of Logo as part of an international computer literacy campaign. The center was generously funded, but then quickly passed from an academic to an economic orientation, whose main goals became that of merchandising French computer equipment in the former French colonies in Africa. In less than a year, Papert, along with Negroponte, had departed from the center. A self-styled "educational utopian," he had no taste for such neoimperialist commercialization.[1]

In seeking to give the computer a significant educational identity, Papert works from a candid awareness of how often the machine is misused in the schools. He is no facile optimist. But the many abuses have not dissuaded him from believing that the computer can dramatically transform the world of education, sparking a revolution "of ideas, not of technology." For Papert, the computer can be "an instrument for teaching everything."[2]

Logo is designed to enter the child's life at a very early stage— conceivably in kindergarten—as an ingeniously accessible programming language. Papert has been at pains to point out that Logo is not just for children; it is intended as a general-purpose language equally applicable at sophisticated levels. But its distinctive feature is its availability to youngsters, and that is where it has found its main audience and market. Very little general-use software has been produced in Logo. In its educational applications, Logo is fully interactive; students can see the immediate result of the commands they give on the video screen. Usually, they start with simple geometrical graphics, using key-stroke commands to move a marker called a turtle. (Originally, there was an actual mechanical turtle connected to the computer which moved across the floor as directed. Most schools now use Logo without the toy, but the little arrow on the screen continues to be called a turtle.) The geometrical figures selected by the students are shaped by trial and error into little programs for drawing squares, circles, pentagons, etc. The language for executing the program is simple: the word *to* (as in "to circle," "to square") marks a command. Students choose their own names for these programs, which can, in turn, become subroutines within larger, more complicated programs.

Because the computer responds at once to every Logo command, students can study and correct their programs as they go along. This correct-as-you-go process is at the heart of Logo's instructional approach. Children see their mistakes; these become "bugs" that must be "debugged" by thinking back through the program and finding strategies to clear the inconsistencies. Papert emphasizes the educative importance of "the powerful idea" of debugging. It is an alternative to the tyranny of right answers which so often burdens the computer. He says,

> The question to ask about the program is not whether it is right or wrong, but if it is fixable. If this way of looking at intellectual products were generalized to how the larger culture thinks about knowledge and its acquisition, we all might be less intimidated by our fears of "being wrong."

Papert regards this as a primary benefit of the computer as an "object to think with." Because it encourages the student to try things and see how they turn out, then to correct and adjust, Logo is called a "discovery-learning" approach.

In this process of self-correcting programming, students are being made to "think about thinking." They are becoming "psychologists and epistemologists." Papert observes, "This powerful image of child as epistemologist caught my imagination while I was working with Piaget. . . . I came away impressed by his way of looking at children as the active builders of their own intellectual structures." It then became Papert's goal to use the computer as a way of helping children self-consciously build such structures. Piaget divided the child's mental development into "concrete" and "formal" stages, the latter (for example, mathematical thinking) requiring more maturity and so coming later in life. In Papert's view, the concrete, hands-on use of the computer can give the child a much earlier introduction to the formal stage of development.

There is a problem here in Papert's scheme. It is not at all clear that the students are "thinking about thinking" in a comprehensive way that might, for example, acquaint them with how an artist rather than a geometer thinks about spatial problems. Rather, they seem to be critically reflecting upon a certain kind of thinking, namely (as Papert calls it), "procedural thinking." Debugging, after all, involves finding the false step in a step-by-step logical sequence. Does debugging in this special sense apply to any other style of thought? Could one imagine a way to debug a fairy tale or a game of hide-and-seek? How would one debug a drawing of a dinosaur?

Papert likes to claim that Logo, because it is transparently interactive at every step, amounts to letting the child program the machine, rather than having the machine program the child, as in many computer exercises. He speaks of the child "teaching the machine." But it is unclear that in this respect Logo is any different from other programming languages. True, students write the program, but they must do so on the machine's terms. They must stay within the machine's language and logic—or the machine will tell them, "I don't know how to . . ." Students are free to call a square a box, and they can instruct the machine to turn the box so many degrees this way or that. But they cannot order the computer to put a Hobbit in the box, or to make the box grow wings and fly away to Middle Earth. Logo grants the children control over an experimental "microworld" in which to do their programming; but the microworld is not the full terrain of the human imagination. It is, at last, a two-dimensional computer screen which can only display the capacities of the program. Logo has a repertory of just so many colors, so many shapes (an airplane, a truck, a rocket, a ball, a box, etc). It is well suited to geometrical play but not to fantasy that oversteps those narrow boundaries. As I read Papert's words, I found myself haunted by the image of the prisoner who has been granted complete freedom to roam the "microworld" called jail: "Stay inside the wall, follow the rules, and you can do whatever you want."

Through Logo, Papert believes the child "acquires a sense of mastery over a piece of the most modern and powerful technology." Like many computer enthusiasts, he is much concerned with power; the word *powerful* appears prominently throughout *Mindstorms*. In one of the most developed Logo workbooks (Daniel Watt's *Learning with Logo),* the phrase *powerful idea*—taken from Papert—appears as a little flag that punctuates the presentation in each chapter. But as with all computer exercises, the mastery comes through adapting to the machine's way of doing things. The same ambiguous relationship between power and dependence remains in Logo as in other computer curricula; the same illusion of control hovers over Papert's microworlds.

Most Logo curricula start with turtle geometry and soon end off after a small but useful repertory of basic programs has been learned. This may be enough to give the child a substantial taste of programming. But Papert's vision of Logo in the classroom is far more ambitious. He believes it can be used throughout the curriculum. It is at this point that Logo, the most fully elaborated of all the computer educational programs, reveals the pitfalls that enthusiasts may overlook.

Consider, for example, how the Logo curriculum seeks to embrace art.* Children are told that they can draw "anything." Accordingly, the exercise begins with a free-hand sketch. Now such a sketch, if it were done with care and imagination, might qualify with most teachers as, in and of itself, an art lesson. But with Logo, this is only a preliminary stage. The child is next instructed to *simplify* the sketch by analyzing it into a number of component geometrical forms. A truck, for example, becomes a big box and a small box sitting atop two circles for wheels. The constructivist artist Piet Mondrian might have approved of such exercises in geometrical abstraction, but even this is still preliminary. Logo actually takes hold with the next step, which is to write a program that will direct the computer to draw these boxes and circles on the video screen with everything in its correct place. This is tricky and is sure to involve lots of trial and error. Finally, when all the components are programmed,

---

* Throughout the remainder of this chapter, I will be following the lesson plans developed in Daniel Watt's *Learning with Logo* (New York: McGraw-Hill, 1983). Watt has worked extensively with Papert and the MIT Logo Group and has taken his lessons into schools for testing and revision. The material cited here on art and poetry comes from chapters 6 and 13.

the whole combination can be tucked away in a single command, TO TRUCK. When it is given, the cursor quickly draws a truck. If all goes well, it will look like this:

And here is the program that drew the truck, with all its subprograms, each of which was worked out as a separate exercise and then incorporated in the total program:

```
TO  TRUCK
BIGBOX
    SUBPROGRAM: REPEAT  4  [FORWARD  60  RIGHT  90]
                END
MOVEOVER
    SUBPROGRAM: RIGHT  90  FORWARD  60  LEFT  90
                END
SMALLBOX
    SUBPROGRAM: REPEAT  4  [FORWARD  30  RIGHT  90]
                END
MOVEBACK
    SUBPROGRAM: LEFT  90  FORWARD  60  RIGHT  90
                END
WHEELS
    SUBPROGRAM: RIGHT  90
                RCIRCLE  5
                FORWARD  90
                RCIRCLE  5
                BACK  90
                LEFT  90
                END
```

Similarly, a Logo drawing of a flower becomes a series of curves programmed to be repeated through 360 degrees, and a Logo drawing of a person is a stick figure.

Unquestionably, the children who learn to produce programs for these designs have thought their way through a demanding exercise. They may be on their way to becoming first class computer programmers. What they haven't done is to learn anything about art; rather, they have been deliberately diverted from the skill of manipulating an artistic medium (crayon, pencil, brush) and the enjoyment of freely creating a picture. If their interest has been sustained through the exercise, it cannot be by the aesthetic pleasure of the task or the result, both of which are rigidly minimal. It can only be by the challenge of the programming, at which some students may be very good.

So then: can Logo teach art? Only if art is defined as what Logo can do in the way of art, which is not much. Logo does not allow the artistic imagination to romp; the child who would like to draw a horse, or a space monster, or a clown that does not look like a collection of boxes and circles is going to be out of luck. Nor does Logo allow the hand to use a pencil to sweep and shade and dance across the page. Art, like everything else Logo teaches, comes down to fingers stroking a keyboard, a mind working out a program. In a perverse sense, this may be an excellent lesson in computer science, especially in the artificial intelligence research that underlies Logo; the children learn the grand reductive principle: If the computer cannot rise to the level of the subject, then lower the subject to the level of the computer. Possibly, in the Information Age, children will find themselves living in a society where that principle has become the rule in all fields touched by the computer. Logo might then be seen as a useful preparation for "real life."

Logo gains its comprehensiveness in the classroom by finding similar ways to intrude something, *anything* the computer can do into whatever interest the child may have. Suppose the children want to dance. What does a computer have to do with that? In one videotaped Logo class I observed, students were encouraged to turn their dancing into an exercise in choreography, but not in their heads or muscles. Instead, after each few steps, they would run to the computer to stroke the keys, as if doing that made dancing real and serious. This clearly has nothing to do with the free kinesthetic play of the body, with twirling and tumbling and expressing. In the Logo classroom, the dance becomes what the computer can handle: geometrical patterns, angles, counting . . . so many steps this way, half-turn, so many steps that way. The exercise lacks the full plasticity of the body, the quality of the music, the emotional tone. But it does yield a program, and for that the children are praised. The lesson is a success.

Or take poetry. Here the student is directed to make up vocabulary lists for each part of speech: article, noun, verb, etc. Each list is then subjected to a randomizing process as part of a program for stringing words together in some specified order. Listing procedures like this are one of the special characteristics of the AI programming language called LISP, to which Logo is closely related.

At first, the result of working with randomized lists is apt to be nonsense: "A computer swims," "A refrigerator flies." So the students are told to try grouping words that "go together." This instruction is tossed off casually enough, but it is actually a mind-boggling demand if one takes it seriously. What words always "go together"? The lesson plan suggests grouping sports words, animal words, nature words. Nature words, for example, turn out to be "snakes," "drifts," "is hidden," "sleeps," "creeps," "murmurs."

The teacher is not encouraged at this point to make some cautionary remarks about the limitations of computer procedures like this. But unless that happens, something about the elusive, essentially protean nature of language will be obscured. For what the Logo lesson now demands is a linguistic absurdity. Language, by virtue of its metaphorically playful origins, simply does not fall into such categories. To which group—sport, animal, or nature—do the words "bat" and "fly" belong? It is precisely this problem of connecting words to well-defined contexts that govern their meaning which has made machine translation so nearly impossible. Behind the problem lies the interesting speculation that language, with whose fluidity and unruliness programmers have such difficulties, arises from the poetic endowment of the mind and continues to bear the stamp of its origin. That possibility may be much to the point for the benefit of budding young poets. If the sort of groupings the Logo lesson now requires were a real part of language (rather than a temporary classroom fiction) the art of metaphor and simile would not be possible. When, after all, do words for "tiger" and "fire" go together? Maybe only in the line "Tiger! Tiger! burning bright . . ."

In any case, the *Learning with Logo* workbook suggests that by following this instruction, the students may finally get results on the computer that approach some kind of coherence: "Loudly the swirling misty swirling sea sleeps." Or sometimes, the result may be intriguingly haiku-like:

> Each limpid pond
> One bird faces over the frosty fir
> Wild blue moon

This leads to the speculation, "because the words go well together, it almost seems like poetry. And if we chose our sentence pattern carefully, maybe it will *be* 'poetry.'"

Now, at some point, more inquisitive children may wonder how an electrical box can be expected to write anything that deserves to be thought of as a poem, no matter how accidentally coherent. Aren't poems *about* something? Don't they have a *meaning* that comes out of somebody's life? When the children make up poems, their own minds would not seem to be doing anything at all like the poem-program. They mean to *say* something, and that something preexists the words as a whole thought. They are not simply shuffling parts of speech through arbitrary patterns.

The Logo curriculum anticipates this question. And this is where the real lesson gets taught. In his manual *Learning with Logo*, Daniel Watt explains it this way:

> When I see a computer can produce a poem, it makes me stop and think just a little. . . . You and I know that the computer was just following a procedure. The procedure tells it to select certain types of words according to a fixed pattern. It selects the words from several long lists of different types of words:

nouns, verbs, adjectives, etc. . . . But wasn't I doing the same thing when I wrote my poem? I was following a procedure, too. The only difference was that I had a much larger choice of patterns and a bigger list of words in my head from which to choose. . . . How is that different from what the computer was doing?

At this point, the child may raise a question about the poetic importance of feelings and meanings, asking if a computer can craft a real poem from nothing more than raw linguistic materials. "Can it?" asks the Logo teacher: "I do believe that a very clever programmer could make a computer program complicated enough to write poems that would seem so 'human' that a poetry expert might have difficulty telling the difference."

The lesson goes on to give examples of more poetry simulations, but there is no hint at any point of what might be involved in "choosing our sentence patterns carefully"—which is, indeed, the whole befuddling secret of speech itself. Instead, the implication is that "poetry procedures" are not all that difficult to work out; indeed, they are just around the corner.

Some computer scientists with big computers are programming them to turn out poems, mystery stories, and other kinds of "literary works." Will there ever be a time when you won't be able to tell the difference between something written by a computer and something written by a person? Someday you may have a chance to try to answer that question for yourself.

The words are kept simple, but behind them there is a theory of mentality that emerges straight from the core of artificial intelligence doctrine. In this case, the children learn that creating literature is nothing but filtering vocabulary through linguistic formulas. Instead of dwelling awhile on the power and insight of a poet or two, the better to acquaint the children with another sensibility, the lesson hastens to teach the data processing model of thought. This leads inevitably to the conclusion that the human mind and the computer are functionally equivalent, with the computer—at least the "big computers" that belong to the scientists—well on its way toward catching up in actual performance. Thus, by allying oneself with the machine and working on its terms at strange conceptions of art and poetry, one may be able to appropriate some of its power.

As with all research in artificial intelligence, it is difficult to be sure in what spirit this program within the program is put forward. Is it another tiresome display of disciplinary chauvinism on the part of the technicians and logicians, determined to demonstrate the supremacy of their methods in the world of intellect? Or is it a sincere misconception about the nature of human creativity? In either case, the children are being exposed to a conception of art which is at once ludicrous and false. They are gaining their computer literacy at the risk of becoming cultural cripples.

Papert himself has been careful to keep the connection between Logo and artificial intelligence doctrine somewhat more tenuous. He defends his curriculum as a protracted lesson in procedural thinking, but he emphasizes that learning "to think like a computer" is mainly intended to make students self-conscious about the way the mind works more generally.

> I have invented ways to take educational advantage of the opportunities to master the art of *deliberately* thinking like a computer, according, for example, to the stereotype of a computer program that proceeds in a step-by-step, literal, mechanical fashion. . . . By deliberately learning to imitate mechanical thinking, the learner becomes able to articulate what mechanical thinking is and what it is not. The exercise can lead to greater confidence about the ability to choose a cognitive style that suits the problem.

He continues,

> I have clearly been arguing that procedural thinking is a powerful intellectual tool and even suggested analogizing oneself to a computer as a strategy for doing it. . . . The advice "think like a computer" could be taken to mean *always* think about everything like a computer. This would be restrictive and narrowing. But the advice could be taken in a much different sense, not precluding anything, but making a powerful addition to a person's stock of mental tools. . . . True computer literacy is not just knowing how to make use of computers

and computational ideas. It is knowing when it is appropriate
to do so.

That would seem reasonable enough. But the problem is, Logo
wants to be a comprehensive educational tool that can be tied into
everything. It can only do that by connecting everything the child
learns with procedural thinking, even when that makes no sense.
Moreover, if the other cognitive styles that Papert alludes to enter
the classroom at all, they do so simply as ideas in someone's head.
Procedural thinking arrives on board an expensive piece of equipment that has been aggressively merchandised to the schools as a
panacea. The teachers who offer computer instruction have similarly
been expensively trained. The financial investment alone guarantees
computer literacy will be given plenty of emphasis over as much
educational ground as possible. In addition, there is an air of urgency
surrounding the machine; the public believes the computer is associated with a skill the children must be taught for their employability.
Taken as a whole, these factors are bound to skew the curriculum
toward heavy computer prominence.

If the Logo curriculum prevails under these circumstances, the
schools may indeed be doing a great deal to help students to think
like computers. In contrast, who will teach them to think any other
way? Where, for example, will the cognitive style called art come in?
Curricula in art are notoriously underdeveloped as it is. Will the
schools now have more or less time and money to balance the computer model of thought? How will these countervailing intellectual
influences make themselves felt? The danger is that they will also be
sought in the computer, the better to get one's money's worth out of
the machine. Art will become Logo art, which, after all, does exist in
Papert's programming repertory. If that happens, it would be worse
than teaching no art at all.

That danger may seem to computer enthusiasts to be somebody
else's problem, not theirs. They may see their mission as limited to
opening the schools to a magnificent educational device. But they
may be misconceiving their own interests as mathematicians and
logicians in an ironic way. As Papert argues, Logo is intended to
teach procedural thinking. Now, there is no doubt that the mind can
be rigorously trained to think this way, and that it is a handy skill
for a range of projects—once the project has been envisioned intuitively as a whole and then chosen as a worthwhile activity. These

two tasks—envisioning things as meaningful wholes, deciding what is worthwhile—are what the mind primarily and naturally does. In time and importance, they take precedence over the mapping out of procedures: ends before means. Experts in artificial intelligence have somewhat come to understand this in their struggle to cope with the phenomena of purposeful activity and common sense in our lives. They have come to see these as meaningful wholes which somehow, intuitively, seem to divide themselves up into countless subsidiary activities. There might almost be something more musical than mathematical to the matter: an orchestration of parts that contributes to the thematic whole. Accordingly, AI researchers have sought to develop programming languages that allow for the "hierarchical self-nesting" of subroutines within larger patterns or frames of purposeful conduct. Even such commonplace projects as planning a meal or baking a cake are now understood to be enormously complex, integrated structures of routines within routines, loops within loops.[3] But none of the routines makes any sense except within the context of a chosen project. Planning things out step by step (programming) within that project is a strictly secondary activity—one that may not always be necessary. Art and poetry obviously have little to do with drafting formal, logical sequences. No skill that involves physical coordination is mastered in that way. This is why no one ever learned to ride a bicycle or play a piano by simply reading a book on the subject and memorizing the rules. If a cook, a carpenter, or the captain of a ship had to write out all the procedures that went into their day's work, they would die of old age before they got the job done.

For that matter, even mathematics—Logo's strong point—may not have much to do with procedural thinking, at least not at its highest levels, where the joy and the creativity of the field are to be found. Mathematicians I have met (as distinct from computer scientists) seem quite willing to admit that they work by strange fits and starts of inspiration, by hunches, guesses, insights, by the sudden formation of surprising gestalts. How else to explain the fact that they ever get stuck trying to solve a problem, since all the logic they need is presumably there in their heads? How to explain the more interesting fact that, after being stuck for weeks, months, years, they may at last break through to a solution: the "ah ha!" experience. I know mathematicians who claim to sleep on a problem and wake up with the answer. What is that all about? Probably the question is better left to the psychologists than the logicians.

The computer model of thought may distort the fundamental nature of mathematics as much as it does art. As a mathematician of my acquaintance once remarked, "The computer people don't seem to realize that higher mathematics was created by a mystic named Pythagoras. It wasn't invented to measure things; it was meant to be a vision of God." It is not difficult to imagine what artists and poets might have to say about Logo in their fields; but how many mathematicians would agree that mathematics is the same as programming?

As Papert realizes, it is extremely difficult to think procedurally; students have to be lured into it cleverly and then work at it with great persistence. Has it ever occurred to Logo educators that there may be a reason for the seeming strain of the exercise? It may be because the mind does not always and spontaneously solve problems in that way, especially the young and growing mind. Children may be much more absorbed at feeling their way through the major contours of mental life. They may be preoccupied with learning about the nature of human projects and the way adults decide among them. Envisioning things as meaningful wholes, choosing among them: this may be the first order of intellectual business for children. Careful, logical plotting of procedures may be premature for them, and so a distraction. Which is not to say that some of them may not be made interested in the specific task of programming a few geometrical problems. These can be made entertaining puzzles in their own right —like solving riddles or playing board games.

Computers "think" procedurally because it is the best they can do. Therefore, the people who program them have to think that way. But this is a special skill that we may value only because we have a machine in our lives that requires it. If we bring that machine into the classroom, will children be learning anything of basic importance about the natural habits and talents of mind? Or will they, by programming computers, simply be learning how to think like computer programmers?

In spite of my reservations about Logo, I would not vote against its use as a means of teaching basic programming skills. There are children who will be good at programming and who will enjoy developing their talents. They should have the chance—provided the schools can afford the costs without losing quality in other areas. In the case of Logo, those costs are apt to be high because it is perhaps the most machine-time intensive of all approaches to computer literacy. There have to be a lot of machines available for the students to get the full benefit.

But precisely because it stems from a comprehensive and ambitiously conceived pedagogical theory, Logo should serve to warn us of the danger posed by the computer in the classroom. That danger would seem to be obvious: once there, the computer may be used to teach what it is inherently incapable of teaching—except in the form of a bad caricature. Many in the computer science establishment may not recognize that such a danger exists. Their data processing model of the mind encourages them to bring the computer into all areas of the curriculum.

What can one do in the face of this formidable pressure but fall back on the one absolute principle in educational philosophy? *Never cheapen.* Any method, any device, any pedagogical philosophy that depreciates the subject taught should be viewed with suspicion and used with caution. A curriculum in computer literacy that aspires to the generality of Logo runs the real risk of cheapening whole areas of intellect. One would hope that teachers recognized that risk when it entered the classroom. And having recognized it, one would hope they retained enough professional authority against the data merchants and the computer enthusiasts to speak out and draw some defensive perimeters around the minds of the young.

OF IDEAS AND DATA

■

IDEAS COME FIRST

■

In raising these questions about the place of the computer in our schools, it is not my purpose to question the value of information in and of itself. For better or worse, our technological civilization needs its data the way the Romans needed their roads and the Egyptians of the Old Kingdom needed the Nile flood. To a significant degree, I share that need. As a writer and teacher, I must be part of the 5 to 10 percent of our society which has a steady professional appetite for reliable, up-to-date information. I have long since learned to value the services of a good reference library equipped with a well-connected computer.

Nor do I want to deny that the computer is a superior means of storing and retrieving data. There is nothing sacred about the typed or printed page when it comes to keeping records; if there is a faster way to find facts and manipulate them, we are lucky to have it. Just as the computer displaced the slide rule as a calculating device, it has every right to oust the archive, the filing cabinet, the reference book, if it can prove itself cheaper and more efficient.

But I do want to insist that information, even when it moves at the speed of light, is no more than it has ever been: discrete little bundles of fact, sometimes useful, sometimes trivial, and never the substance of thought. I offer this modest, common-sense notion of information in deliberate contradiction to the computer enthusiasts and information theorists who have suggested far more extravagant definitions. In the course of this chapter and the next, as this critique unfolds, it will be my purpose to challenge these ambitious efforts to extend the meaning of information to nearly global proportions. That project, I believe, can only end by distorting the natural order of intellectual priorities. And insofar as educators acquiesce in that distortion and agree to invest more of their limited resources in information technology, they may be undermining their students' ability to think significantly.

That is the great mischief done by the data merchants, the futurologists, and those in the schools who believe that computer literacy is the educational wave of the future: they lose sight of the paramount truth that *the mind thinks with ideas, not with information.* Information may helpfully illustrate or decorate an idea; it may, where it works under the guidance of a contrasting idea, help to call other ideas into question. But information does not create ideas; by itself, it does not validate or invalidate them. An idea can only be generated, revised, or unseated by another idea. A culture survives by the power, plasticity, and fertility of its ideas. Ideas come first, because ideas define, contain, and eventually produce information. The principal task of education, therefore, is to teach young minds how to deal with ideas: how to evaluate them, extend them, adapt them to new uses. This can be done with the use of very little information, perhaps none at all. It certainly does not require data processing machinery of any kind. An excess of information may actually crowd out ideas, leaving the mind (young minds especially) distracted by sterile, disconnected facts, lost among shapeless heaps of data.

It may help at this point to take some time for fundamentals.

The relationship of ideas to information is what we call a *generalization.* Generalizing might be seen as the basic action of intelligence; it takes two forms. *First,* when confronted with a vast shapeless welter of facts (whether in the form of personal perceptions or secondhand reports), the mind seeks for a sensible, connecting pattern. *Second,* when confronted with very few facts, the mind seeks to create a pattern by enlarging upon the little it has and pointing it in the direction of a conclusion. The result in either case is some general statement which is not in the particulars, but has been imposed upon them by the imagination. Perhaps, after more facts are gathered, the pattern falls apart or yields to another, more convincing possibility. Learning to let go of an inadequate idea in favor of a better one is part of a good education in ideas.

Generalizations may take place at many levels. At the lowest level, they are formulated among many densely packed and obvious facts. These are cautious generalizations, perhaps even approaching the dull certainty of a truism. At another level, where the information grows thinner and more scattered, the facts less sharp and certain, we have riskier generalizations which take on the nature of a guess or hunch. In science, where hunches must be given formal rigor, this is where we find theories and hypotheses about the physical world, ideas that are on trial, awaiting more evidence to strengthen, modify, or subvert them. This is also the level at which we find the sort of hazardous generalizations we may regard as either brilliant insights or reckless prejudices, depending upon our critical response: sweeping statements perhaps asserted as unassailable truths, but based upon very few instances.

Generalizations exist, then, along a spectrum of information that stretches from abundance to near absence. As we pass along that spectrum, moving away from a secure surplus of facts, ideas tend to grow more unstable, therefore more daring, therefore more controversial. When I observe that women have been the homemakers and childminders in human society, I make a safe but uninteresting generalization that embraces a great many data about social systems past and present. But suppose I go on to say, "And whenever women leave the home and forsake their primary function as housewives, morals decline and society crumbles." Now I may be hard pressed to give more than a few questionable examples of the conclusion I offer. It is a risky generalization, a weak idea.

In Rorschach psychological testing, the subject is presented with a meaningless arrangement of blots or marks on a page. There may be many marks or there may be few, but in either case they suggest no sensible image. Then, after one has gazed at them for a while, the marks may suddenly take on a form which becomes absolutely clear. But where is this image? Not in the marks, obviously. The eye, searching for a sensible pattern, has projected it into the material; it has imposed a meaning upon the meaningless. Similarly in Gestalt psychology, one may be confronted with a specially contrived perceptual image: an ambiguous arrangement of marks which seems at first to be one thing but then shifts to become another. Which is the "true" image? The eye is free to choose between them, for they are both truly there. In both cases—the Rorschach blots and the Gestalt figure—the pattern is in the eye of the beholder; the sensory material simply elicits it. The relationship of ideas to facts is much like this. The facts are the scattered, possibly ambiguous marks; the mind orders them one way or another by conforming them to a pattern of its own invention. *Ideas are integrating patterns* which satisfy the mind when it asks the question, What does this mean? What is this all about?

But, of course, an answer that satisfies me may not satisfy you. We may see different patterns in the same collection of facts. And then we disagree and seek to persuade one another that one or the other of these patterns is superior, meaning that it does more justice to the facts at hand. The argument may focus on this fact or that, so that we will seem to be disagreeing about particular facts—as to whether they really *are* facts, or as to their relative importance. But even then, we are probably disagreeing about ideas. For as I shall suggest further on, facts are themselves the creations of ideas.

Those who would grant information a high intellectual priority often like to assume that facts, all by themselves, can jar and unseat ideas. But that is rarely the case, except perhaps in certain turbulent periods when the general idea of "being skeptical" and "questioning authority" is in the air and attaches itself to any dissenting, new item that comes along. Otherwise, in the absence of a well-formulated, intellectually attractive, new idea, it is remarkable how much in the way of dissonance and contradiction a dominant idea can absorb. There are classic cases of this even in the sciences. The Ptolemaic cosmology that prevailed in ancient times and during the Middle Ages had been compromised by countless contradictory observations over many generations. Still, it was an internally coherent, intellectually pleasing idea; therefore, keen minds stood by the familiar old system. Where there seemed to be any conflict, they simply adjusted and elaborated the idea, or restructured the observations in order to make them fit. If observations could not be made to fit, they might be allowed to stand along the cultural sidelines as curiosities, exceptions, freaks of nature. It was not until a highly imaginative constellation of ideas about celestial and terrestrial dynamics, replete with new concepts of gravitation, inertia, momentum, and matter, was created that the old system was retired. Through the eighteenth and nineteenth centuries, similar strategies of adjustment were used to save other inherited scientific ideas in the fields of chemistry, geology, and biology. None of these gave way until whole new paradigms were invented to replace them, sometimes with relatively few facts initially to support them. The minds that clung to the old concepts were not necessarily being stubborn or benighted; they simply needed a better idea to take hold of.

THE MASTER IDEAS

■

If there is an art of thinking which we would teach the young, it has much to do with showing how the mind may move along the spectrum of information, discriminating solid generalizations from hunches, hypotheses from reckless prejudices. But for our purposes here, I want to move to the far end of the spectrum, to that extreme point where the facts, growing thinner and thinner, finally vanish altogether. What do we find once we step beyond that point into the zone where facts are wholly absent?

There we discover the riskiest ideas of all. Yet they may also be the richest and most fruitful. For there we find what might be called the *master ideas*—the great moral, religious, and metaphysical teachings which are the foundations of culture. Most of the ideas that occupy our thinking from moment to moment are not master ideas; they are more modest generalizations. But from this point forward I will be emphasizing master ideas because they are always there in some form at the foundation of the mind, molding our thoughts below the level of awareness. I want to focus upon them because they bear a peculiarly revealing relationship to information, which is our main subject of discussion. *Master ideas are based on no information whatever.* I will be using them, therefore, to emphasize the radical difference between ideas and data which the cult of information has done so much to obscure.

Let us take one of the master ideas of our society as an example: *All men are created equal.*

The power of this familiar idea will not be lost on any of us. From it, generations of legal and philosophical controversy have arisen, political movements and revolutions have taken their course.

It is an idea that has shaped our culture in ways that touch each of us intimately; it is part, perhaps the most important part, of our personal identity.

But where did this idea come from? Obviously not from some body of facts. Those who created the idea possessed no more information about the world than their ancestors, who would, doubtless, have been shocked by such a pronouncement. They possessed far less information about the world than we in the late twentieth century may feel is necessary to support such a sweeping, universal statement about human nature. Nevertheless, those who shed their blood over the generations to defend that assertion (or to oppose it) did not do so on the basis of any data presented to them. The idea has no relationship whatever to information. One would be hard pressed even to imagine a line of research that might prove or disprove it. Indeed, where such research has been attempted (for example by inveterate IQ theorists), the result, as their critics are always quick to point out, is a hopeless distraction from the real meaning of the idea, which has nothing to do with measurements or findings, facts or figures of any kind. The idea of human equality is a statement about the essential worth of people in the eyes of their fellows. At a certain juncture in history, this idea arose in the minds of a few morally impassioned thinkers as a defiantly compassionate response to conditions of gross injustice that could no longer be accepted as tolerable. It spread from the few to the many; finding the same insurgent response in the multitude, it soon became the battle cry of an era. So it is with all master ideas. They are born, not from data, but from absolute conviction that catches fire in the mind of one, of a few, then of many as the ideas spread to other lives where enough of the same experience can be found waiting to be ignited.

Here are some more ideas, some of them master ideas, each of which, though condensed in form, has been the theme of countless variations in the philosophy, religious belief, literature, and jurisprudence of human society:

Jesus died for our sins.

The Tao that can be named is not the true Tao.

Man is a rational animal.

Man is a fallen creature.

Man is the measure of all things.

The mind is a blank sheet of paper.

The mind is governed by unconscious instincts.

The mind is a collection of inherited archetypes.

God is love.

God is dead.

Life is a pilgrimage.

Life is a miracle.

Life is a meaningless absurdity.

At the heart of every culture we find a core of ideas like these, some old, some new, some rising to prominence, some declining into obsolescence. Because those I list here in terse formulations are verbal ideas, they might easily be mistaken for intended statements of fact. They have the same linguistic form as a point of information, like "George Washington was the first president of the United States." But of course they are not facts, any more than a painting by Rembrandt is a fact, or a sonata by Beethoven, or a dance by Martha Graham. For these too are ideas; they are integrating patterns meant to declare the meaning of things as human beings have discovered it by way of revelation, sudden insight, or the slow growth of wisdom over a lifetime. Where do these patterns come from? The imagination creates them from *experience*. Just as ideas order information, they also order the wild flux of experience as it streams through us in the course of life.

This is the point Fritz Machlup makes when he observes a striking difference between "information" and "knowledge." (He is using "knowledge" here in exactly the same way I am using "idea"—as an integrating pattern.) "Information" he tells us, "is acquired by being told, whereas knowledge can be acquired by thinking."

> Any kind of experience—accidental impressions, observations, and even "inner experience" not induced by stimuli received from the environment—may initiate cognitive processes leading to changes in a person's knowledge. Thus, *new knowledge can be acquired without new information being*

received. (That this statement refers to subjective knowledge goes without saying; but there is no such thing as objective knowledge that was not previously somebody's subjective knowledge.)[1]

Ideas, then—and especially master ideas—give order to experience. They may do this in deep or shallow ways; they may do it nobly or savagely. Not all ideas are humane; some, which bid to become master ideas and may succeed, are dangerous, vile, destructive. Hitler's *Mein Kampf* is a book filled with toxic ideas that were born of vengefulness and resentment. Yet they became, for a brief interval, the master ideas of one troubled society. No one who ever read that book and hated it did so because they thought the author had gotten some of his facts wrong; no one who ever read it and loved it cared about the accuracy of its information. The appeal of the book, whether accepted or rejected, was pitched at a different level of the mind.

Here are some more ideas that, at least in my view, are just as toxic:

Society is the war of each against all.

Self-interest is the only reliable human motivation.

Let justice be done though the heavens fall.

The only good Indian is a dead Indian.

Nice guys finish last.

The end justifies the means.

My country right or wrong.

It is precisely because some ideas—many ideas—are brutal and deadly that we need to learn how to deal with them adroitly. An idea takes us into people's minds, ushers us through their experience. Understanding an idea means understanding the lives of those who created and championed it. It means knowing their peculiar sources of inspiration, their limits, their vulnerabilities and blind spots. What our schools must offer the young is an education that lets them make that journey through another mind in the light of other ideas, including some that they have fashioned for themselves from their own experience. The mind that owns few ideas is apt to be crabbed and narrow, ungenerous and defensive in its judgments. "Nothing is more dangerous than an idea," Emil Chartier once said, "when it is the only one we have."

On the other hand, the mind that is gifted with many ideas is equipped to make its evaluations more gracefully. It is open and welcoming to its own experience, yet capable of comparing that experience discriminately with the lives of others, and so choosing its convictions with care and courtesy.

EXPERIENCE, MEMORY, INSIGHT
■

One of the major liabilities of the data processing model of thought is the way in which it coarsens subtle distinctions in the anatomy of the mind. The model may do this legitimately in order to simplify for analytical purposes; all scientific models do that. But there is always the danger—and many computer scientists have run afoul of it—that the model will become reified and be taken seriously. When that happens on the part of experts who should know better, it can actually falsify what we know (or should know) about the way our own minds work.

Take, for example, the significant interplay between experience, memory, and ideas, which is the basis of all thought. I have been using the word *experience* here to refer to the stream of life as it molds the personality from moment to moment. I use the word as I believe most artists would use it; more specifically, it is experience as it would be reflected in the literary technique called stream of consciousness.

Experience in this sense is the raw material from which moral, metaphysical, and religious ideas are fashioned by the mind in search of meaning. This may seem like an imprecise definition, especially to those of an empiricist inclination. In the empiricist tradition "experience" has come to be the equivalent of information. It is the sensory data which we collect in neat, well-packaged portions to test propositions about the world in a strictly logical way. When the empiricist philosophers of the seventeenth and eighteenth centuries defined experience in this way, they were in search of a form of knowledge that would serve as an alternative to statements that were meant to be accepted on the basis of authority, hearsay, tradition, revelation, or pure introspective reasoning. Experience was intended to be that kind of knowledge which was firsthand and personally tested. It was also meant to be available for inspection by others through *their* experience. Hence, it was *public* knowledge and, as such, free of obfuscation or manipulation. This, so the empiricists argued, was really the only kind of knowledge worth having. Unless all the rest could be verified by experience, it probably did not deserve to be regarded as knowledge at all.

But experience of the kind the empiricists were after is actually of a very special, highly contrived variety. Modeled upon laboratory experimentation or well-documented, professional research, it exists almost nowhere except in the world of science—or possibly as evidence in a court of law. We do not normally collect much experience of this sort. Rather, we ordinarily take in the flow of events as life presents it—unplanned, unstructured, fragmentary, dissonant. The turbulent stream passes into memory where it settles out into things vividly remembered, half remembered, mixed, mingled, compounded. From this compost of remembered events, we somehow cultivate our private garden of certainties and convictions, our rough rules-of-thumb, our likes and dislikes, our tastes and intuitions and articles of faith.

Memory is the key factor here; it is the register of experience where the flux of daily life is shaped into the signposts and standards of conduct. Computers, we are told, also have "memories," in which they store information. But computer memory is no more like human memory than the teeth of a saw are like human teeth; these are loose metaphors that embrace more differences than similarities. It is not the least of its liabilities that the cult of information obscures this distinction, to the point of suggesting that computer memory is superior because it remembers so much more. This is precisely to misinterpret what experience is and how it generates ideas. Computers "remember" things in the form of discrete entries: the input of quantities, graphics, words, etc. Each item is separable, perhaps designated by a unique address or file name, and all of it subject to total recall. Unless the machine malfunctions, it can regurgitate everything it has stored exactly as it was entered, whether a single number or a lengthy document. That is what we expect of the machine.

Human memory, on the other hand, is the invisible psychic adhesive that holds our identity together from moment to moment. This makes it a radically different phenomenon from computer memory. For one thing, it is fluid rather than granular, more like a wave than a particle. Like a wave, it spreads through the mind, puddling up here and there in odd personal associations that may be of the most inexplicable kind. It flows not only through the mind, but through the emotions, the senses, the body. We remember things as no computer can—in our muscles and reflexes: how to swim, play an instrument, use a tool. These stored experiences lodge below the level of awareness and articulation so that there is no way to tell someone how we drive a car or paint a picture. We don't actually "know" ourselves. In an old bit of folk wisdom, the daughter asks her mother how she bakes such a good apple pie. The mother, stymied, replies: "First I wash my hands. Then I put on a clean apron. Then I go into the kitchen and bake a good apple pie."

Moreover, where we deal with remembered experience, there is rarely total recall. Experiences may be there, deeply buried in our brain and organism, but they are mostly beyond recollection. Our memory is rigorously selective, always ready to focus on what matters to us. It edits and compacts experience, represses and forgets— and it does this in ways we may never fully understand. As we live through each present moment, something immediately before us may connect with experiences that call up vivid sensory associations, pains, pleasures; these in turn may make us laugh, they may leave us sad, they may bring us to the point of nausea or deep trauma. Some of what we have experienced and stored away in memory may derive from our speechless childhood; some may be phantoms of prenatal recollection. Much is drawn from private fantasies never reported to anyone, hardly admitted to ourselves.

We may say that we remember what "interests" us; but we may also perversely conceal or recompose things that are too threatening to face. The recollections we retain are mysteriously selected, enigmatically patterned in memory. There are hot bright spots filled with rich and potent associations; there are shadowed corners which may only emerge vividly in dreams or hallucinations; there are odd, quirky zones that delight to fill up with seemingly useless, chaotic remnants—things we remember without knowing why, even items (insistent song lyrics, irritating advertising jingles) we would just as soon erase if we could . . . but we can't. If we could draw a full anatomy of memory in all its elusive variety, we would have the secret of human nature itself. The shape of memory is quite simply the shape of our lives; it is the self-portrait we paint from all we have experienced. It is not the computer scientist but a literary artist like Vladimir Nabokov who can tell us most about the strange dynamics of experience. He writes:

> A passerby whistles a tune at the exact moment that you notice the reflection of a branch in a puddle which in its turn and simultaneously recalls a combination of damp leaves and excited birds in some old garden, and the old friend, long dead, suddenly steps out of the past, smiling and closing his dripping umbrella. The whole thing lasts one radiant second and the motion of impressions and images is so swift that you cannot check the exact laws which attend their recognition, formation, and fusion. . . . It is like a jigsaw puzzle that instantly comes together in your brain with the brain itself unable to observe how and why the pieces fit, and you experience a shuddering sensation of wild magic.[2]

Experience, as Nabokov describes it here, is more like a stew than a filing system. The ingredients of a lifetime mix and mingle to produce unanticipated flavors. Sometimes a single piquant component—a moment of joy, a great sorrow, a remembered triumph or defeat—overpowers all the rest. In time, this stew boils down to a rich residue of feelings, general impressions, habits, expectations. Then, in just the right circumstance—but who can say what this will be?—that residue bubbles up into a well-formed insight about life which we may speak or paint or dance or play out for the world to know. And this becomes, whether articulately or as an unspoken existential gesture, an *idea*. Certainly, this has much to do with the climate of opinion in which we find ourselves, the traditions we share, the autobiographical momentum of our lives. But how these will combine in any given mind at any given moment and what they will produce is wholly beyond prediction. The stew of personal experience is too thick, too filled with unidentifiable elements mixed in obscure proportions. What emerges from the concoction can be genuinely astonishing. Which is only to observe what all culture tells us about ourselves: that we are capable of true originality. History teems with such marvelous examples of invention and startling conversion. Paul of Tarsus struck blind on the road to Damascus rises from the trauma to become the disciple of a savior he had never met and whose followers he had persecuted; Tolstoy, falling into an episode of suicidal depression, disowns his literary masterworks and strives to become an ascetic hermit; Gandhi, driven from the white-only compartment of a South African train, renounces his promising legal career to don a loincloth and become the crusading mahatma of his people. This is experience at work, mysteriously shaping new ideas about life in the depths of the soul.

So too all of us, as we bear witness to the emerging convictions of others, confront what they say and do with the full force of our experience. If there is a confirming resonance within us, it may be because our lives have overlapped those we encounter. But it may also be that the power of the encounter in itself—then and there in a single moment—shatters the convictions of a lifetime, and we have the sense of beginning anew, of being reborn. For there are such instances of people being unmade and remade by charismatic confrontation and the pressures of crisis. It may even be the case that these gifts of originality and sudden conversion play a crucial evolutionary role in the growth of culture. Perhaps this volatility of mind is what saves human society from the changeless rigidity of the other social animals, the ants, the bees, the beasts of the pack and the herd. We are gifted as a species with a crowning tangle of electrochemical cells which has become an idea-maker. So spontaneously does this brain of ours make ideas and play with ideas that we cannot say much more about them than that they are there, shaping our perceptions, opening up possibilities. From moment to moment, human beings find new things to think and do and be: ideas that erupt seemingly from out of nowhere. We are remarkably plastic and adaptable animals, and the range of our cultural creativity seems unlimited. It would be a great loss if, by cheapening our conception of experience, memory, and insight, the cult of information blunted these creative powers.

There are computer scientists who seem well on their way toward doing that, however. They believe they can simulate our originality on the computer by working out programs that include a randomizing element. (The Logo program for poetry which we reviewed in the previous chapter is an example of this.) Because this makes the output of the program unpredictable, it has been identified as "creative." But there is all the difference in the world between such contrived randomness and true originality. Again, the data processing model works to obscure the distinction. In the human mind, an original idea has a living meaning; it connects with experience and produces conviction. What the computer produces is "originality" at about the level of a muscular spasm; it is unpredictable, but hardly meaningful.

Of course, there are other forms of experience that come to us more neatly packaged and labeled: things learned by rote or memorized verbatim, precise instructions, procedures, names, addresses, facts, figures, directions. What such experiences leave behind is much like what fills computer memory: *information* in the proper sense of the term. Our psychological vocabulary does not clearly distinguish these different levels and textures of memory; we have simply the one word for the remembrance of things past. We *remember* a phone number; we *remember* an episode of traumatic suffering that changed our lives. To sweep these different orders of experience under the rubric *information* can only contribute to cheapening the quality of life.

"The heart has its reasons," Pascal tells us, "which reason cannot know." I would take this to mean that the minds of people are filled with ideas which well up from deep springs of mixed and muddled experience. Yet these ideas, hazy, ambiguous, contradictory as they may be, can be, for better or worse, the stuff of strong conviction. In a debate that involves such "reasons," information is rarely of much use. Instead, we must test and sample in the light of our own convictions, seeking the experience that underlies the idea. We must do what I dare say you are doing now as you read these words, which are convictions of mine presented for your consideration. You pause, you reflect, probing to discover what my moral and philosophical loyalties might be. As you try to get the *feel* of the ideas I offer, you cast about in your recollections to see if you can find there an echo of the experiences I draw upon. You may loiter more over nuances and shades of meaning than over matters of fact. Here and there you may detect distant implications or hidden assumptions that you may or may not care to endorse. Possibly you sense that some of your fondest values are challenged and you hasten to defend them.

There is no telling how this critical rumination will turn out, but one thing should be obvious: none of this is "data processing." It is the give and take of dialogue between two minds, each drawing upon its own experience. It is the play of ideas, and all the information in all the data bases in the world will not decide the issues that may stand disputed between us.

THE EMPIRICIST GAMBIT

Once they focus on the matter, many people will find the primacy of ideas so obvious that they may wonder why it has to be raised as a bone of contention at all. How have the computer scientists managed to subordinate ideas to data so persuasively? This is an intriguing historical question to which we might do well to give some attention.

Earlier in this chapter, I made reference to the empiricist school of philosophy and the way in which it has chosen to reinterpret the meaning of experience. Let us return for a moment to the impact of empiricism upon Western philosophy, for it plays a significant role in the cult of information.

Some four centuries ago, in that turbulent transitional zone that leads from the Renaissance to the modern period, the realm of knowledge in the Western world was a relatively small island of certainty surrounded by a sea of accepted mystery. At its far, unfathomable reaches, that sea merged with the mind of God, the contents of which might only be approached by an act of faith. On the island, the major bodies of thought were the scriptures, the works of the Church fathers, a handful of surviving Greek and Roman masters, and possibly a small select group of Jewish and Arab thinkers. Over several centuries of the medieval period, these sources had been worked up, often by way of brilliant elaborations, into an august repertory of knowledge that was held to answer all the questions the human mind could expect to have answered.

In such a culture, there is no such category as "information"; facts count for very little where whatever can be known is already known and has been assimilated to well-known truths. Instead of information there is confabulation: constant, sometimes inspired play with familiar ideas that are extended, combined, reshaped. By the latter part of the sixteenth century, this intellectual style was becoming more and more incompatible with the social and economic dynamism of Western society. For one thing—a dramatic thing—

new worlds were being discovered, whole continents and cultures that were unaccounted for by any existing authority. These were *discoveries*. And if there could be geographical discoveries, then why not new worlds of the mind as well? Francis Bacon used just that comparison to justify his restless quest for a "New Philosophy." He, Descartes, Galileo, Giordano Bruno were among the first to match their culture's expansive passion for physical discovery with a corresponding intellectual daring.

These seminal minds of the seventeenth century hit upon an exciting cultural project. Their proposition was this: Let us devise a kind of inquiry which will have the power to discover *new things* about the world—about its forces, and structures, and phenomena. This will be a way of thinking that will be the equivalent of the great voyages of discovery that have found new worlds across the seas. This style of inquiry, they decided, should involve rigorous, well-targeted interrogation of nature by close observation and experimentation. It should be undertaken in a spirit of total objectivity, avoiding all assumptions and presuppositions. It should simply try to see things as they really are. The result of this new method will be a growing body of solid, reliable facts, usually measurements, which have heretofore been overlooked. Then, if an observer sets about scrupulously collecting these facts, they will eventually speak for themselves, shaping themselves into great truths as vast in their scope as the size of the whole universe.

We can now recognize this method (the *novum organum*, as Bacon called it) as the distant beginning of the modern scientific world view. No one can fail to appreciate its historical contribution; but we also have enough historical perspective to know how very misconceived that method was. In its narrow focus on facts, it left out of account the crucial importance of theoretical imagination, hypothesis, speculation, and inspired guesswork—without which science would not have had its revolutionary impact. Looking back from our vantage point, we can clearly see theoretical imagination at work in the minds of Galileo, Newton, Kepler, Boyle, Hook, contours of thought which were there but which they were too close to notice. We have learned that great scientific breakthroughs are never assembled piecemeal from lint-picking research. At times, limited, fine-grained investigation may succeed in raising important doubts about a scientific theory; but it must at least have that theory before it as a target or a baseline. Without some master idea that serves that function, one would not know where to begin looking for facts. Science is structured inquiry, and the structures that guide its progress are ideas.

There was, however, a good reason why the founding fathers of modern science should have erred in the direction of overvaluing facts at the expense of ideas. In Galileo's day, the dominant ideas about nature were derived from a few sacrosanct authorities—either Christian theology or Aristotle. In order to free themselves from this increasingly restrictive heritage of tired, old ideas, these daring minds were moved to call *ideas themselves* into question. So they recommended a new point of departure, one which seemed innocuously neutral and therefore strategically inoffensive to the cultural authorities of the day: they would concentrate their attention on the clear-cut indisputable facts of common experience—the weights and sizes and temperatures of things. Facts first, they insisted. Ideas later. And this proved to be a persuasive approach. It brought to light any number of terrestrial and astronomical novelties that could not be adequately explained by Aristotle, the Bible, the Church fathers—or perhaps had never been noticed by them at all. If the mission of the early empiricists is viewed in its historical context, it can be recognized as a clever philosophical gambit whose purpose was to break down ethnocentric barriers and ecclesiastical authority. In this, it finally succeeded. By encouraging a bold skepticism about all inherited ideas, it liberated the restricted intellectual energies of Western society. Its connection with the birth of modern science will always endow it with a special status.

The trouble is, the very success of the empiricists has helped to embed a certain fiercely reductionistic conception of knowledge in our culture, one that drastically undervalues the role of the imagination in the creation of ideas, and of ideas in the creation of knowledge, even in the sciences. In our time, minds loyal to the empiricist love of fact have seized upon the computer as a model of the mind at work storing up data, shuffling them about, producing knowledge, and potentially doing it better than its human original. Those who see the world more or less in this way represent one pole in an argument which had already been joined in the days of Plato, Aristotle, and Democritus. Which is more "real," things or the ideas we have of things? Does knowledge begin in the senses or in the mind?

It is hardly my intention to try to adjudicate that argument here. I only wish to emphasize that the data processing model of the mind is not some purely objective "finding" of contemporary science. It grows from a definite philosophical commitment; it represents one side in an ancient debate, still with us and still unsettled. The empiricist side of that debate deserves to be respected for the rich contribution it has made to our philosophical heritage. We would not want to do without it. But I have found it interesting, whenever I am in the company of those who hold a rigorously empirical position, to remind them of a paradox: their viewpoint is itself an *idea*. It is an idea about ideas . . . and about knowledge, experience, and truth. As such, it is not based on fact or information, because it is this very idea which defines information in the first place. There is ultimately no way around ideas, then. They are what the mind thinks with, even when it is attacking the primacy of ideas.

For that matter, the computer is also an idea, just as all machines are. It is an idea about number, and classification, and relationship —all realized in the form of a physical invention. The proposition that the mind thinks like a computer is an idea about the mind, one that many philosophers have taken up and debated. And like every idea, this idea also can be *gotten outside of*, looked at from a distance, and called into question. The mind, unlike any computer anyone has even imagined building, is gifted with the power of irrepressible self-transcendence. It is the greatest of all escape artists, constantly eluding its own efforts at self-comprehension. It can form ideas about its own ideas, including its ideas about itself. But having done that, it has already occupied new ground; in its next effort to understand its own nature, it will have to reach out still further. This inability of the mind to capture its own nature is precisely what makes it impossible to invent a machine that will be the mind's equal, let alone its successor. The computer can only be one more idea in the imagination of its creator. Our very capacity to make jokes about computers, to spoof and mock them, arises from our intellectual distance from them. If there is anything that frustrates the technician's talent, it is open-ended potentiality.

NO IDEAS, NO INFORMATION

■

From the viewpoint of the strict, doctrinaire empiricism which lingers on in the cult of information, the facts speak for themselves. Accumulate enough of them, and they will conveniently take the shape of knowledge. But how do we recognize a fact when we see one? Presumably, a fact is not a mental figment or an illusion; it is some small, compact particle of truth. But to collect such particles in the first place, we have to know what to look for. There has to be the idea of a fact.

The empiricists were right to believe that facts and ideas are significantly connected, but they inverted the relationship. *Ideas create information,* not the other way around. Every fact grows from an idea; it is the answer to a question we could not ask in the first place if an idea had not been invented which isolated some portion of the world, made it important, focused our attention, and stimulated inquiry.

Sometimes an idea becomes so commonplace, so much a part of the cultural consensus, that it sinks out of awareness, becoming an invisible thread in the fabric of thought. Then we ask and answer questions, collecting information without reflecting upon the underlying idea that makes this possible. The idea becomes as subliminal as the grammar that governs our language each time we speak.

Take an example. The time of day, the date. These are among the simplest, least ambiguous facts. We may be right or wrong about them, but we know they are subject to a straightforward true or false decision. It is either 2:15 P.M. in our time zone, or it is not. It is either March 10, or it is not. This is information at its most irreducible level.

Yet behind these simple facts, there lies an immensely rich idea: the idea of time as a regular and cyclical rhythm of the cosmos. Somewhere in the distant past, a human mind invented this elegant concept, perhaps out of some rhapsodic or poetic contemplation of the bewilderingly congested universe. That mind decided the seemingly shapeless flow of time can be ordered in circles, the circles can be divided into equal intervals, the intervals can be counted. From this insight, imposed by the imagination on the flux of experience, we derive the clock and the calendar, the minutes, days, months, seasons we can now deal with as simple facts.

Most of our master ideas about nature and human nature, logic and value eventually become so nearly subliminal that we rarely reflect upon them as human inventions, artifacts of the mind. We take them for granted as part of the cultural heritage. We live off the top of these ideas, harvesting facts from their surface. Similarly, historical facts exist as the outcroppings of buried interpretive or mythic insights which make sense of, give order to the jumbled folk memory of the past. We pick up a reference book or log on to a data base and ask for some simple information. When was the Declaration of Independence signed and who signed it? Facts. But behind those facts there lies a major cultural paradigm. We date the past (not all societies do) because we inherit a Judeo-Christian view of the world which tells us that the world was created in time and that it is getting somewhere in the process of history. We commemorate the names of people who "made history" because (along other lines) we inherit a dynamic, human-centered vision of life which convinces us that the efforts of people are important, and this leads us to believe that worthwhile things can be accomplished by human action.

When we ask for such simple points of historical information, all this stands behind the facts we get back as an answer. We ask and we answer the questions within encompassing ideas about history which have become as familiar to us as the air we breathe. But they are nonetheless human creations, each capable of being questioned, doubted, altered. The dramatic turning points in culture happen at just that point—where new idea rises up against old idea and judgment must be made.

What happens, then, when we blur the distinction between ideas and information and teach children that information processing is the basis of thought? Or when we set about building an "information economy" which spends more and more of its resources accumulating and processing facts? For one thing, we bury even deeper the substructures of ideas on which information stands, placing them further from critical reflection. For example, we begin to pay more attention to "economic indicators"—which are always convenient, simple-looking numbers—than to the assumptions about work, wealth, and well-being which underlie economic policy. Indeed, our orthodox economic science is awash in a flood of statistical figments that serve mainly to obfuscate basic questions of value, purpose, and justice. What contribution has the computer made to this situation? It has raised the flood level, pouring out misleading and distracting information from every government agency and corporate board-room. But even more ironically, the hard focus on information which the computer encourages must in time have the effect of crowding out new ideas, which are the intellectual source that generates facts.

In the long run, no ideas, no information.

COMPUTERS AND PURE REASON

■

THE LIGHT IN PLATO'S CAVE

■

Up to this point, we have been concentrating on the computer's capacity to store and retrieve seemingly limitless amounts of data. This is one of the machine's most impressive and useful powers; it is the feature that stands foremost in the minds of those who hail the advent of the Information Age. They are emphasizing the computer's ability to access data bases, of which there are already thousands in existence, and to channel this wealth of material into people's homes and workplaces.

But when we speak of the computer as a "data processor," it is easy to overlook the fact that these two words refer to two separate functions that have been united in the machine. The computer *stores* data, but it can also *process* these data—meaning it can manipulate them in various ways for purposes of comparison, contrast, classification, deduction. The data may be numbers which are being run through mathematical processes; but they may also be names, addresses, medical records, personnel files, technical instructions which are also being run through a program to be sorted, ordered, filtered, or placed in some designated sequence. Thus, when a computer is ordered to run a spreadsheet scenario for a business, it draws upon all the data it holds for that business (inventory, overhead, earnings, seasonal performance, etc.), but it also massages the data, shaping them as the program instructs. Even a simple mailing list may reorganize the material in its data bank in response to a program designed, for example, to segregate names by zip code in order to upscale the subscription list of a magazine or to edit out names on the basis of credit rating, ethnicity, age, etc.

These two operations have become so integrated in the performance of most computers that they are rarely thought of any longer as separate functions. Yet they are, and each may be given a separate evaluation. *Storing* data connects the computer with the job of record keeping; it dates back to the ledgers and filing cabinets which electronic data banks are now replacing. In this capacity, the computer mimics the faculty of memory. *Processing* data, on the other hand, represents a different line of technological descent. Here the computer dates back to the adding machine, and in this capacity, it mimics the power of human reason. For many computer enthusiasts, this second line of development is the real significance of the machine. They value its ability to work through lengthy logical-mathematical procedures with blinding speed and absolute precision. For them, this is the computer's closest approximation to the human mind.

In Chapter 4, we touched upon Seymour Papert's Logo computer curriculum. Logo is an example of a computer application that has very little to do with data; the value Papert sees in it is its capacity to teach "procedural thinking," and so to discipline the rational faculties in a way that a mathematician would find important. He believes children should be taught to "think like a computer" because he believes computers have somewhat the capacity to think like human beings and so can help children learn that mental skill.

I have argued that those who celebrate the computer as an information keeper and provider tend to underrate, if not ignore the value of ideas, assuming, as many strict empiricists have, that information somehow compiles itself automatically into knowledge without the active intervention of theoretical imagination. Yet, ironically enough, the second line of technological descent that flows into the computer—that which has to do with procedural thinking—derives from a very different philosophical tradition, one which is intimately connected with the power of pure reason. Along this rationalist line of descent, the computer draws upon a class of ideas which has proved to be uniquely persuasive and long-lived, even though it has no connection whatever with data or with human experience of any kind. These are *mathematical ideas:* ideas discovered in the light of unaided reason, fashioned from the logical structure of the mind itself.

In the history of philosophy, it is mathematics that has again and again been used as an example of a priori knowledge, knowledge which supposedly has no connection with sensory experience, with the data of observation and measurement. As Bertrand Russell observes:

> Mathematics is . . . the chief source of the belief in eternal and exact truth, as well as in a supersensible intelligible world. Geometry deals with exact circles, but no sensible object is *exactly* circular; however carefully we may use our compasses, there will be some imperfections and irregularities. This suggests the view that all exact reasoning applies to the ideal as opposed to sensible objects; it is natural to go further, and to argue that thought is nobler than sense, and the objects of thought more real than those of sense perception.[1]

The classic formulation of this idea about mathematical ideas is that of Plato, for whom geometry served as the model of all reliable knowledge. Plato assumed that geometrical ideas are born into the mind as our one sure foundation for thought. In the darkness and confusion of life, we have the certainty of mathematics to guide us. In his famous Allegory of the Cave, Plato portrays the human race as a population of wretched slaves confined by their physical mortality to a tenebrous dungeon where they can see nothing but a blurred show of animated shadows; they know nothing that is not impermanent and illusory. In their squalid prison, there is but one distant glimmer of illuminating sunlight. Only the true philosopher discerns it; it is the power of pure reason, which gives us, especially in the form of mathematics, a knowledge of eternal verities, the pure forms that transcend the flux of time and the frailty of the flesh.

Over the centuries, in a variety of ways, philosophers have taken issue with Plato's theory of knowledge and the mystique which it lends to mathematics. Still, for all the criticism, there remains a haunting quality to mathematical ideas, a trust in the clarity of numbers and of mathematical logic that lingers on in modern science and which survives in cybernetics and information theory. Plato's mysticism may have been banished from these new sciences, but the spell of geometrical certainty remains. For, ironically enough, the machine that gives the cult of information its greatest strength is grounded in a body of ideas—mathematical ideas—which has nothing to do with information, and which might conceivably be seen as the best proof we have to offer of the primacy of ideas.

As computers have grown "smarter" (meaning faster, more capacious, more intricate in their programming) over the past two decades, computer scientists have often exhibited some uneasiness with the name of their machine. As most recent textbooks in computer science hasten to tell students in the first chapter, the computer is no longer merely a computing instrument; it has transcended its lowly origins to become a form of artificial intelligence in the broadest sense. Thus, Margaret Boden observes,

> It is essential to realize that a computer is not a mere "number cruncher," or supercalculating arithmetic machine, although this is how computers are commonly regarded by people having no familiarity with artificial intelligence. Computers do not crunch numbers; they manipulate symbols. . . . Digital computers originally developed with mathematical problems in mind, are in fact general purpose symbol manipulating machines. . . .
>
> The terms "computer" and "computation" are themselves unfortunate, in view of their misleading arithmetical connotations. The definition of artificial intelligence previously cited—"the study of intelligence as computation"—does not imply that intelligence is really counting. Intelligence may be defined as the ability creatively to manipulate symbols, or process information, given the requirements of the task in hand.[2]

It is certainly true that computers have evolved a long way from being super adding machines. But it is also true that, in large measure, the reputation which computer science and computerized forms of "intelligence" have acquired in our popular culture borrows heavily upon the age-old mystique of mathematics. Insofar as computer scientists believe that computers are "machines who think" and that may someday think better than people, it is because of the machine's historic connection with what the scientists and technicians have always taken to be the clearest, most productive kind of thinking:

mathematics. The promise that many enthusiasts see in the computer is precisely that it will, in time, produce a form of intelligence which will apply the exactitude of mathematics to every other field of culture. The computer's repertory of symbols may no longer be limited to numbers; nevertheless, the hope remains that its more sophisticated programs will be able to manipulate symbols with the logical rigor of mathematical reasoning. Fritz Machlup makes the point that the word *computation* has taken on a vastly extended usage, now covering whatever computers can do as symbol manipulators. This leads to a good deal of public confusion. When, for example, a cognitive scientist speaks of artificial intelligence programs, and people "read a sentence or clause to the effect that 'mental processes are computational processes,' they are most likely to think of processes of numerical computation—but would be wrong."[3]

It is, however, this very error which works to enhance the prestige of the computer by making it all too easy to believe that whatever runs through a computer thereby acquires the ironclad certainty of pure mathematics. Though they would blush to associate themselves with Plato's mysticism, many opportunistic figures in computer science and especially artificial intelligence have exploited that error for all it is worth in the confused public mind.

It is curious how, at times in the most unpredictable way, something of the old Platonic spirit surfaces in the world of computer science. Plato was convinced that it was the corruption of the flesh that separates us from the highest forms of knowledge. So he recommended the study of geometry as a sort of purgation of the senses that would elevate the mind above the body's mortality. We can see exactly this same alliance of the ascetic and the mathematical in the following passage from Robert Jastrow's study of "mind in the universe":

> When the brain sciences reach this point, a bold scientist will be able to tap the contents of his mind and transfer them into the metallic lattices of a computer. Because mind is the essence of being, it can be said that this scientist has entered the computer, and that he now dwells in it.
>
> At last the human brain, ensconced in a computer, has been liberated from the weakness of the mortal flesh. . . . It is in control of its own destiny. The machine is its body; it is the machine's mind. . . .

It seems to me that this must be the mature form of intelligent life in the Universe. Housed in indestructible lattices of silicon, and no longer constrained in the span of its years by the life and death cycle of a biological organism, such a kind of life could live forever.[4]

In this disembodied form, Jastrow imagines that the computer will transform us into "a race of immortals."

THE OLD MATHEMATICAL MAGIC
■

The mathematical model of absolute certainty is one of the undying hopes of our species. As tough-minded as most scientists might be (or wish to appear to be) in their response to the old mathematical magic, that Platonic dream survives, and no place more vividly than in the cult of information. Data—the speed and quantity of their processing—may be what the cult most often emphasizes in its celebration of the computer. But quite as important as the data is the mathematical precision with which the computer's programs manipulate the information fed into them. This is what computer scientists mean by the term *effective procedure*. We are told that a computer can do anything for which an "effective procedure" is given. The phrase means "a set of rules (the program) unambiguously specifying certain processes, which processes can be carried out by a machine built in such a way as to accept those rules as instructions determining its operations."[5] The search for such a procedure would be pure whimsey were it not for the fact that there is one field of thought which offers us a model of just such strict logicality: mathematics, the field that produced the computer in the first place. When limited to the realm of what *can* be treated with such logical rigor, the computer functions at its full strength. But the further we stray from that realm, the more rapidly its powers fade.

Unfortunately, not all computer scientists are willing to concede that point. They forget—and help the public forget—that mathematical ideas are of a very special kind. They are *formal* ideas, meaning they are built from axioms by unambiguously specifiable rules. They can be analyzed into parts, and the parts are ultimately logical principles and postulates that lend themselves to mechanical manipulation. The value of mathematical ideas lies precisely in this analytical clarity and nonambiguity. Within their field of proper application, they have the power to confer logical transparency; they strip away ambiguity to reveal the skeletal structure that connects parts, stages, and procedures. They can be programmed. This is because, by an astonishing exercise of the human imagination, mathematical systems have been developed outside the real world of daily experience, which is more often than not blurred, fuzzy, and infinitely complex.

Since there are areas of the real world that appear to approximate formal order, there are portions of mathematics that can be applied to that world in order to isolate its more measurable and rule-abiding elements. Where that happens, we have the realms of theoretical and applied science. And so here too computers can be highly useful in channeling large amounts of information through scientific and technical programs. But even here we should bear in mind that there are underlying ideas of a nonmathematical kind (we might call them insights or, perhaps, articles of faith) that govern all scientific thought. Take our basic conviction that there is a rational order to nature, a pattern which the mind can grasp. This is the most fundamental of scientific ideas. But what is it based upon? It is a hunch or a desperate hope worked up perhaps from fleeting perceptions of symmetries or regularities in nature, recurring rhythms and cycles—all of which are continually dissolving in the "buzzing, booming confusion" of daily life. But working with that idea as a kind of filter, we screen out the exceptions and distractions and find deeper regularities which begin to look like an *order* of things. But what kind of order? Our science has chosen to look for the order of numbers. We work from Galileo's potent idea that "the great book of nature is written in the language of mathematics." But we might have chosen another kind of order. There is the order of music (thus the astronomer Kepler spent most of his life searching for the harmony of the spheres); there is the order of architecture and of drama; there is the order of a story (a myth) told over and over; there is the order of a god's behavior, where we watch for reward and punishing, wrath and mercy. Which order is the most important? Making that choice is also an idea to be selected from all the possibilities.

Very nearly the whole of modern science has been generated out of a small collection of metaphysical, even aesthetic ideas such as:

The universe consists of matter in motion. (Descartes)

Nature is governed by universal laws. (Newton)

Knowledge is power. (Bacon)

None of these ideas is a conclusion arrived at by scientific research; none of them is the result of processing information. Rather, they are premises that make scientific research possible and lead to the discovery of confirming data. Once again, these are master ideas about the world, and like all master ideas, they transcend information. They arise from another dimension of the mind, from a capacity for insight that is perhaps akin to the power of artistic and religious inspiration.

There is no question but that in the area of mathematical and scientific ideas, the computer supplements the mind significantly. It can carry out calculations at blinding speed; it can make hypothetical projections; it can offer amazingly flexible graphic representations; it can produce complex simulations that stretch the imagination. This is quite a lot for a machine to offer. Yet it may be that even in the sciences, the computer's proficiency as an information processor has its liabilities. At least one leading scientist has raised a provocative warning about the use of computers in astronomy. Sir Bernard Lovell writes:

> I fear that literal-minded, narrowly focused computerized re-
> search is proving antithetical to the free exercise of that
> happy faculty known as serendipity. . . . Would the existence
> of radio galaxies, quasars, pulsars and the microwave back-
> ground ever have been revealed if their discovery had de-
> pended on the computerized radio observations of today? . . .
> The computers act as very narrow filters of information; they
> must be oriented to specific observations. In other words,
> they have to be programmed for the kinds of results that the
> observer expects. Does this mean, then, that computers are
> antiserendipitous? And if they are, should we not be troubled
> that they may be obscuring from our understanding further
> major features of the universe?[6]

THE SEDUCTIONS OF SOFTWARE
■

There is a predictable response to the argument I have been making here. It would insist that computers can *also* be programmed with nonmathematical ideas. Indeed, this is done all the time. For this is what a "program" is: an algorithm, a set of instructions that organizes information for some purpose. The ideas that animate programs may be too obvious to merit comment, as in the case of a family budget program that operates from the assumption that bankruptcy is undesirable and should therefore be avoided. (The program may then even dramatize the warning with a sharp command or a blinking signal.) Or the idea may be as brutally simple as the goal of the video game which dictates that Ms. Pacman should eat without being eaten.

Many programs are a great deal more complex than that. There are integrated management packages that claim to do the jobs of an entire office staff and perhaps a vice president or two. There are computer games that are fiendishly complicated, to the point of requiring as much intuition as calculation—meaning the complexities of strategy outdistance logical analysis. The trouble is, in the world of computer science *both* the ideas that govern the program *and* the data that are put through the program have come to be included within the concept of "information." The cult of information has gained a great deal for its mystique by bringing the program as well as the data within its province. But this can be a disastrous confusion. For it is like saying that there is no difference between, on the one hand, the architectural design of a building (the blueprints) and, on the other, all the measurements of all the materials that will be used in constructing that building. The materials and their measurements comprise a vast mass of detailed information that might usefully be entered into a computer under various convenient and cross-referenced headings and then called up for review at the push of a button. Yet it is the design of the building that holds this shapeless chaos of quantities together and gives it meaning. This is what answers the question, What is all this information about? It is also the design, once it is before us, that allows us to ask even more important questions which the data in the computer's memory cannot possibly answer. Do we really want to build this structure in the first place? Does it have a sensible relationship to its site, its neighborhood, its environment? Is it beautiful? Is it practical? Will it work? Will it make us proud? Will we feel at home in it? Does it have warmth, nobility, a human scale, a sense of its time and place that will make it welcome to those who must live with it and work within it?

We might discuss the design in all these respects without any measurements of any materials being given at all. (Even the true meaning of "human scale" may not always be a matter of size, but often of the character of the environment.) We are then talking about the *idea* of the building, as we had it in mind or perhaps as it might exist in a mere doodle on a scrap of paper. Nowadays the doodle might be done by the architect with an electronic stylus on a video screen, but the distinction holds: the idea comes first, the idea contains the data, the idea governs the data.

Once we reflect upon the matter, we cannot fail to see that the data and the program that processes the data stand on different levels, the one subordinate to the other. Why is it, then, that they have both come to be called "information"?

In part, this may have to do with the fact that whatever gets fed into a computer is at once translated into binary numbers. The numbers become bits, the letters of words become packages of bits called bytes. The binary code then comes to be seen as a comprehensive "language" that homogenizes all that it expresses. In some universities, the systems used to help make the translation (BASIC, PASCAL, LISP, etc.), metaphorically referred to as "programming languages," can now be substituted for the study of French, German, Russian . . . the faster to make the students computer literate. These are not, of course, languages at all; they are coding systems. But in the computer's electronic metabolism, the omnivorous bit devours everything—numbers, words, geometrical forms, graphics, music— into long strings of ones and zeros. Does this not, then, erase the distinction between data and idea? As I was once told by a computer expert, "information" is anything that can be entered into the machine as off/on, yes/no.

Now, if there were such a thing as a conscious transistor, this might be the odd way in which such an alien entity would see the world: as an infinite collection of undifferentiated "ones" and "zeros." But the fact that a transistor could not tell the difference between the bits that are data and the bits that are ideas, does not mean that *we* are free to blur this vital distinction. For if we do, we risk surrendering our intelligent control over the programs that now govern more and more of our lives. Every piece of software has some repertory of basic assumptions, values, limitations embedded within it. In no sensible meaning of the word are these "information." Crude as they may often be, they are ideas about the world, and, like all ideas, they must be kept in clear, critical view.

In early 1985, a financial columnist ran an experiment that involved four of the most widely used computer financial planning programs. A hypothetical middle-class family was invented and its financial resources, needs, plans, preferences were run through the programs. The result was four strikingly different sets of recommendations, covering such options as investments, savings, liquidity, insurance, retirement.[7] Why? Because the advice of each plan was programmed with different assumptions, a fact which none of the services mentioned. For the user, it simply seemed to be a matter of entering personal financial information and getting a printout which had every appearance of absolute authority.

This illusion of mathematical certainty becomes especially pronounced in the current obsession with spreadsheets in the business community. Since the first spreadsheet software was published by David Bricklin of the Harvard Business School in the late 1970s, this form of computerized accounting has become what Steven Levy calls a "virtual cult" among the entrepreneurs.[8] A useful way of modeling and projecting financial decisions, the spreadsheet like all programs is built upon an underlying matrix of assumptions. Some of these are ideas about people, their tastes and motivations; some are value judgments that place priorities upon various courses of action. All require some form of numerical weighting and factoring, perhaps of a crude or foolish kind. Then, too, even in the business world there are imponderable matters of good will, morale, satisfaction with one's enterprise, moral conduct; all these demand attention, yet, because they resist quantification, may find no place in the spreadsheet program. The vice of the spreadsheet is that its neat, mathematical facade, its rigorous logic, its profusion of numbers, may blind its user to the unexamined ideas and omissions that govern the calculations. As Levy observes, "Because the spreadsheet looks so authoritative—*and it was done by a computer, wasn't it?*—the hypothetical model gets accepted as gospel." It is, once more, an example of the mathematical mystique obscuring clear, critical evaluation of the underlying program.

We may not care to bear down on the matter, but even in the simplest video games our children play, there can be questionable ideas at work. The games are clearly dominated by ruthless competition and willful destruction. *Winning* is what matters, *killing* is what is valued. Many of the games are profoundly sexist, drawing on stereotypic macho images that appeal to adolescent boys—the main clientele for the video arcades. In contrast, one firm, which has published a series under the title "Computer Games for Girls," has imbued its software with conventional ideas of femininity, such as avoiding bloodshed, cooperating, taking time to clean up and pick flowers. Girls play the game as partners, not competitors; their games involve rather little hand-eye coordination.[9] It is commendable that the firm has tried to include girls in its market, but its games also deal in sexist stereotypes.

In a sensitive critique of video games, Ariel Dorfman concludes that the vast majority of them carry assumptions and goals that contribute to a form of "psychic numbing."

> Those who play videogames and leave their sensitivity and ethics aside when they deal with fictitious extinction on the blithe screen, when they militarize their free time, do so in the same society which contemplates mass murder as deterrence, corpses as statistics, forty million dead as victory, permanent escalation as peace.[10]

Perhaps most child's play throughout history has revolved around violent excitements, especially that of adolescent boys whose conception of manhood is still sadly underdimensioned. But surely the computer, with its hypnotic graphics and lightning fast responses (an enemy world spectacularly destroyed at the flick of a joystick), makes that wretched reflex of the pubescent glands more bedazzling and therefore more seductive.

It is only when we strike a clear distinction between ideas and information that we can recognize that these are radically different levels of discourse requiring different levels of evaluation. In most cases, we may be able to assess the data that flow through the program as either "right" or "wrong," a question of fact that yields to standard research methods. But the ideas that govern the data are *not* information; nor are they sacrosanct matters of mathematical logic. They are philosophical commitments, the outgrowth of experience, insight, metaphysical conviction, which must be assessed as wise or foolish, childlike or mature, realistic or fantastic, moral or wicked. That critical project spans the full range of computer software, from the video game that places the fanciful annihilation of a galaxy beneath the power of a child's thumb to the computerized war machine that places the real choice of genocide before our presidents and generals. Weighing such matters up in the critical scales requires an education which standard computer literacy will never provide.

Since information technology has been with us, its discriminating users have recognized the principle of GIGO: garbage in—garbage out. The computer can do no better than the quality of the information selected by a human intelligence to be entered into it. But this principle needs to be extended to another level. The mathematical rigor of the computer may mislead some into interpreting GIGO as what Ashley Montague once construed it to mean: garbage in—*gospel* out. We need another principle that makes us aware of the fallibilities which may be embedded in the programs that lie waiting inside the machine to receive the information. Even when the data are well selected, they may be ambushed by intellectual "garbage" of another order hiding in the depths of the program.

AN ALIEN INTELLIGENCE
■

> However much intelligence computers may attain now
> or in the future, theirs must always be an intelligence
> alien to genuine human problems and concerns.
> Joseph Weizenbaum[11]

The genius of computer science lies in its remarkable capacity to elaborate extremely complex programs out of extremely primitive building blocks. Not many computer users may realize that ultimately everything the machine does is derived from the rapid manipulation of a few basic logical relationships, like those expressed in the words *and, or, both, neither, implies.* There is very little any computer program produces that cannot be traced back to a small collection of simple rules, such as:

This is the same as *that;* put *these* together.

This is not the same as *that;* put *this* someplace else.

If *this* is so, then *that* is so; move right along.

If *this* is so, then *that* is not so; *that* can be eliminated.

Either *this* or *that;* make a choice.

And so on.

These are the kinds of two-choice rules that translate neatly into the zero/one notation of binary numbers and move smoothly through the off/on channels of electrical transistors. Thus, we get a nice three-tiered synergistic sandwich: *effective procedures* (the idea of the program) based upon *binary arithmetic,* based upon the *physical stop-go traffic of electrons* through semiconductors. This is an intriguing interplay that connects humanly useful operations with an invisible substratum of nonhuman physical phenomena. When the programming rules that govern this interplay are densely packed into long sequences and run by at blinding speed, what the computer does no longer looks simple at all. Especially when probabilities, priorities, and weightings have been calculated into the program, it may look something like a cunning little intelligence at work, deliberating, choosing, deciding. Yet, it is an intelligence that its designers know is operating by strict mathematical rules and physical laws. Understandably, then, some computer scientists have wondered how much farther such procedures might be extended into the realm of intellect. How many faculties of the human mind—its intuition, creativity, judgment—might be simulated by running data through the sort of formal processes that characterize mathematical thinking?

The study called artificial intelligence (AI) represents such a quest: to find ways to program as many kinds of thoughts as possible so that a computer can simulate them. It is a challenging pursuit which has produced programs of much greater sophistication than its critics would have predicted ten or twenty years ago, when the field was first making its way into the universities. Among its highly touted achievements are the several "expert systems" that can serve as valuable aids to physicians, geologists, chemists, and geneticists. Essentially, these systems are programs that represent a composite of how experts in certain fields would work their way through a problem. For example, a physician might enter a collection of symptoms into a computer which will then sort them through and suggest the diagnosis on which several specialists might agree. The logic of the matter is simple: where the specialists have seen *this,* and *this,* and *this* in their patients, they have usually come to the following conclusion. Of course, the specialists may also have picked up a few things intuitively from the patient's general look—slouching posture, glazed eyes, sallow cheeks—that are difficult to include in the program. Or, the specialists being specialists, they may have overlooked something vital outside their field of expertise. It is dubious that even such an ingenious system will ever be able to function except in an advisory capacity to flesh and blood physicians who must ultimately rely upon their own judgment—to the point of bearing the ultimate responsibility in a malpractice suit.

As impressive as such advances are, AI continues to fall short of what its enthusiasts have been promising since the study began in the early 1950s. As we have seen, AI has been peculiarly characterized by extravagant, often propagandistic claims in its own behalf, with the result that authorities in the field have contributed as much to the folklore of computers as the advertisers, promising machines that would translate languages, understand speech, process visual images, make legal, political, and financial decisions, and, in general, outstrip human intelligence in every application. Thus, in 1959, Herbert Simon and Allen Newell were predicting that "in the visible future" their research would produce computers with problem solving powers "coextensive with the range to which the human mind had been applied."[12] Marvin Minsky was prepared to hazard even more ambitious forecasts:

> In from three to eight years, we will have a machine with the general intelligence of an average human being. I mean a machine that will be able to read Shakespeare, grease a car, play office politics, tell a joke, have a fight. At that point, the machine will begin to educate itself with fantastic speed. In a few months, it will be at genius level, and a few months after that, its power will be incalculable.[13]

That prediction was made in 1970. Even Minsky's colleagues at the MIT artificial intelligence laboratory found it extravagant; more judiciously, they predicted such results would take another *fifteen years* at the outside. By then, they thought Minsky was probably right in believing that computers would be in a position to "decide to keep us as pets."

The reason for such conscienceless self-advertisement is not difficult to identify. There is a great deal of money at stake. Along with its more recently born companion discipline cognitive science, AI has been one of the most richly funded fields of academic research over the past two decades. Its public image and its fortunes have fluctuated greatly over that period, depending on the success of its efforts, but currently AI is back in the public eye and placed high on the military-industrial payroll. It has become the great hope of the computer industry as it seeks to produce a new generation of more sophisticated merchandise—the so-called fifth generation. AI is now being looked to for the great breakthroughs that will yield supersmart machines in every walk of life, from talking refrigerators to the automated battlefield. Some observers estimate that by the mid-1990s, AI will be at the center of a market worth $50 billion a year, *if* all the promised inventions materialize. As one commentator has put it (Michael Bywater writing in the London *Observer* in November 1985), "artificial intelligence is a two-word phrase which makes US Department of Defense officials salivate when they hear it."

AI and cognitive science have played along opportunistically with this new wave of speculative investment, associating their professional interests with the sky's-the-limit commercial hype that helps fund its research. Major corporations like IBM, Digital Equipment, and Data General, along with the Pentagon's Defense Advanced Research Projects Agency (DARPA), have been making lucrative arrangements with leading universities to stimulate the necessary research. These developments have not gone uncriticized from within the computer science profession. Some worry that military-industrial money on the current scale will vastly distort the priorities of research; others are concerned (rather belatedly) about the ethical implications that arise from the alliance between information technology and the Pentagon. But more basically still, there are those who charge that AI has been oversold to a degree that flirts with outright fraud. The field may be nowhere near capable of producing what it advertises. This challenge was raised at the 1984 meeting of the Association for Computing Machinery by Lewis M. Branscomb of IBM, who observed, with respect to AI, that "the extravagant statements of the past few years have become a source of concern to many of us who have seen excessive claims by researchers in other fields lead to unreasonable expectations in the public."

The charge was put even more pointedly by Herbert Grosch, formerly of IBM:

> The emperor—whether talking about the fifth generation or AI—is stark naked from the ankles up. From the ankles down, the emperor is wearing a well worn and heavily gilded pair of shoes called expert systems. They are useful, but we've had them for over thirty years. All that the fifth-generation boys have done is relabel them.[14]

The problems that AI has encountered in pursuing its inflated claims are illuminating, if for no other reason than that they reveal the limitations of the mathematical mind when it strays beyond the boundaries of pure reason—or rather seeks to extend those boundaries into the real world.

At the outset—as soon as the first postwar generation of computers began to move in on the universities—the computer scientists were elated by the rapid progress they had made in programming their machines to play games of strategy like tic-tac-toe, checkers, and chess. The strategy for tic-tac-toe was quickly mastered by the computers, as it has been by most ten year olds. The game of checkers also yielded its few secrets rapidly. Since the first chess program was developed in 1957, computerized chess strategies have been worked up to the "high expert" level of play.[15] These successes were highly encouraging. If the machine could do so well at such demanding tasks, then what could it not do?

But as it turns out, AI has run into its toughest problems at another, much humbler level of mental activity. While computers do impressively well with games of strategy, they continue to be stymied in the areas of life where "common sense" and "natural languages" are decisive. For example, suppose the task is to develop a program that will deal with the following pedestrian scenario:

You want to find out what's happening in the world. How can

this be done? Let us say by reading the morning newspaper. Where is the morning paper? Somewhere on the front lawn. Then, obviously, you should go out, pick it up, and bring it in the house. Correct. Unless it is raining. If it is raining, you don't wish to get wet. How can this be avoided? By putting on a raincoat, then going out and picking up the paper.

This is an actual research project that was funded for study by the Alfred P. Sloan Foundation at the Computer Science Division of the University of California at Berkeley. It involved developing an effective procedure that deals in some sensible sequence with determining if it is raining, how hard it is raining, putting on a raincoat, going outside, picking up the paper—all of this in a simulated form obviously; the computer does not leave the lab to go scrambling around the campus to find a real newspaper.[16]

Not much of a problem, it would seem. But for the computer, this tiny slice-of-life adventure must be scripted into an enormously long and detailed program, with many a bug and glitch along the way. And if the choice of using an umbrella is worked into the situation, or the need to decide *how* wet one might be willing to get before using either umbrella or raincoat, the program becomes a jungle of conflicting contingencies. Is this how the human mind deals with such a common-sense problem? Certainly not. Yet it is the only way a computer can do it—and not very well at that.

An ironic, but deeply significant truth emerges from research like this. The most valuable thing that AI and cognitive science may be proving is the severe limitation of mathematical logic over a vast range of problems in the real world. We simply do not seem to get through much of our life by way of effective procedures. We may have a computer that can come close to stalemating a grandmaster at chess, but the machine may still not be smart enough to come in out of the rain. This suggests that there is a radical discrepancy between the way a machine simulates thinking and the way people actually think. In fact, that discrepancy could even include those areas, like mathematics and chess, where computers produce their most impressive results. As we suggested in our discussion of Logo in Chapter 4, it may not be the case that people play chess or do mathematics the way machines do. In these activities, too, the human mind may often work in the same quirky, informal, fuzzy way it functions when it decides (without seeming to think about it) that there is no point in fetching a sopping wet newspaper off the front lawn anyway, and so settles for turning on the radio to catch the news.

The sort of effective procedures that have been developed in mathematics and chess are the best AI has to offer us as an approach to the understanding of human thought. If they are as alien to real thinking as some critics believe, then that is all the more reason to be on one's guard about the way software manipulates data. For the mathematical rigor of the procedure may not even be the result of *real* mathematics, but of a crude mechanical caricature of the mathematical mind at work. In which case, the old mathematical magic which lies at the root of information technology may be misleading to the point of deception. A computer mimics a quality of mind, but inappropriately, claiming an authority it does not deserve.

The vice that always hovers over AI and cognitive science is to insist that what an effective procedure leaves out doesn't really matter or can be fed in later as part of some yet-to-be-developed program. Thus, with respect to computerized tasks that may need a certain emotional flavoring, Marvin Minsky assures us,

> We'll be able to program emotions into a machine once we can do thoughts. We could make something that just flew into a rage right now, but that would be a brainless rage. It wouldn't be very interesting. I'm sure that once we can get a certain amount of thought, and we've decided which emotions we want in a machine, that it won't be hard to do.[17]

Facile remarks like this are based upon the fact that every human activity can be reduced to *some* kind of formal description—if we eliminate all the unprogrammable ambiguities, subtleties, and imponderables. For example, a computer can be programmed with key words that trigger sets of rules that invoke a selection of "frames" representing "romantic love," "familial love," "Platonic love." If the romantic love frame is activated, the machine can print out "I love you," or better still, "I *really* love you," followed by "parenthesis-sigh-parenthesis." It can even be loaded with an anthology of great love poems which it then quotes.

For some AI experts, the brutal simplification involved in such an effective procedure may be seen as a first step in a lengthy search for something more authentic. The danger is that, at some point, the search becomes frustrating and is given up, but the first step is not repealed. Because the first step is so logically rigorous, it comes to be seen as reliable: a true advance or maybe the goal itself. Which is like accepting a rough caricature as an adequate substitute for a studied protrait—or even for the real person behind the likeness.

THE FLIGHT FROM REALITY

∎

The examples given here of AI at work in highly contrived laboratory experiments may seem harmlessly academic, even a bit amusing, since the projects under study are so far removed from real life. We might conclude that if everyday common-sense activities cannot be successfully duplicated by AI, then the research will never get beyond the drawing board and may eventually join the ranks of such failed efforts as the search for perpetual motion or the universal solvent.

But that is not quite how the world works when powerful institutions are out to maximize their influence and their profits. AI is now penetrating our economic life in a variety of highly consequential ways as part of the massive economic conversion to high tech. It is common knowledge that a great and increasing amount of shop-floor automation has been introduced into the manufacturing sector with a view to robotizing the assembly lines. This effort to save labor costs by more and more mechanization is being steadily stepped up through the chain of industrial command, through the highly skilled and supervisorial levels. At every stage along the way automative technology is based on the same assumption that guides research in chess playing and common-sense problem solving in the AI laboratories: namely, that effective procedures can be developed for what skilled or semiskilled workers, and perhaps even for what foremen and managers do in the production process. The public at large now readily believes this can be done; after all, we have read glowing reports and seen impressive films of automated factories at work. The propaganda of industry and government keeps telling us it can be done and that the result will be more and cheaper productivity. Thanks to high tech, high-priced human labor will be automated out of the wage market and American industry will once again become competitive in the world.

But there is at least a small body of dissenting literature on the subject of automation, especially with respect to the effort to replace highly skilled crafts by such major industrial programs as integrated computer assisted manufacturing (ICAM). The doubts all have to do with problems that arise when computer scientists seek to reduce a skilled machinist's work to a formal, numerically controlled process: in other words, to play chess with people's labor. It is being discovered that nothing about such work is as simple as it may seem at first sight from the distant and lofty viewpoint of the computer scientist. Skilled work requires far more adaptability, experienced judgment, intuition than anyone has yet been able to program. The hour-to-hour reality of the shop floor is simply not a chess board.

In a remarkable and detailed study, David Noble has collected an impressive body of evidence—including the nitty-gritty experience of industrial workers themselves—that highlights the many expensive but usually well-disguised failures that continue to plague the drive toward total automaticity.[18] But the effort to create workerless factories continues, with one level of corrective technology being heaped upon another in the search for "adaptive control." The pursuit is well funded by industry and by the military and represents a "sweet problem" for the computer scientists, especially for AI researchers, who remain ever ready to claim the power to do miracles. Noble observes,

> Adaptive control is the attempt to make machines fully self-correcting, through the use of sophisticated sensors, delicate feedback mechanisms, and even "artificial intelligence." Such devices, it is hoped, will automatically compensate for all variations and changing conditions, and render machining a totally automatic, self-contained process, one amenable to remote management control.

The result of this costly and determined campaign to build "the factory of the future" is a workerless production process loaded with "sensors, monitors, counters, alarms, self-actuated repair devices" which is more and more prone to breakdown or malfunction. The factories become like those advanced military weapons systems—the

F-16 fighter, the AEGIS cruiser, the Maverick antitank missile—which have reached a level of complexity and delicacy that finally overwhelms the ability of those who must use them.[19] "The greater complexity required to adjust for unreliability," Noble comments, "merely adds to the unreliability." He calls the effort "a flight from reality"—the reality of how the human mind and organism actually work, which is nothing like the data processing model even in the supposedly dull mechanical routine of the production process.

When AI is described as "an alien intelligence" by critics like Joseph Weizenbaum, it may seem that this is a sentimental response to the cold logic of the computer. Certainly many AI defenders have tried to construe the criticism in that way and so to dismiss it as a mere "cry of the heart." But it may also be the case that an alien intelligence is one that simply cannot do most of the jobs it is supposed to do because it is not in touch with the reality we must all live within. So it seeks to create *another* reality, one that can meet the rarefied specifications of pure reason. Which is precisely what Plato did when he established the first academy and retired there to contemplate the design of his ideal republic. He was frank to admit that no society could achieve the geometrical perfection he sought without becoming an autocracy. His philosophical utopia never reached beyond the boundaries of the academy; there was not the wealth or power to build it.

The domineering exponents of pure reason are still with us today in the form of the computer scientists, wielding the age-old mystique of mathematics for all it is worth. And having invented a machine that embodies that mystique, they have found the social forces that have the power to make their utopia a serious political proposition.

THE FIFTH GENERATION . . . AND BEYOND
∎

Those who toil in the ranks of AI and cognitive science are nothing if not persistent. As often as their promises have fallen flat, they have renewed them with ever more bravado. They are a dogged lot. What Marvin Minsky promised in 1970 to achieve in "three to eight years" ("a machine with the general intelligence of an average human being" and not long after of "genius level") is still on the AI agenda, now more actively touted than ever because there have been technological breakthroughs and conceptual innovations. Currently, one can find all these breakthroughs and innovations packaged together under the label "the fifth generation," the supersmart computers so long predicted and now—almost—at hand.

In a much publicized survey of these new technological horizons, two prominent computer scientists appear to have arrived at some of the same conclusions I have been presenting in these pages: namely, that computer-processed information and human ideas are "separate entities" that function at significantly different mental levels. But the scientists go on to develop this distinction in a remarkable and revealing way. In their study *The Fifth Generation*, Edward Feigenbaum and Pamela McCorduck agree that the raw information which computers can now process so abundantly may have little value after all; it can even overwhelm us.

So they argue that in order to have "intellectual leverage," information must be "well-engineered." By this they mean, it must be "constantly selected, interpreted, updated, and adapted as circumstances change." Now this is more or less what I have identified as the function of ideas: to winnow the data and organize them. Information that has been "engineered" in this way becomes what Feigenbaum and McCorduck define as "knowledge," and this, they tell us, is what our emerging economy of "knowledge workers" must have.

Within the cult of information, this would seem to be an important concession. It amounts to saying that information processing is not everything. This is rather as if a devout Calvinist (with whose single-minded rigor computer science sometimes shares a curious similarity) were caught flirting with the heresy that faith alone will not bring salvation but must be supplemented by good deeds. Yet— again in the style of Calvinist theologians hastening to preserve the sovereignty of God—Feigenbaum and McCorduck quickly devise a way to rescue the omnipotence of the computer. There lies before us, they announce, a *"new* computer revolution," which will lead us through "the transition from information processing to knowledge processing." That transition will be achieved by the next (the fifth) generation of computers. These remarkable machines will be nothing like the computers we have come to know; they will be KIPs—

knowledge information processors. KIPs will have the power to "subsume the confusion of details, data points, and ever-changing information under orderly, general, and plausible interpretations."

It is difficult to understand what "interpretation" means in this context. Ordinarily, an interpretation is what results when we apply some moral, aesthetic, or ideological judgment—an idea—to an intellectual problem. This is usually what people take issue with in one another's interpretations. For example, we might have a Marxist interpretation of *The Wealth of Nations,* or a Freudian interpretation of Hamlet, or an existentialist interpretation of Marx and Freud. The clash of such ideas among thoughtful people is pretty much what fills and enlivens our cultural life. We compare and contrast our differing views of things, using the ideas that our experience has given us to select, filter, and shape the facts at hand. The result is, at best, fruitful dialogue; at worst, bitter argument, perhaps violence.

What are we to make, then, of the prediction that KIPs will produce "orderly, general, and plausible interpretations" so that "the burden of producing the future knowledge of the world will be transferred from human heads to machine artifacts"?[20] In the fifth generation, may we expect to have Marxist and Freudian and existentialist computers, possibly arguing among themselves? Or will the new computers, lacking the living experience that leads to such commitments in life, work out their own peculiar nonhuman interpretations of things, perhaps based upon various chemical modifications of their silicon?

The prospect of machine interpretation is not only whimsical; it is absurd. Interpretation belongs solely to a living mind in exactly the same way that birth belongs solely to a living body. Disconnected from a mind, "interpretation" becomes what "birth" becomes when it does not refer to a body: a metaphor. But Feigenbaum and McCorduck are not speaking metaphorically. They are speaking literally, and they *think* they are saying something meaningful. If they were, what a nightmare that would be. Bad enough to have computer enthusiasts insisting that the information which gets processed through computers is unassailably correct. Imagine being confronted with machine interpretations that were held to be just as authoritative. We might then find ourselves reading *the* correct "interpretation" of the latest presidential press conference, hot off the computer. Granted that in one sad respect this might make life easier for troubled minds that can no longer make sense of the world. But for whom besides the defeated and resigned is it a "burden" to produce the knowledge of the world? There are surely more than a few of us left who enjoy thinking.

Feigenbaum and McCorduck recognize—commendably—that the mind needs something more than raw information to think with. But their notion of knowledge is deeply perplexing. While they realize that knowledge has something to do with selecting, judging, interpreting, they fail to grasp the role ideas play in this process, which is no doubt why they believe that a new generation of computers can be transformed into knowledge-producing machines.

An idea (or the information that flows from an idea) becomes knowledge when it gathers to itself a certain broad consensus in the society. Knowledge is a status conferred upon an idea by that consensus. How does this consensus come about? It occurs when a sufficient number of people agree that an idea is true. And how do they arrive at that conclusion? By applying some shared idea about truth to the matter under discussion. For example, in medieval times, there was the widely shared idea that truth could be found at that point where the teaching of scripture, the authority of the Church fathers, and (possibly) the logic of Aristotle harmoniously intersected. Leading minds like the Schoolmen of the period argued various matters along these lines, seeking that intersection. If an idea—such as that of original sin, or the trinitarian nature of God, or the arrangement of the planets in the cosmos—passed through the filter of these authorities, it became "knowledge." Some three centuries later, when direct empirical verification became the prevailing idea of truth, this "knowledge"—once accepted by learned and honest minds—came to be regarded as questionable and at last faded out of the culture.

A society's criterion of truth is among its master ideas. Arguments about the criterion are, therefore, the most interesting and usually the most heated. Every society that is not wholly isolated or moribund is normally filled with many competing ideas about truth, each with its own loyal following. These days, we witness lively, often nasty exchanges between evangelical Christians and their "secular humanist" opponents where issues are hotly in dispute because the criteria of truth are hopelessly at odds between the camps. For the one, the Bible is the supreme, if not the sole measure of truth on faith, morals, history, geology, biology. For the other, the Bible is simply an old book filled with many defunct ideas. These and other contending ideas of truth jostle and struggle and collide with one another all about us each day; or they mix and mingle and ally. The result is that ever-troubled and turbulent thing we call civilized life, where one person's information is another's nonsense, one person's knowledge is another's superstition. Usually there is a mainstream consensus that the priesthood, or the academies, or some other dominant institution reflects and enforces, and this is generally what gets labeled as "knowledge." But in a lively culture, that consensus is always under pressure and at hazard from dissenting elements.

If the Information Age continues into a fifth (or a tenth) generation to come, when the computers will have become microscopic in size and jammed full with millions of times the data they now hold, there is no chance whatever that we will mechanize the dilemmas of cultural debate and hard personal choice. Ideas produce knowledge, and human minds—quite mysteriously—create ideas. Who would want it any other way?

The fifth generation of AI-enriched computers is now beginning to work its way into practical applications. Rich contracts have gone out from the military and the corporations to tap the latest research. But even before the fruits of these investments have been harvested, there are rumors of a new generation of information technology under study. One might wonder how much further AI and cognitive science can be pushed, since they already promise to surpass the limits of human intelligence itself. Still, the Japanese are reported to be pioneering a more distant, barely imaginable frontier. The Japanese Science and Technology Agency has announced that it has formed a joint project with several Japanese high tech companies to open a "sixth generation" of computerized telecommunications research. Under the direction of Hiroo Yuhara of Uniden Corporation, the project is examining various forms of parapsychological and extrasensory perception to see whether these occult forces of the mind can be harnessed.[21]

Yuhara believes the human body possesses sensors that can act as electrical transmitters. These might be connected to computers by way of a magnetic link. The result would be "the ultimate modem": the extrasensory powers of the human psyche integrated in some ethereal way into the global telecommunications grid. As the Science and Technology Agency puts it, computer ESP carries industrial research forward into "the study of man's spiritual activities."

Just as the Japanese initiative in fifth generation technology spurred the Americans and Europeans into action, surely this new effort will have the same inspiring result. Perhaps before long we will have a new discipline in the computer laboratories: artificial clairvoyance. And the military, having bought so much of the rest of the Star Wars scenario and wanting "the Force" to be with them, will no doubt rush forward to provide the research funds.

THE COMPUTER AND THE COUNTERCULTURE

■

BIG BLUE AND THE GUERRILLA HACKERS

■

Until the mid-1970s, the prevailing public image of information technology was austere and exotic. It focused on a mysterious, highly expensive machinery that belonged in the exclusive care of trained technicians. Its operations had to be discussed in the esoteric language of information theory, with the aid of much mathematics. As an extension of the human mind, the computer was coming to be seen as a necessary adjunct of all advanced scientific thought and high-level decision making, a role that still further distanced it from public access. Its reputation as a rival to human intelligence may have had much to do with science fiction exaggerations (like the rebellious computer HAL in the film *2001*), but there was already a lively discussion abroad about the way in which automation would soon revolutionize the assembly line and the white collar workplace by taking over an ever larger range of skilled employment. There was very little the public knew about computers that did not make the machines seem elite and intimidating.[1]

Perhaps most dramatically of all, by way of saturation television coverage, the nation had been many times treated to the sight of the

Johnson Mission Control Center in Houston, where massed ranks of technicians seated before massed ranks of computers supervised the triumphs of the still glamorous space program. Oddly, the television presentations from the center always featured panoramic vistas of computer screens, as if the machines were the stars of the event. The technicians, turned away and faceless, seemed to be no better than anonymous, almost servile attendants taking their cues from the machines. As a result of this familiar national scene, it was becoming nearly impossible to imagine scientists and engineers out of the company of scintillating video terminals where arcane calculations raced by at a breathtaking pace. The computer, rapidly assimilated to the scientific mystique, was bidding to dominate it.

Quite as intimidating as such media imagery was the social fact that the province of information technology was still under tight corporate control. Indeed, it was dominated by the most elite and private of corporations: IBM, a high tech colossus that stood astride the world, suave, aloof, and imperial. Since the war years, "Big Blue," as IBM was known in the industry, had grown into the quintessential embodiment of the technocratic business style. As close to a world monopoly as any firm had ever come, its control of the industry was assumed to be efficient to the point of infallibility. By the mid-1960s, it owned two-thirds of the information technology business. What it did not own largely survived by its sufferance, salvaging the crumbs that IBM let fall from its plate. So large and domineering was IBM that it was not regarded as anybody's "competition"; rather, it was the "environment" within which everybody else did business. Other companies surrounded IBM like the vassals of the crown; their business was mainly to do what IBM chose not to do or to produce plug-in compatibles for IBM equipment.

True to its lordly stature, IBM had brought the postwar organization man ethos to its perfection. It was run like a taut ship whose disciplined crew was coolly ruthless in the marketplace, fanatically loyal to the firm, machine-tooled to fit the corporate chain of command. But at some point in the 1960s, infallible Big Blue made a miscalculation. The possibility was at hand for making small, low-priced computers. This could be done as simply as by detaching existing terminals from their mainframes and upgrading them into autonomous data processors. Such machines would have minimal memory and could only run reduced programs, but they would be more compact and cheaper than even the minicomputers then being used in offices and laboratories. In effect, they could be household appliances. IBM nevertheless elected to keep its money and brains concentrated on the development of large-scale computers. This was, of course, where most of its thriving military and civilian market lay: with expensive mainframe machines and their accessories. Perhaps, in part, IBM's decision also sprang from the fact that the company saw the future of information technology in its own corporate image: rigidly hierarchical and centrally controlled. IBM had never conceived of selling computers to the general public. It preferred to sell big, often custom-tailored machines to big customers. Or better still, it would lease its products, keeping them under its own control. IBM's machines went out to the world as locked black boxes; their inner architecture was proprietary, meant to be accessible only to company engineers. Where Big Blue would not lead, other major computer firms were not prepared to tread; its decision to maintain its elitist style thus allowed a chink to open in the walls of the industry's citadel.

The chink was the microcomputer, a highly affordable, table-top machine suitable for home and personal use. IBM and the other major firms were not unaware of the technical feasibility of such a computer. Computers had been getting steadily smaller as they grew more powerful, and all the while becoming progressively cheaper. Engineers at IBM and other companies had hand-tooled in-house prototypes of computers small enough to be carried in a briefcase. But was there a significant market for such a device? Big Blue judged not. Others thought differently.

The most important of these "others" was the growing population of young computer enthusiasts who had been gathering along the fringes of computer research for the better part of a generation. In his study *Hackers: Heroes of the Computer Age*, Steven Levy traces their origins back to the MIT computer laboratory of the late 1950s, where gifted students were often allowed to congregate, sometimes staying on through the night to run the equipment. Most of these early computer addicts were cut from the Tom Swift mold: adolescent mechanical geniuses capable of improvising brilliantly out of scraps and patches for the sheer love of solving sweet problems. Among them were to be found the inventors of the first computer games and toy robots, novelties they did not even trouble to patent. By the late 1960s, some of these youthful talents had found their way into the lower echelons of the computer industry. There, a few of them were already experimenting with primitive microcomputers, all of which would be shelved by the companies they worked for.

In the folklore of computer history, the early hackers are remembered as a special breed. Reportedly, many of them were socially gauche to the point of being unworldly. They are the archetypal "nerds" of the profession. As a group they possessed even less political consciousness than commercial savvy; they were purely technicians from first to last. But by the end of the 1960s, there was another species of hacker on the horizon, emerging mainly on the West Coast from the ranks of the antiwar movement. These were the radical or guerrilla hackers, who were destined to give the computer a dramatically new image and a political orientation it could never have gained from Big Blue or any of its vassals in the mainstream of the industry. At their hands, information technology would make its closest approach to becoming an instrument of democratic politics.

AN ELECTRONIC POPULISM
∎

In the spring of 1970, a small group of dropped-out computer scientists who had been involved in the war protest movement at the University of California at Berkeley came together in the midst of the Cambodia crisis to discuss the politics of information. They constituted one of the earliest gatherings of socially concerned hackers. They deplored the fact that the computer was being monopolized for profit and power by the same military-industrial complex that already controlled every other major technology. Yet they were also convinced that their profession held the key to a vital participatory democracy. That key was information. In the words of *People's Computer Company,* a radical hacker newspaper that began publication in late 1972: "Computers are mostly used against people instead of for people, used to control people instead of to *free* them. Time to change all that—we need a . . . people's computer company." [2]

What, then, was to be done? The solution for the Berkeley hackers was Resource One, "a community computer utility" quartered in an artist's warehouse collective in the industrial sector of San Francisco. Its founders made the following argument:

> Both the quantity and content of available information is set by centralized institutions—the press, TV, radio, news services, think-tanks, government agencies, schools and universities—which are controlled by the same interests which control the rest of the economy. By keeping information flowing from the top down, they keep us isolated from each other. ... Computer technology has thus far been used ... mainly by the government and those it represents to store and quickly retrieve vast amounts of information about huge numbers of people. ... It is this pattern that convinces us that control over the flow of information is so crucial.[3]

Several corporations and foundations contributed small grants to Resource One; most importantly, Transamerica Corporation gave the effort its centerpiece: an IBM XDS-940 time-share computer, an overaged behemoth of a machine that was well on its way toward obsolescence. Resource One refurbished the machine and advertised it as a true public utility, in the hope that political activists would make use of it and the skill of its operators to run voter surveys, collect social statistics, organize mailing lists. An "urban data base" became an early high priority; it would coordinate data from the census, election returns, land use, property valuations. Also on the agenda were a social services referral directory and an accounting service for nonprofit community groups.

Resource One hulked along for a few years sustained mainly by the sweat capital of its organizers, but it never found enough support or use to give it the prominence it sought. The problem, so some frustrated members speculated, was a technical one. The technology was too restricted; it needed to get out into the community, where people could gain hands-on experience with this exotic machine. Accordingly, a new project was spun off: Community Memory, which was envisioned as a network of small computer terminals distributed throughout the Bay Area. The terminals would be available free of charge and linked to the Resource One central data bank and processing unit. Some anticipated a much larger project: a nationwide alternative information system that would use the

AT&T long lines to link together cities and campuses across America. The objective was to create "a direct democracy of information."

Community Memory got its first operational terminal established in August 1973; it was located in a heavily trafficked record store near the University of California campus in Berkeley. The terminal proved popular as an electronic bulletin board; it also carried a lot of hearsay, therapeutic outpouring, gossip, and graffiti. The terminal shifted places a few times; a couple more were added along the way, one at a San Francisco branch library in a working-class community. But when Resource One went broke in 1975, Community Memory soon followed it into bankruptcy, though it was to resurface some ten years later with a network of three terminals, still operating at the bulletin board and graffiti level: amusing, marginally helpful, an improvement over the three-by-five card on a corkboard, but hardly an instrument for significant social change even in as politicized a locale as Berkeley.

As halting as these efforts were, they struck a new populist chord in the public perception of information. They identified the computer as, potentially, a "radical social artifact." In the words of Michael Rossman, one of the project's theoreticians:

> Community Memory . . . is *convivial* and *participatory* . . . A CM system is an actively open ("free") information system, enabling direct communications among its users, with no centralized editing of or control over the information exchanged. . . . Such a system represents a precise antithesis to the dominant uses both of electronic communications media, which broadcast centrally-determined messages to mass passive audiences; and of cybernetic technology, which involves centralized processing of and control over data drawn from or furnished to direct and indirect users. . . . The payoff is efficient, unmediated (or rather self-mediated) interaction, eliminating roles and problems that develop when one party has control over what information passes between two (or many) others. This freedom is complemented by the way the system democratizes information-power, for no group of its users has more access to its main information than the least user has.[4]

From the viewpoint of those who launched Resource One and Community Memory, information was much more than an industrial necessity or a commercial commodity. It was the life's blood of democratic politics, and as such too precious to be conceded to corporate and government control. For political activists who had spent the Vietnam and Watergate years protesting the secrecy, the coverups, the news management of the government, the computer looked like the antidote to technocratic elitism—provided its power could be made universally accessible. But how was this to be done? Resource One had tried to bring the people to the computer—a single, esoteric, mainframe machine; Community Memory had tried to being the computer to the people in the form of smaller, user-friendly terminals. Neither approach had developed much social momentum. But meanwhile, the technology itself was changing in ways that suggested another strategy for the creation of an electronic populism. By the mid-1970s, the microcomputer, which IBM had written off as a poor investment, began to look more and more like an affordable tool that might attract a sizable population of users on the open market. Suppose, then, the technology were to be brought into the homes of America like radios, television sets, stereo record players. Would that not offer the distribution and the access necessary to break the corporate-government monopoly of information processing?

THE HEROIC AGE OF
THE MICROCOMPUTER
■

From its beginning, the microcomputer was surrounded by an aura of vulgarity and radicalism that contrasted sharply with the mandarin pretensions of the high tech mainstream. This is because so much of the new, smaller-scaled technology was left to be developed outside the corporate citadel by brash, young hackers—especially in California, where the socially divergent types had gathered along that strip of the San Francisco peninsula which was coming to be called Silicon Valley. By the mid-1970s, small groups of these hackers had begun to meet in informal rap sessions where computer lore was freely swapped like gossip over the cracker barrel in a country store. The feel of these meetings was deliberately down-home: a self-conscious rejection of the stilted corporate style. The names told a good deal about the spirit of the times. One start-up company of the period called itself the Itty-Bitty Machine Company (an alternative IBM); another was Kentucky Fried Computers.

Here was an ambience where scruffy and unshaven types in jeans could freely congregate to discuss the machines they were developing in attics and garages. The Homebrew Computer Club in Menlo Park (near the Stanford University campus and industrial park) was the most colorful and productive of these funky town meetings. It has since taken on legendary proportions in memoirs of the period. It was at Homebrew that Stephen Wozniak unveiled his new microcomputer in 1977. The name he gave it—the Apple—brought a new, organic, slightly rustic quality with it that was meant to soften the hard edge of the technology, to make it plain-folks and friendly. The name also recalled the old Beatles' record company. (Still another anecdote derives the name from the fruitarian diet which Steven Jobs, Wozniak's partner, had brought back from his mystic sojourn in India.)

The breed of hacker that assembled at places like Homebrew had been huddling along the borders of the high tech world for several years. Many of them were university dropouts and veterans of recent countercultural politics in the Bay Area. In the words of one participant-observer, the style "had its genetic coding in the sixties, in anti-establishment, anti-war, pro-freedom, anti-discipline attitudes."[5] The perception of computers and information the guerrilla hackers brought to their work was a weird amalgam of political insurgency, science fiction, do-it-yourself survivalism, and pure fun and games. If they had not actually read the works of E. F. Schumacher, their motto nonetheless might have been "small is beautiful"—if for no other reason than that "small" was all they could afford to build for themselves. Similarly, if they had not studied the theories of Ivan Illich, their search was for an Illich-style "convivial" technology that built a community of interest and need among users. Mixed with these more serious veins of thought, there was more than a touch of whimsey, a taste for childlike fantasy that saw the computer as a sort of magic box that might emerge from a sword and sorcery tale. Thus, the first microcomputer to circulate through the hacker underground —it appeared in 1975 as a mail order kit packaged by a couple of overworked computer freaks in Albuquerque—was named the Altair, after an alien planet in the "Star Trek" television series.

As primitive as the Altair kit was, it became what haughty IBM had never imagined that an economy-sized data processor could be: "an absolute, runaway, overnight, insane success."[6] It soon became a featured item in the *Whole Earth Catalog*, a further boost for its sales. The guerrilla hackers were prime examples of the *Catalog's* worldview, an ethic of rugged self-reliance and pioneer adventure. In its initial issue in 1968, the *Catalog* had announced itself to the world as "an outlaw information service," intended for a disaffiliated readership of freaks and rebels. For the most part, the *Catalog* featured the wares of simple living and rustic ways: woodburning stoves, wigwams, buckskin clothing, techniques of midwifery and backyard horticulture. But from its inception, it had also been fascinated with certain forms of high tech: stereo systems, cameras, synthesizers, and, as early as its first issue, computers. The *Catalog* was, after all, inspired by the work of Buckminster Fuller, the maverick engineer who had patented the geodesic dome.

The dome might, in fact, be seen as the harbinger of the sort of populist technology that the microcomputer would one day become in the eyes of its inventors. Thanks to Fuller's special gift for grandiloquent obfuscation, the dome had acquired a metaphysical aura that appealed to countercultural tastes. Not only did Fuller make it seem cheap and easy to build, daring to live in, and culturally divergent in style, but he insisted that its basic stuctural unit—the tetrahedron—somehow resonated with the geometric logic of the cosmos. As a result, in the later 1960s, a cult grew up around the dome; Fuller's disciples, beginning with Stewart Brand, the editor of the *Whole Earth Catalog,* touted this piece of eccentric engineering as uniquely a *people's* technology, the emblem of a cause. Indeed, there were those who predicted that whole communities of domes might soon appear on the outskirts of major cities like barbarian encampments, harbingers of a new culture. Several years further along, the microcomputer, an invention of Fulleresque mavericks toiling away in back porch workshops, came to be seen in the same light—as a technology of liberation.

By a quirky coincidence that might only be imaginable in California, this insurgent vision of information technology was shared, or at least occasionally voiced, by the governor who happened to be in office at the time the talents of the Homebrew Computer Club were beginning to take on major industrial proportions. Jerry Brown was among the first American politicians to pick up on the promise of high tech. As one might guess, the governor's interest, like that of California governors before and since, was solidly rooted in the sort of big military-industrial contracts that are the staple of the state's economy. But Brown had the knack of being able to associate himself, if only obliquely and ambiguously, with a range of offbeat values and countercultural types. He was an outspoken opponent of nuclear power and a strong environmental champion. He was known to keep company with Zen Buddhists, rock stars, and Schumacher-style economists; early on, he had enlisted Stewart Brand as a confidant and advisor. In Sacramento, he had created a State Office of Appropriate Technology, where ambitious schemes for solar and wind energy, urban homesteads, and organic farming were being brainstormed. And when it came to the computer, he could throw off such remarks as:

> More people are spending more of their time on collecting, analyzing, and processing information, and that is an entirely different culture from what we've known. . . .

> By pressing a button, you'll get more and more information on the decision-making going on. . . . Information is the equalizer and breaks down the hierarchy.[7]

There was an interval in the early 1980s—it did not last longer than a few intoxicating years—when, in California at least, the guerrilla hackers seemed on the brink of making over the Information Age on their own terms. Emerging from their musty garages and sweeping across the high tech landscape, they had succeeded in throwing the corporate giants of the industry off balance. Their achievement was more than a matter of marketing, though that was a large part of the story. The microcomputer makers had found a buying public the major companies had overlooked. But their profits stood on a base of solid technical innovation. From the first Apple machine onward, the microcomputer hackers had made a virtue of the limited data storage capacity at their disposal by developing an interactive connection between the keyboard and the videoscreen. The user could see at once what was going on in the machine. This enhanced the computer's game-playing ability; but far more importantly, it set up a new, almost conversational relationship between user and machine in which many began to see inviting educational possibilities. When this capacity for instant interaction was combined with Stephen Wozniak's ingenious disk drive for the Apple II, the world of floppy disk software suddenly blossomed, soon to become an industry in its own right with an outreach far beyond hackers and professionals. Even Big Blue would have to come to terms with a technological breakthrough of this importance; it would have to revise its plans and enter the personal computing competition in earnest. But IBM was well behind in the race, and it lacked the guerrilla hackers' entrepreneurial daring and unbuttoned innovational style. Their invention, the microcomputer, was a runaway sensation that looked as if it might change the American way of life at every level—including the manners and morals of the marketplace.

The hackers even had a friend (of sorts) in the governor's office who could speak for their vision and command a national, mainstream audience. The heady exuberance of the period vibrated through the annual trade fairs of the new industry, starting with the first held in Marin County in 1977, where the astonishing Apple II was first unveiled. These events were becoming latter-day countercultural gatherings in the San Francisco Bay Area. Those who attended still speak of their experience of excited wonder as they walked among the exhibits surveying the technological power that seemed to be before them for the taking. All the while, throughout Silicon Valley, new firms, clever new products, bright new social possibilities were springing up too fast to be counted. And the money was pouring in. Apple Computer astounded its founders by doing $200,000 worth of business in 1976. The next year, it sold $7 million worth of Apples. Five years later, it had come within sight of the billion dollar mark. In the meantime, it had gone public on the stock market, instantaneously transforming its backers into multimillionaires.

At the zenith of his success, Stephen Wozniak, cofounder of Apple and now a countercultural Horatio Alger, decided it was time to put all the money to good use. Dropping out of the company, he decided to revive the flagging spirit of the dissenting 1960s. He set about producing a big outdoor rock festival—bigger than Woodstock and wholly dedicated to the unfolding promise of the Information Age. There were two of these events, one in 1982, the second in 1983. Together they cost Wozniak $20 million of his own money. From all around the country, the rebels, the dropouts, the surviving hippies, the rock stars came to mingle with the new wealth of Silicon Valley and to create . . . who could say what revolutionary possibilities?

They were called the US Festivals.

REVERSIONARIES AND TECHNOPHILES
■

Utopian visions of the future have generally been divided between two philosophical camps. The first—it might be called the *reversionary* scenario—has begun by wishing the industrial world away. The nineteenth century socialist leader and artist William Morris typifies this viewpoint. Anguished by the moral horrors of Victorian factory life and the aesthetic horrors of mass production, Morris (in his *News from Nowhere*) envisaged a postindustrial future that recreated the preindustrial past, a society of villages, family farms, and tribal settlements. His ideal economy was based on the handicrafts; government was an informal communal arrangement among virtuous bucolics.

In contrast, other utopians—the *technophiles*—have enthusiastically embraced the urban-industrial system, hoping to see it mature into a wholly new order of life in which science and technology have permanently mastered the forces of nature and have undertaken to redesign the planet. This is the future predicted by Francis Bacon in his *New Atlantis* and by H. G. Wells in his *Shape of Things To Come*.

The future which the guerrilla hackers envisioned is unique in its determination to synthesize these two seemingly contradictory images. They wanted to have it both ways. Committed by their tastes and talents to the expansion of high tech, they had no hesitation in seeking to play through the full repertory of computer electronics and global telecommunications. But the new technology would be contained within an organic and communitarian political context. Somehow the folksy, funky ways of the Homebrew Computer Club and Community Memory would be preserved. Things would be kept decentralized and humanly scaled; indeed, the computer would make that very result possible. It would undergird a new Jeffersonian democracy based, not upon the equal distribution of land, but upon equal access to information. The destiny of the microcomputer was to create a global culture of electronic villages cradled in a healthy natural environment—the sort of world one found scattered through the pages of the *Whole Earth Catalog*. In this charming and idealistic scenario, one pictures the computer terminal as a sort of hearth or campfire around which, by way of their modems and satellite transmitters, the clans gather to exchange gossip and graffiti with their counterparts half a world away. So rustic was some of the imagery of this worldview that one might almost believe the computer was a new kind of plow. There was, for example, the poem which Richard Brautigan wrote in the later 1960s. Its title, "All Watched Over by Machines of Loving Grace," was later appropriated by Loving Grace Cybernetics, the company that set up the Berkeley Community Memory experiment in 1973.

> I like to think (and
> the sooner the better!)
> of a cybernetic meadow
> where mammals and computers
> live together in mutually
> programming harmony
> like pure water
> touching clear sky
>
> I like to think
> (right now, please!)
> of a cybernetic forest
> filled with pines and electronics
> where deer stroll peacefully
> past computers
> as if they were flowers
> with spinning blossoms
>
> I like to think
> (it has to be!)
> of a cybernetic ecology
> where we are free of our labors

and joined back to nature,
returned to our mammal
brothers and sisters,
and all watched over
by machines of loving grace [8]

The computer was not the first or the only piece of advanced technology to be assimilated to this hybrid reversionary-technophiliac vision. Earlier on, as we have seen, there was a similar fascination with Buckminster Fuller's geodesic dome, which became for many of those in the counterculture of the 1960s and 1970s a sort of futuristic wigwam. The one major effort of the period at building a village of domes—it was called Drop City, located on the outskirts of Trinidad, Colorado—was described by its founders as a "weed-patch commune." Its domes were assembled out of junked cars from the nearest dump. While it lasted from 1965 to about 1975, Drop City sought to be an easy amalgamation of sophisticated engineering and tribal simplicity. [9] Along these same lines, there was the zany media metaphysics of Marshall McLuhan, who saw television and the computer as the electronic building blocks of a "global village" that would be cozy and participative, yet technologically sophisticated. There was the architect Paolo Soleri, who believed that the solution to the ecological crisis of the times would be found in his megastructural "arcologies"—ant-heap cities in which the urban billions could be neatly compacted. There was Gerard O'Neill, who barnstormed the country whipping up enthusiasm for the wildest scheme of all: the creation of self-contained space colonies, a "high frontier" where the pioneer spirit might be reborn.

At one point or another during the 1960s and 1970s, each of these became countercultural favorites; O'Neill especially became for a few years the pet project of Stewart Brand and the *Co-Evolution Quarterly,* successor to the *Whole Earth Catalog.* [10] Permeating each of these visionary schemes, one sees the same interplay of values and fantasies, the same hope that the technophiliac road forward will lead to a reversionary future. When H. G. Wells envisioned Things to Come, he saw a gleamingly sterile urban world run by a benevolent technocratic elite. But for many in the counterculture, the result of high industrial technology would be something like a tribal democracy where the citizenry might still be dressed in buckskin and go berry picking in the woods.

At times, this wished-for synthesis of rustic savvy and advanced technology seemed to stem from nothing more than some very slippery metaphors. Thus, McLuhan's conception of the urbanized mass media, pressed to its extreme, becomes a "village." For O'Neill, the space rocket and satellite, developed on a gargantuan scale, return us to a "frontier," which its enthusiasts seemed to think might be something like the world of the log cabin and wood-burning stove. The fans who organized the L-5 Society to promote O'Neill's ideas liked to imagine vistas of homesteads and organic gardens stretching for miles inside their orbiting steel canisters, plus no end of weightless fun and games skydiving and wind surfing in zero gravity. Even Soleri's high-rise human beehives were seen as a way of preserving the threatened wilderness in its pristine condition—though one can only shudder at the prospect of tens of thousands of his arcological tenants lined up at the elevator shafts, waiting to get to the picnic grounds.

Finally, for the surviving remnants of the counterculture in the late 1970s, it was digital data, even more so than domes, arcologies, and space colonies, that would usher the world into the postindustrial promised land. The personal computer would give the millions access to the data bases of the world, which—so the argument went —was what they most essentially needed in order to become a self-reliant citizenry. Computerized networks and bulletin boards would keep the electronic villages in touch, exchanging the vital data that the power elite was denying them. At the same time, clever hackers would penetrate the classified data banks that guarded corporate secrets and the mysteries of state. Who would have predicted it? By way of IBM's video terminals, AT&T's phone lines, Pentagon space shots, and Westinghouse communications satellites, a worldwide movement of computer-literate rebels would arise to build the organic commonwealth. They might even outlast the total collapse of the high industrial system that had invented their technology. For there was a bleak vision of thermonuclear holocaust deeply mixed into the survivalist instincts of the counterculture. It can be seen in one of the more bizarre expressions of the guerrilla hacker worldview, that of Lee Felsenstein, a founder of the Homebrew Computer Club and Community Memory, later the designer of the Osborne portable computer. Felsenstein's technological style—emphasizing simplicity and resourceful recycling—arose from an apocalyptic view of the industrial future. As he saw it,

The industrial infrastructure might be snatched away at any time, and the people should be able to scrounge parts to keep his machine going in the rubble of the devasted society; ideally, the machine's design would be clear enough to allow users to figure out where to put those parts.

As Felsenstein once said, "I've got to design so you can put it together out of garbage cans."[11]

DOMES, DATA, AND DOPE
∎

It is important to appreciate the political idealism that underlay the hopes of the guerrilla hackers. It is quite as important to recognize that the reversionary-technophiliac synthesis on which those hopes were grounded is as naive as it is idealistic. So much so that one feels the need of probing deeper to discover the secret of its strange persuasiveness for so many bright minds. For how could anyone believe something so unlikely?

If we delve a bit further into the origins of the counterculture—back to the late 1950s and early 1960s—we find what may be the most revealing connection between its reversionary and technophiliac values. In the beginning was the music—always the major carrier of the movement: folk, then rock and roll, then rock in all its permutations. Early on, the music, as it was performed in concert and in the new clubs of the period, took on a special mode of presentation, which has now come to be taken for granted on the popular music scene: it was electronically amplified. Its power was borrowed from the apparatus. The youthful audience that crowded the clubs may have looked grungy in the extreme; it may have come brandishing emblems of disaffiliation from industrial society. But that audience wanted its music explosively amplified and expertly modulated by the best means available; it wanted to feel the beat through its pores. Therefore, the music needed machines. And as time went on over the next decade, the music would need more and more machines as the aesthetic tastes of the period summoned a whole new recording technology into existence that began to replace the performers and their instruments with sound engineering of the most complex kind, and finally with various kinds of digital enhancement. The style of the performers may at times have sought to be raw, unadorned, "natural." As in the case of Bob Dylan, it may have wanted to come across with an unwashed and uncouth authenticity. But the technicians were steadily taking control of the music. They would make sure it came out sounding *professionally* unwashed, *expertly* uncouth.

Just as a sound experience, with nothing added, rock was supposedly sufficient to produce mind-blowing results. As one rock connoisseur of the period put it,

> By itself, without the aid of strobe lights, day-glo paints, and other subimaginative copouts, [rock] engages the entire sensorium, appealing to the intelligence with no interference from the intellect. . . . Rock is a tribal phenomenon . . . and constitutes what may be called a twentieth century magic. [12]

But soon enough, the audience wanted the strobe lights and the day-glo paints as well: ecstasies for the eye as well as the ear. Hence the light shows that became an adjunct of rock performances everywhere. The shows were more than a visual accompaniment to the music. They were seized upon at once as a way of reproducing and/or occasioning psychedelic experience. They were the visible signature of dope. And from the outset, the premier dope of the era was LSD, which was itself a technology, a laboratory product that emerged from the advanced research of the Swiss pharmaceutical house of Sandoz and Company.

In the early postwar period, LSD and other laboratory hallucinogens belonged to a small, elite public made up primarily of top dollar psychiatrists and their high society clientele. At that time, before LSD had acquired a criminal aura, mainstream publications like *Time* and *Life* were prepared to celebrate its many therepeutic benefits. But by the early 1960s, the hallucinogens had found another, less respectable public; they were being touted among the beat poets and dropped out youth in the streets of Haight-Ashbury and Greenwich Village as the salvation of our troubled culture. Soon Timothy Leary was proselytizing for dope across America; in the San Francisco Bay Area, as of 1966, Ken Kesey and his Merry Pranksters were blithely dosing whole audiences on this mysterious elixir (or promising to do so) at such public events as the Acid Tests and the Trips Festival.

The assumption underlying these mass distribution efforts was blunt and simple: dope saves your soul. Like the Catholic sacraments, it takes effect *ex opere operato*—by its very ministration. Once this promise crossed wires with the growing interest in oriental mysticism, the psychedelics had been launched as a cultural force. It seemed clear that the research laboratories of Western society—including those of the giant pharmaceutical corporations—had presented the world with a substitute for the age-old spiritual disciplines of the East. Instead of a lifetime of structured contemplation, a few drops of homebrewed acid on a vitamin pill would do the trick. It was the shortcut to enlightenment.

"Better Things for Better Living Through Chemistry" ran the slogan of the Dupont Company. And thousands of youthful acidheads were ready to agree. They had heard the music; they had seen the colored lights; they had sampled the dope. Nothing did more to tilt the counterculture toward a naive technophilia than this seductive trio of delights. If the high tech of the Western world could offer so great a spiritual treasure, then why not more?

Here is the reason why Buckminster Fuller, Marshall McLuhan, and the others struck such a responsive chord among the countercultural young. Acid and rock had prepared an audience for their message, and prepared it in an especially persuasive way that undercut the cerebral levels. For the psychedelics are a powerful, even a shattering experience. Combined with the music and the lights in a total assault upon the senses, they can indeed make anything seem possible. They can induce a sense of grandeur and a euphoria that may make the grimmest political realities seem like paper tigers. At the same time, the experience connects—or so its proselytizers always insisted—with primordial mystical powers of the mind that still flourish, or *might* still flourish, in exotic quarters of the globe, among native practitioners and traditional peoples like Carlos Castaneda's legendary Don Juan. This experience, purchased out of the laboratories of our industrial culture, somehow allied its disciples with the ancient, the primitive, the tribal. Here, then, we find the same surprising blend of the sophisticated-scientific and the natural-communal that Buckminster Fuller claimed for the geometry of the geodesic dome and that the Silicon Valley hackers would eventually claim for the personal computer.

In a 1985 interview, Stewart Brand is quoted as saying, "This generation swallowed computers whole, just like dope." There may be more literal truth to the metaphor than he intended. [13]

DECLINE AND FALL

∎

The meteoric history of the microcomputer "revolution" might be summarized in two sensational advertising efforts. At the beginning of 1984—and in recognition of the year's Orwellian association— Apple Computer ran a million dollar, one minute television spot commercial during the broadcast of the Superbowl game. The ad was meant to be seen only once, strategically located toward the climax of the fourth quarter—an unprecedented extravagance which, in itself, provoked a great deal of comment in the media. Echoing the theme of the year, the commercial showed the face of Big Brother glowering down from a monumental television screen, haranguing a pathetic mass of uniformed minions. Whatever else the scene signified, it represented the monolithic corporate structure of the computer industry, most obviously the dominance of IBM, by then Apple's foremost competitor, and moving up fast in the home computer market. Suddenly, from the ranks of Big Brother's cowering audience, a rebellious spirit emerges. It is a muscular young woman. She rushes forward and flings a Thor-sized hammer at the screen. It shatters. The enslaved millions are free.

These are powerful images of defiance and liberation. With some allowances for histrionic exaggeration, the commercial catches the spirit of the guerrilla hackers who launched the Apple Company with such high hopes for the electronic populism they might help encourage.

But by the end of 1984, things had significantly changed in the microcomputer industry. Its sales had stalled; its market seemed to be all but saturated. One sees the crisis reflected in Apple's major year-end advertising effort. Again, with much fanfare, the company did something unprecedented in its extravagance. It bought out every inch of advertising space in the November election special issue of *Newsweek* and filled the pages with its own copy. The theme of the issue was boldly announced as being "the principle of democracy as it applies to technology: one person, one computer"—in this case, Apple's new Macintosh. But what was it Apple now had to say in behalf of the personal computer? Throughout the magazine, it featured the fictitious story of a clever young entrepreneur (a "yuppie," as he is designated), presumably one of IBM's former chattels, now able to exercise the freedom which Apple has won for him. He has a hot idea and wants to go into business. A sharp, well-informed tycoon, he selects Apple computers and software to design his product and keep his accounts. And what is his product? "Splendora Gourmet Baby Food."

Quite a descent from the idealistic attack upon Big Brother that opened the year. But no doubt a more realistic assessment of where the microcomputer market was to be found.

By early 1985, Steven Jobs, then still president of Apple, was prepared to admit what many critics had long suspected: that the market for the home computer had been vastly overestimated. Lacking the specific, well-recognized use that every household appliance must have, it had been turned into a bewilderingly all-purpose machine, many of whose proposed applications (balancing checkbooks, storing recipes, filing addresses) were plain silly. Too many people—and they were perhaps the major part of those who could afford to buy the machine in the first place—had brought their computer home without any idea of how they would put it to use. The instructions that came with the hardware (quaintly called "documentation" —already a sign of technical mystification) were often incomprehensible; too many times, the computer made simple things inanely complex. And then, no matter how carefully users might select their software from the bewildering clutter that fills the stores, within a few months there was always bound to be something newer and better on the market. The cost, with all the accessories and necessary programs included, was never as cheap as advertised. Indeed, the home computer never gets wholly and completely bought; there is always one more thing to add on in order to get the full benefit. At least where the ordinary consumer is concerned, the prolific dynamism of the computer industry—new companies, new products, whole new concepts—was proving to be self-defeating. *Now* seems never the time to buy.

Facing up to the sagging prospects of the home market, Jobs was prepared to believe that the future of the microcomputer lay in the office and the school. If that much is true, it still marks out a prodigious territory for information technology, one that will continue to exert a powerful influence over our lives. But this is a dramatic change in the career of the personal computer. As of the mid-nineties, the ideal of an electronic populism based on the near-universal distribution of personal computers was badly faded. Apple Computer, the champion of the cause, suffering the same killing market pressures as IBM, had gone into partnership with the dreaded Big Blue. Economic recession makes strange bedfellows. The giants of the industry have all proved to be financially vulnerable, making large-scale mergers and corporate colossalism the wave of the future.

Some still hope gamely for great, liberating things from the Internet and local bulletin boards. Critic Jon Katz, writing in *Rolling Stone* in the Spring of 1993, called "digital news" the "purest journalistic medium since smoke signals...the first medium the whole planet can be connected to at once." True enough for those who put the technology to that use. And yet all the bright possibilities seem so disturbingly compatible with corporate control and commercial exploitation. The data merchants have not, after all, given up on the home and individual consumer market; they have simply diverted it to more trivial and lucrative uses. Every time computer prices drop, people still rush to buy, but once they get their machines home, what they are given to do with them is less and less what principled hackers had in mind. If the Apple II landmarked the high, idealistic hopes of the seventies, what are we to make of the Apple Newton MessagePad of the nineties—an electronic notebook costing hundreds of dollars that takes days to "learn" its owner's handwriting and many minutes to record a luncheon date?

Upscale commercial networks like CompuServe and Prodigy may find a growing public for stock market reports and video-shopping services. They may also offer sanitized equivalents of talk-radio—which is rarely a forum of reasoned discourse. And no doubt games will continue to thrive—including adult games that gravitate toward classier, 3D and virtualized forms of erotic fantasy. Perhaps, in this era of megabyte financial strategies and AIDS, the computer will find a future guerrilla hackers could never have predicted. It will become the ideal medium for economic vandalism and safe sex.

THE POLITICS OF INFORMATION

∎

NOTHING BUT THE FACTS

Facts alone are wanted in life. Plant nothing else, and
root out everything else. You can only form the minds
of reasoning animals upon Facts: nothing else will ever
be of any service to them.

Mr. Gradgrind in *Hard Times*
by Charles Dickens

Without the computer, the cult of information would be unthinkable. Yet well before even the most primitive data processing machinery existed, there was one well-organized political movement
that precociously recognized the persuasive force of facts and figures
in the modern world. These were the English Utilitarians of the early
nineteenth century, the true-believing disciples of the eccentric philosopher Jeremy Bentham. Their career as one of the most far-reaching intellectual influences of modern times offers an instructive
critical model. All the essential elements of the cult of information
are there—the facade of ethical neutrality, the air of scientific rigor,
the passion for technocratic control. Only one thing is missing: the
computer. The Benthamites lacked a spectacular machinery that
could dazzle the public with godlike authority and win its bewildered
acquiescence. Ultimately, this absence of an intimidating technology
made their ideological bias apparent. They can therefore serve as a
case study, reminding us that information is never neutral; it is political through and through.

The Benthamites are one of the first distinctly modern movements in political philosophy; they are inextricably part of an industrial system. The very name they took for themselves—Utilitarianism —reflects the hard-headed practicality, the unsentimental assertion of material values that dominated the new economic order of their day. England was the first society to enter the age of the machine and the factory. It did so gropingly, blindly, by fits and starts. Through the early nineteenth century, industrial towns were springing up like strange, overnight growths on the land, producing convulsive dislocation. The population of the society mushroomed in numbers and began to shift massively across the countryside. Whole new forms of labor, property, marketing, invention rose suddenly into existence, and with them new social values, new political forces. The Utilitarians were among the first to grasp the historical importance of this swift, confusing transformation and to send up a cheer for what many others saw as a social calamity. Also, intuitively, they grasped that in societies as chronically dynamic as England was becoming, the control of facts—or even the *apparent* control of facts —begets power. It creates the impression of competence; it confers the very ability to govern.

In an industrial society, change is the order of the day. But change destroys old certainties; it bewilders and makes anxious. In the midst of the seeming chaos that arrived with the industrial revolution, the Utilitarians boldly seized the philosophical initiative, insisting that change could become progress if it was used as the opportunity for reform. And the secret of reform was the control of facts, lots of facts. In their own time, the Utilitarians were also known as "philosophical radicals" precisely because they were among the strongest champions of reform in all fields—law, economics, education, welfare, prisons, sanitation. In their many campaigns for public improvement, intensive fact-finding was always the first order of business. They were driven by the conviction that the facts, if gathered in sufficient quantity, could be trusted to speak for themselves. Line them up on the page, and they will reveal waste, corruption, inefficiency, wherever it exists.

The historian G. M. Young describes what he calls "the Benthamite formula" as consisting of "inquiry, legislation, execution, inspection, and report."[1] The inquiry, inspection, and report stages of that formula gave rise to the great public investigations of the Victorian period by parliamentary and royal commissions. Today, we take it for granted that governments are in the business of collecting data. But this was a strange new idea in Bentham's time, when no society as yet even troubled to take an accurate census. The Utilitarians changed all that. "In a few years," Young observes, "the public mind had been flooded with facts and figures bearing on every branch of national life ... No community in history had ever been submitted to so searching an examination." It was not unusual for a single Victorian commission to produce several printed volumes crammed with data and statistics. And if the inquiry resulted in the creation of a new administrative agency, as was usually the case, then the record keeping would snowball, as year by year the government's fact finding continued. Before the century was halfway through, these vast quantities of information were being compiled into the famous Victorian Blue Books, the densest collection of social statistics in human history.

The Blue Books were the source from which Karl Marx would later draw all the damning evidence he needed for his indictment of capitalism. He did not feel he had to budge from his desk at the British Museum in order to do the job. All the data he required were there in black and white before him. By Prime Minister Gladstone's time at the end of the century, thanks to the ingrained Benthamite style, the practice of politics had been dramatically reshaped. "Knowledge of the facts," Young observes, "and an apt handling of figures was ... the surest proof of capacity" in public life. Gladstone, whose carefully wrought budgets were the new world standard of modern statecraft, was perhaps the first politician to build a career on the magisterial control of social statistics. He would make an admirable showing these days in an American presidential debate, spouting numbers in all directions.

In their fascination for the collection of data, the Utilitarians may be seen as the distant heirs of Francis Bacon. Bacon's interest, of course, was science; Bentham's was legal affairs and economics. But there is a connection between the two. Just as Bacon believed that little bits and pieces of data would conveniently arrange themselves into laws of nature, so the Utilitarians believed that the social facts produced by sound inquiry would instantly prove the failures of existing laws and institutions, and so point directly to the obvious solution. This conviction lent the Utilitarians a certain brash but refreshing air of supreme confidence. They stood ready to investigate everything with a sharp, critical eye, no matter how time-honored and hoary with tradition. They reveled in their intellectual insurgency, delighting to show up the folly and confusion of ancient customs, of which there were many still actively alive in English society. They took courage from their peculiar weapon: the fact, the omnipotent fact, against which neither sentiment nor emotional rhetoric could stand.

Yet despite their stance of studied objectivity, the Utilitarians actually worked from a definite political ideology, a not-so-very-hidden agenda of ideas and ideals that served to animate the information they collected. It is important to underscore this aspect of their work because it reveals the inevitable interplay of ideas and information. In the case of Bentham's followers, this can be seen vividly in their most ambitious official fact-finding campaign: the nationwide survey of the British Poor Law in 1833. This was the largest investigative project every undertaken. The inquiry covered the nation, descending to such fine points as weighing out the bread and gruel served in poorhouses across the land.

We now know that the Utilitarians who served on this great inquiry were determined from the outset to scuttle the system. So they assiduously documented the waste, the inconsistency, the ineptitude of the Old Poor Law. That was hardly difficult to do. The Poor Law was, in reality, not a single law but a centuries-old jumble of statutes and regulations for dealing with every form of social dependency: the sick, the aged, the handicapped, the jobless, the orphaned, the insane. Over the generations, this all-purpose program had compounded into an incoherent tangle of contradictions and improvisations. The Utilitarians, documenting the mess, quickly convinced the government that the law should be replaced by a new, uniform, centralized, and far cheaper program of their own design. They won their point. The result was the draconian workhouse system we find depicted in the novels of Charles Dickens. While the Poor Law Commission sought to make its survey look totally neutral—a purely professional inquiry based on principles of sound economy—it was shaped from the beginning by a well-structured social philosophy, based, for example, on the assumption that poverty was a form of criminal parasitism which deserved to be punished and that too generous a system of relief will only corrupt the people's will to work. Lurking behind the investigation was a perfectly dismal vision of human nature and a grim obsession with cash values. The Utilitarians firmly believed that the poor must be whipped to work. This made them the allies of factory owners, who had reduced the conditions of labor to an inhuman level. It would be no exaggeration to say that, with the lash of pure fact in their hands, the Benthamites helped produce the work force of the industrial revolution.

Thus, the Utilitarians, who made so important an early contribution to the cult of information, were as morally and politically motivated as any political pressure group. They might be seen as the forerunners of all the think tanks and policy study centers of our day which continue to fill the political arena with ideologically biased pronouncements decked out to look like purely academic exercises. Indeed, it was because the Utilitarians linked their passion for social research to a coldblooded, unfeeling social philosophy that they succeeded in making their principled concern for the facts obnoxious to a more humane spirit like Dickens. In *Hard Times,* his classic tale of an early industrial town, Dickens takes the Utilitarians severely to task, portraying them as heartless drudges and hypocrites who believe that facts are more real than flesh. Dickens's stereotypic Utilitarian is Mr. Gradgrind the schoolmaster, who believes the essence of education is filling his pupils' minds with as much information as possible. Facts, nothing but facts. It is the school system, as Dickens shrewdly recognized, that forms the mind of the times. And in Mr. Gradgrind's school, there is no room for anything but atomistic data and quantities.

What is a horse? he asks his pupils. The answer gets down to the facts of the matter.

> Quadruped. Graminivorous. Forty teeth, namely twenty-four grinders, four eye-teeth, and twelve incisive. Sheds coat in the Spring; in marshy country, sheds hoofs too. Hoofs hard, but requiring to be shod in iron. Age known by marks in mouth.

If computers had existed in his day, Mr. Gradgrind would have hastened to fill his school with them. They would have delivered all the data he wanted at the stroke of a key, perhaps with animated graphics in a three-dimensional simulation. But his purely statistical quadruped would still have been no living creature.

DATA GLUT

■

The new power is not money in the hands of the few,
but information in the hands of the many.
John Naisbitt, *Megatrends*

When it comes to data mongering, our politics has become a Utilitarian dream come true. The relentless fact finding that Bentham and his followers recognized as a necessity of life in an urban-industrial society has been permanently installed in an ever-growing contingent of government agencies and bureaus. With the advent of the computer, it has grown into a major service industry of the private sector. Decision makers both private and public now enjoy limitless supplies of information delivered with lightning speed.

We might learn a valuable and seemingly obvious political lesson from the early example of the Utilitarians at work in the arena of public policy. Namely, it is not facts that determine policy, but more often policy that determines the facts—by selection, adjustment, distortion. Nevertheless, it is part of the folklore of the Information Age that the computer, especially in the form of the personal computer, will bring us a democratic renaissance. The machine that makes an abundance of data available to every man and woman in their home is supposedly destined to be a liberating force. The idea traces back to Marshall McLuhan, who predicted in the mid-1960s that the several electrical media would transform the planet into a global village where "instant information creates involvement in depth."

McLuhan primarily had television in mind; he insisted that people sitting passively in front of cathode ray tubes, watching a steady display of images from around the world, were somehow becoming more participative citizens. Computer enthusiasts have expanded the idea to a new use of the video screen: its capacity to function interactively with its viewer, producing an endless supply of material from data bases everywhere in response to the viewer's demand. "The computer will smash the pyramid," John Naisbitt tells us. "We created the hierarchical, pyramidal, managerial system because we needed it to keep track of people and things people did; with the computer to keep track, we can restructure our institutions horizontally."

This prospect is surely based on an odd diagnosis of our social ills. It assumes that the body politic is starving for lack of information and that only the computer can make good that shortage. One must picture the newsstands, the bookstores, the libraries of the nation picked clean by a population that has consumed their precious stores of data and now hungers for more than these sources can provide.

Obviously this is not so. The public has hardly exhausted the information that is now readily available to it. For the price of subscribing to one of the country's better newspapers and a few well-selected magazines, most households could easily and cheaply increase their information supply severalfold. For that matter, a letter to one's representatives in Washington will bring a spate of free government publications filled with information in any field one cares to name: committee hearings, special reports, brochures, booklets. All of this, the reams of research and statistics pumped out by official agencies both state and federal, is available to any interested citizen. Some of what these sources send may be reliable, some of it not. There is no way around the problem of personal evaluation. After all, many of the data base services accessed by computer have been compiled from the same sources. A government report that gets written up in the *New York Times* and is then digested into the NEXIS data base does not automatically gain credibility by being computerized. As for official secrets and classified data, which may often be what citizens most need, these are not apt to be accessible except to clever hackers who can infiltrate well-guarded government files. Ironically, computers that can violate personal privacy do not assure public access.

One might argue that if the public took advantage of all the information the U.S. Post Office could deliver to its front door from public and private providers, it would soon be awash in data.[2] In some of the world's totalitarian societies, the great political problem may be an official censorship that works to choke off the flow of information. In ours, the problem is just the opposite. If anything, we suffer from a glut of unrefined, undigested information flowing in from every medium around us. Here is a problem the Utilitarians never foresaw: that there can be *too much* information. So much that the forest gets lost among the trees. The result is then a new variety of politics in which governments do not restrict the flow of information but flood the public with it. One is reminded of Orwell's *1984*, where Big Brother's ubiquitous loud speakers steadily drone on with bewildering statistics of production and consumption. To be sure, in *1984* the information was monolithic; there was no critical competition. But where competing sources do exist, as in our society, the strategy of government is not to censor but to counter fact with fact, number with number, research with research. It even becomes advantageous to have lots of contention about facts and figures, a statistical blizzard that numbs the attention.

In the view of some computer enthusiasts, data glut is no worse than an unfortunate, temporary imbalance in the system. So John Naisbitt tell us, "We have for the first time an economy based on a key resource that is not only renewable but self-generating. Running out of it is not a problem, but drowning in it is. Data is now doubling every twenty months." However, he confidently predicts, the problem will soon be corrected. How? By computers. "Information technology brings order to the chaos of information pollution and therefore gives value to data that would otherwise be useless." More specifically, an "on-line information selection business" is fast appearing; it will serve to filter the glut and organize it to our personal specifications.

What Naisbitt has in mind are various specialized data bases and bibliographic services to which home computer users can subscribe, often at a hefty price. By one count, there were some 2,200 data bases on the market in early 1985. [3] But these services are "selective" only in the sense that they arrange material by subject matter, in the same way that a library card catalog or newspaper index does. Nothing about quality, honesty, or pertinence is implied by the service. Ultimately, data bases, like all reference aids, are the creation of people who have decided what should or should not be entered into the system. Data base compilers are also capable of mistakes due to boredom and burnout. The mysterious, oracular character of the computer—its impersonal, efficient operation—may disguise that fact from many users, but it remains so. The companies that assemble data bases are apt indiscriminately to include anything that offers their service the look of respectable expertise; certainly they will include official sources and statements, congressional hearings, government reports and documents. Suppose, then, one wants to research the debate over the MX missile. A computerized data base will dutifully deliver everything it holds on the subject, including all the Pentagon materials that have been produced for public consumption. Any more refined "selection"—say, with respect to who's making sense and telling the truth—must inevitably be left up to users. If they are inclined to trust their government in such matters, access to a standard data base like NEXIS or the Bibliographic Reference Service will only strengthen the government's case in their view. If they are prone to be mesmerized by a flashy show of facts by experts in the field, they will still be the victims of data glut. No data base will ever be invented that answers to the command: "Show me everything that is true and relevant."

What computer enthusiasts overlook is the fact that data glut is not some unforeseen, accidental fluctuation of supply, like a bumper crop of wheat. It is a strategy of social control, deliberately and often expertly wielded. It is one of the main ways in which modern governments and interest groups obfuscate issues to their own advantage; they dazzle and distract with more raw data than the citizenry can hope to sort through. Since the Kennedy–Nixon debates of 1960, the prevailing rhetorical style of our political leadership has been to saturate the public attention with information—usually numbers: economic indicators, budgetary projections, social statistics, throw weights, megatonnage, body counts, ratios, percentages, trends.... It worked for Kennedy, who seemed to have a computerized brain. Ever since then, candidates have been reading often senseless or fictitious numbers off the teleprompter at a mile a minute. Politicians to come will continue to do the same for as long as the public stands ready to be impressed or intimidated by a barrage of facts and figures.

The computer did not generate this treacherous style of political discourse. As we have seen, the Utilitarians were masters at it when data processing was no more than a matter of scratching things down with a pen on paper. Behind the style stands the mystique of scientific expertise that lends authority to those who marshal facts in a cool, objective manner. The computer is simply a mechanical embodiment of that mystique; it borrows upon our deference to scientistic jargon and our weakness for machine dependence. But it also allows information to be compiled and manipulated in far more befuddling ways, always with the assumption that whatever comes out of a computer must be reliable.

In the 1980 presidential elections, the American public was confronted by candidate Ronald Reagan with a dire assessment of the national defense. His arguments brimmed with figures. There was supposedly a "window of vulnerability" in our defenses which placed the nation in immediate danger of annihilation. The "window" had been discovered by computer-simulated war games. The Reagan administration used this scenario and the resulting public anxiety to initiate the largest military buildup in history, only later to admit under critical pressure that many of its facts, figures, assumptions, and deductions were erroneous.[4] But by the time the opposition had caught up with the errors and deceptions, the Defense Department had opened a whole new front filled with more studies and scenarios and simulations. It was called the Strategic Defense Initiative: "Star Wars."

It is hardly novel that governments should yield to the temptation of lying or misleading. But to deceive by glutting the public with more expertly engineered information than it can digest is a decidedly new and highly effective twist, one to which the computer makes an indispensable contribution.

ISSUES BEFORE INFORMATION
■

The politics of information makes strange bedfellows. Left, right, and center—by the Sunbelt conservatives, the high tech liberals, the guerrilla hackers—we are assured that information will empower the citizenry and save democracy. But in all cases, we are confronted by sprawling conceptions of information that work from the assumption that thinking is a form of information processing and that, therefore, *more* data will produce *better* understanding. The result is that the computer enthusiasts quickly fall victim to the strategy of data glut and then seek to defend themselves by once again turning to the computer for a solution.

But there is no solution to be found in mechanized methods of organizing the glut. Rather, we must insist upon a new standard of political discourse. In a vital democracy, it is not the quantity but the *quality* of information that matters. What are the criteria of quality? Relevance, coherence, and insight. How do we bring these criteria into play? By shaping information into issues. Issues, in turn, are well formulated when they help to focus attention, raise questions, facilitate criticism, and finally allow us to make choices with the sense that we have intelligently discriminated among all the available options.

Once again we arrive at the all-important distinction between information and ideas. Information is transformed into a political issue when it is illuminated by an idea—about justice, freedom, equality, security, duty, loyalty, public virtue, the good society. We inherit ideas like these out of our rich tradition of political philosophy: from Plato and Aristotle, Machiavelli and Hobbes, Jefferson and Marx. Very little of what these minds offer is connected with information. If it were, the data would long since have been antiquated; but the ideas live on, a rock-solid ethical substructure on which laws, programs, and policies continue to be based, even by politicians who may never have read these thinkers. In addition to discursive philosophy, mythic themes provide some of the most durable ideas in our political repertory. The legendary image of the Biblical prophet Nathan challenging King David in the name of a higher law, the folk memory of Adam and Eve living in an original anarchic equality, have had more to do with stirring revolutionary energies than any body of sociological research. For that matter, wholly fabulous characters in our popular culture—Horatio Alger's virtuous street urchins or the gunslingers of the Old West—have everything to do with the creation of popular political values. The great utopias of More and Bellamy and the dystopias of Huxley and Orwell similarly have nothing to do with "facts"; but these are the living images of the good (or evil) society which sway people's imaginations. Such ideas live on because they are powerful answers to universal political questions; the depth of experience, the quality of thought, the magnitude of the aspirations that went into those answers infuses them with a special persuasiveness. Facts, if they are to be of any value, need to be used in the service of images and ideas like these. When that happens, one good fact can be worth a thousand irrelevant details.

For a number of years, until it stopped circulating, I subscribed to *I. F. Stone's Weekly*, a landmark of American journalism. To its loyal readership, the *Weekly* was of greater value than a dozen ordinary newspapers; none of us would have traded it for free subscriptions to the major news magazines. Yet it was only four pages long. Obviously, it did not carry much information; but it was the work of a razor-sharp political intelligence. Behind it, there was a mind that confronted the affairs of the day, knowing what questions to ask and how to tell the relevant from the worthless. One did not have to agree with Stone in order to appreciate his journalism; one profited from his guidance in showing where the contours of public debate lay. Investigative reporting of Stone's caliber reminds us that news, which is the daily pulse of politics, is never simply information; it is not raw factual material that simply drops out of the world into a data base. It is focused inquiry and interpretation based upon a solid set of ideas about the world: what matters, where is the history of our time heading, what's at stake, what are the hidden agendas, what is the big picture? The answers to these questions are the ideas that determine the value of information. Often what a good journalist must do is cast out tons of obfuscating data glut in order to get down to the living truth.

It is the vitality of issues that saves democracy. At most the computer makes a limited and marginal contribution to that goal. Certainly the snippets and summaries its so-called new services offer (such as the Compuserve Information Service and The Source Newswire, edited from the United Press International) are inconsequential for anything that goes beyond weather and stock market reports. As a political nation, we would be better off if the mainstream public were actively in touch with a few good journals of opinion (left, right, and center) than if we had a personal computer in every home.

ON-LINE COMMUNITIES: THE PROMISE OF NETWORKING
■

There is another, more promising use to which computers can be put besides that of struggling to overcome data glut. Indeed, that has always been a strictly secondary item on the agenda of many politically engaged hackers. The information they have wanted most to access has not been data bases but other people's ideas. Their hope has been that the networking capacity of the technology—the ability to tie personal computers together through the phone lines—might be a means of building communities of citizenly concern. The result would be an expanding forum of opinion and debate. Most notably, Seymour Papert has championed the ideal of "alternative computer cultures," not only among minorities and special interest groups within the advanced industrial societies, but also within and between Third World nations. In large measure, his programming language Logo is meant to help children and meagerly educated adults achieve enough computer literacy so that they can build their own computer culture. His hope is that computer networks might serve to leapfrog the underdeveloped societies into the twentieth century by gaining them access to many kinds of expertise (education, medicine, trade, agriculture) as well as to one another's experience.[5]

Unfortunately, but typically, networking of this kind also gets swept under the sprawling rubric of "information"; yet it is a distinctly different use of the computer, one that offers possibilities well worth exploring. Some of these are already available in a pioneering form. Commercial networks like Compuserve (with some 75,000 subscribers) and The Source (with some 40,000) now make it possible for home computer owners to join together in nationwide teleconferencing on a variety of topics. Compuserve's SIGs (special interest groups) include ongoing discussions of numerous political and social issues. The Source's PARTI conference line has been used by Representative Edward Markey (Democrat-Massachusetts) to solicit views on the nuclear freeze. PARTI has also been called into service by its subscribers following such crises as the Grenada invasion or the Soviet downing of the Korean airliner 007. Teleconferences are similarly available by way of the Electronic Information Exchange System (EIES), run by the New Jersey Institute of Technology, and the University of Michigan's Confer II, both of which can be used either as open discussions among all subscribers or by smaller groups pursuing a specific project.[6]

The cheaper local versions of these national networks are the hundreds of bulletin board systems (BBSs) which can now be found in new, computer-created constituencies that are usually about the size of telephone area codes. For the additional cost of a modem, a terminal program, and possibly a special dedicated phone line, any computer owner can become a "sysop" (systems operator) and run a BBS for any purpose. All one needs to do in order to draw a following is to pass one's phone number around, perhaps by placing it on other, existing bulletin boards in the area. Some of these electronic forums have a political focus; all of them can be used to send out community alerts, raise local issues, and work up discussions of current affairs.[7] One BBS that has been much praised as a model of computerized democracy is The Chariot, organized in the Colorado Springs area by political activist Dave Hughes. He has used his regional network to campaign successfully on several issues before the state and local legislatures. One of Hughes's objectives is to have every elected representative in the state on line for instant communication night and day—though it is difficult to understand why politicians should be more responsive to electronic mail than to ordinary letters.

While they are similar to citizen band radio and to phone-in radio programs, computer networks are in many ways a unique form of communication. There is no other way in which a great number of people over an area as large as the world's telephone system can exchange ideas in so unstructured a way at all hours of the day and night, and even preserve a transcript in the form of hard copy. The mode of discourse—words typed on to a video screen—may be an awkward substitute for face-to-face conversation, but, strangely enough, there are those who find the anonymity of the medium peculiarly attractive. Supposedly, the impersonality which personal computers make possible to networkers has a liberating and leveling effect; it blanks out race, age, gender, looks, timidity, and handicaps and encourages frankness. No doubt it also encourages a certain amount of role playing; networkers, like CB radio broadcasters, tend to use colorful, made-up "handles" rather than their names. That, in turn, can lead to pranks and irresponsible outbursts. Some BBS printouts I have seen carry a striking amount of rather nasty material: racist and sexist slurs, dirty jokes, profanity. The medium weakens toward becoming electronic graffiti. As with phone-in radio, there can be a certain populist vitality to all this. But will cyberspace become a vast collection of solipsistic enclaves where the like-minded exchange E-mail with one another and where we choose our own news of a no-longer shared world? Some observers, like Dan Kennedy writing in the July/August 1993 issue of *The Media Culture Review,* worry that we may be losing our "sense of shared cultural experience." He wonders if "people will travel the information highway with blinders on, reinforcing their prejudices, closed to new ideas." Breaking down the elitism of the media is undoubtedly desirable, but will what replaces that elite represent enlightened public debate? Not all the signs are encouraging.

While there are racist, white power, and American Nazi networks that fall within the constitutional limits of free speech, a child pornography network came to light in 1985 which was transmitting the names and addresses of children who were available for sexual exploitation.[8] The medium never guarantees anything about the quality of its messages.

Still, even as a relatively costly means of communication, networking can do valuable service and surely deserves to be explored fully for all it is worth. I will offer only two cautionary notes that networkers might bear in mind; both are based on historical experience.

First, it is worth remembering that the original computer network—it dates back to the early 1970s—was the ARPAnet, which began as soon as "packet switching" telecommunications was able to link computer terminals across the country. The ARPAnet was developed to allow military computers to transfer data; but almost at once it was appropriated by people—namely, the military contractors and consultants at major laboratories and universities. This unintended, human ARPAnet sprang up spontaneously to exchange information about weapons and strategies among the experts.[9] This is precisely the sort of computer abuse that guerrilla hackers feared; but it is an application invented and utilized by those social forces that have bankrolled most of what computers can do, including networking. Members of the military-industrial complex continue to innovate applications which ordinary citizens will never be able to afford or exploit; in all its most advanced uses, the computer is *their* machine. Using it for more citizenly purposes has always been a matter of outsmarting or outflanking those who dominate the technology.

Second, the promise that networkers see in the computer is much like that offered by citizen band radio in the 1960s and 1970s. While its range was restricted to the immediate locality, CB radio could have been used to build local communities. In this respect, it offered the benefit of actual speech between people: the human reality of tone, nuance, emphasis—all of which are indispensable to the most effective exchange of ideas. CB radio was also cheaper and freer than computer networking since, unlike computers which are restricted to privately owned phone lines, it made use of an open public utility: the broadcast air.

But CB radio was rarely used for anything more politically significant than giving speeding truckers the chance to elude the high-way patrol, a sort of minimally anarchist gesture of rebellion. For the most part, it became another consumer novelty. There are many signs that home computers will repeat that pattern, wasting their promise in frivolous, lightweight uses that have no great political relevance. The shelves of the computer retailers are packed with video games, exercise programs, household budgeting, recipes, horoscopes. It is the proliferation of such funware, gameware, and a great deal of junkware that presently passes for the "information revolution." Similarly, those who package and sell networking services are not apt to have much interest in encouraging controversial political uses. Compuserve is owned and operated by H & R Block, the tax consultants; The Source belongs to the *Reader's Digest*. It is no surprise that networks run by such interests are overwhelmingly taken up with shop talk among hobbyists, travel tips, dating and purchasing services, sexual banter, and long-range "interactive tele-gaming."

At the local level, the major preoccupation of bulletin board subscribers seems to be "user groups." These are networks made up of people who use the same brand of computer and who are in search of advice about the equipment that brought the network into existence in the first place: a strangely incestuous aspect of computing. Beyond this, there are numerous amusements: film and restaurant reviews, jokes, occult lore, soap opera summaries, Dungeons and Dragons. . . . In most of the BBS hard copy I have seen, the gems of thought lie scattered through a dense thicket of trivia, cute limericks, snippets of opinion, off-the-wall outbursts, illegible fragments. I would be inclined to see much of this as simply another source of data glut, requiring more time to sort through and glean than it is worth. Is networking really better than gathering of an evening at a nearby coffeehouse, or pub, or cafe to make conversation?

There is nothing wrong with the sort of diversions that presently fill the networks; but there is nothing magnificent about it either. It leaves one to ponder: what information did the computer enthusiasts think the American public was waiting to receive from this medium before it became an enlightened democracy? And how much of that information really had to be provided by an expensive piece of electrical equipment? Certainly very little of what gets done by way of computer networks *has* to be done that way. For the price of the network subscription fee, the connect time, and the cost of a modem, one could subscribe to a dozen magazines and newsletters. The computer can perhaps function as a flashy replacement for the printed word. It can keep countless bits and bytes of data sizzling across the global power grid. But what has that got to do with rebuilding democracy?

BEN FRANKLIN'S INFORMATION SERVICE

■

Libraries, Literacy, and the Ecology of Mind

THE PUBLIC LIBRARY: THE MISSING LINK IN THE INFORMATION AGE

■

The city, county, and state libraries of our nation represent the oldest, best-developed reference and reading resource available to the general public. A genuinely idealistic institution dedicated to a high standard of public service, the library has been offering intellectual sustenance to our society since the days of Benjamin Franklin; indeed, as a concept, it emerges from the Age of Reason that invented the democratic politics which the Age of Information is now supposed to serve. Yet it is striking that, in the superheated public discussion of computer technology, the library is so rarely mentioned.

To some degree the library may be a missing link between the computer and our society at large because, in the public mind—and perhaps in the minds of many librarians as well—it is too closely associated with print-on-paper to seem compatible with high tech. But this is hardly justified; the library has been reaching well beyond books since it first included magazines in its collection. It has continued expanding the diversity of its holdings ever since; its resources have been gracefully extended to include film, records, audio and videocassettes, maps and charts, graphic materials. There are even toy libraries and, in my hometown, Berkeley, California, a public tool library where one can borrow power drills and jackhammers.

The library's traditional commitment to books hardly precludes its use of electronic apparatus. In fact, a great deal of the material that has gone into the major databases was formerly embedded in the reference books that have long been the librarian's major tools. Accordingly, libraries have followed where their reference sources have led; librarians can and do use computers when they can find the funding to buy into the technology. For that matter, many if not most of the information brokers in the private sector are former librarians who have gone over to a fee-for-service career.

There may be other, more revealing reasons why computer enthusiasts so often leave the library out of account. The computer has been marketed as an appliance for the affluent middle class, like the Cuisinart and the compact disc player. Its use in the library associates it with ideas of public budgeting and thrifty purchasing, of sensible investments meant to serve a distinctly downscale populace addicted to the unspeakably bad habit of *borrowing* books (and collectively owned books at that!) rather than buying them. This institution does not even pay authors royalties. Since its inception, the library has been an offense to private property.

A true citizen's reference service of this kind clearly does not jibe with the thrust toward making information a proprietary benefit available only by license from those who own it, for whatever fee they care to charge for it. In times past, a book which contained information might be a commodity with a price upon it; but a book is cheap. If it finds its way into a public library, the library owns it and it is available free of charge. And whatever it contains—say, the definitions in a dictionary, the thought in an encyclopedia, the statistics in an almanac—is in the public domain. Nobody collects a fee each time you look up a word in *Webster's* or consult the *Britannica*.

Worse still for its high-tech image, the library, in its democratic outreach, contacts a clientele that includes the genuinely poor, whom the data merchants do not regard as any sort of market at all. More than any group of professionals besides social workers, librarians have been forced to deal with poverty. The poverty is there in the form of the homeless who can be found outside the door of every central city library each morning, waiting to get in off the streets. As of 1990, the American Library Association has gone on record supporting a "poor people's services policy resolution" that guarantees "equal access to information for all," if necessary by eliminating fees and overdue charges, by providing classes in basic literacy, and by creating advisory groups composed of low-income persons and antipoverty activists.

Not all elements in the library world support these goals wholeheartedly, especially not those who want to cultivate a more entrepreneurial image of librarians as information brokers. At a Congress for Librarians conference in 1986 dealing with "Unequal Access to Information Resources," Fay Blake of the University of California, Berkeley, Library School was among the outspoken advocates of meeting the needs of the poor, who, she feels, are ill served by most libraries. Yet the poor, she argues, may need information more desperately than any other patrons; it may be a matter of life and death. But where are they to find it? "The specific kinds of information poor people need are least likely to be collected for commercialized databases." She has in mind information about hot meals, shelter, employment, schools, child care, toilets, washbasins, medical care. "Those who need such information can't pay for it, so it ceases to exist."[1]

The fact that librarians even raise issues like this may explain at least in part why the computer industry, which has been prepared to donate its product to upper-middle-class school districts that can seed its future market, has limited its donations to libraries to one minor effort by the Apple company. The need is there, but not the commercial demographics. When was the last time you saw "information" associated with the needs of the distressed and victimized? This is not the image or the reality that the computer industry wants to cultivate. From its viewpoint, information is upscale merchandise priced to the budget of top-dollar professionals and executive decision makers. The electronic marketplace is well stocked with what that public requires: market reports, tips on resorts and restaurants, dating services, consumer news. In the San Francisco Bay Area, one group of hackers at CompuMentor (their fax is (415) 512-

9629) has offered its expertise to local emergency services agencies to help network information about jobs and housing for the homeless, but I suspect we will wait a long while before we have databanks called Welfarex, Pauperserve, or Joblessnet.

It is not hard to understand the reluctance of the data merchants to feature the library in their marketing. They, after all, are out to sell their wares, both hard and soft. Library sales count for little compared to the prospect of putting a privately owned microcomputer into every home or on every office desk. Moreover, if computers—or at least access to them through a specialist's skills—were readily available free of charge in the library, that might dissuade some potential customers from buying.

But even if libraries find little place in the profit-oriented view of an increasingly commercialized information industry, how are we to account for the silence of professional futurologists, like Alvin Toffler and John Naisbitt, who have done so much to spread the folklore of the Information Age? They give the library no attention whatever. Even more curiously, idealistic hackers who still believe in the possibility of creating a global electronic village have come up with no better idea for spreading the benefits of the new technology than bulletin boards and networks based upon the private ownership of the means of computing. Why do these computer buffs give the library so little of their attention?

Might it be that the library is so distinctly a gendered workplace, one of the traditional women's professions? The library is stereotypically associated with a certain prim and mannerly feminine subservience that is bound up with the age-old culture of books. In contrast, high tech deals with powerful machines representing billion-dollar investments. It is an aggressively masculine operation connected to "the art of the deal," with an ambience of high-rolling entrepreneurs and world-beating executives. In the near background are the inspired inventors, genius hackers, and brilliant nerds of the technology: more male types. The sexual stereotype overlaps with the class stereotype, lending the library an unpromising image for ambitious, forward-looking brainstorming.[2]

All this is unfortunate because if computerized information services have any natural place in a democratic society, it is in the public library. There the power and efficiency of the technology can be maximized, along with its popular access. Librarians can have many more databases at their disposal than all but the wealthiest private subscribers can afford to rent. Moreover, their use of those databases is bound to be far more expert than that of the general user. The world of on-line information is a complex place; every database has a different protocol, a different fee structure. Librarians know the peculiarities of the many database services; they know which to try and the best strategies for tapping them quickly. Quite as important as the quantity of resources is the quality of their use, meaning the economy and precision with which they can be exploited. Some databases are tricky; an amateur may wander about in them for many expensive minutes or hours and still draw a blank. It takes hands-on daily experience to go hunting for information in just the right way in just the right places. It is a special skill that few home computer users will ever be able to develop to a professional librarian's level of competence.

Librarians can offer another advantage. By virtue of their training and experience, they know when *not* to use a computer. As a fully stocked information service, the library includes a multitude of standard reference works that are often the best, quickest, cheapest, and sometimes the *only* place to look up a fact. Librarians tell me it is one of the vices of the time that students often limit their research to on-line materials, assuming that the computer is guaranteed omniscient: it lacks nothing and nothing that comes out of it can be less than authoritative. Librarians can help correct for that bias. For that matter, they know how to look beyond their own resources to special archives, to private collections, to authorities and experts in the field. Over the years, most reference librarians have built up a file of such less visible sources. Searches I have had libraries run have extended to queries (by letter or phone) to out-of-the-way government agencies, journalists, hobbyists, and enthusiasts. One search originating at the Los Angeles Public Library culminated in a phone call to the Office of the Joint Chiefs of Staff in Washington where the librarian had a contact. Librarians know what many fanatical hackers overlook: as an information-processing instrument, the computer supplements other sources, it does not replace them.[3]

It should not be thought that the work reference librarians do for the public is limited to an academic and intellectual clientele. In the course of the last generation, many public libraries have expanded their services to include referrals, pamphlets, and contacts that cover a wide range of community social needs: legal assistance, tenants' rights, unemployment benefits, job training, immigration, health, welfare, and consumers' problems. The object is to put disadvantaged members of the public in touch with groups and agencies that can help with daily matters of livelihood and survival. This is not the kind of information one finds in commercial databases; and while the service may overlap the function of some electronic bulletin boards, the library can make it available to those who cannot afford a computer or easily master its intricacies.

How painful it is to realize that so much of the money that might have gone to libraries as tax revenues to buy into the new technology for these noble purposes has instead been diverted into the purchase of home computers, modems, database rentals—an approach that finally buys the public less data for its dollars. This repeats the economic pattern that has degraded Benjamin Franklin's other great contribution to democratizing the dissemination of information: the post office. There too the public utility has been left underfunded, thus persuading consumers to divert their money toward the more expensive telecommunications and overnight delivery systems of profit-seeking entrepreneurs.

These examples should remind us that making the democratic most of the Information Age is a matter not only of technology but also of the social organization of that technology. If many libraries cannot provide the first class information services they would like to offer, it is only for lack of the funds to do so. They cannot buy the equipment, rent the sources, or hire and train the personnel.

PRIVATIZING
THE PUBLIC'S RIGHT TO KNOW
■

In the libraries of the nation, we have an existing intellectual network spread across the society, stationed in almost every neighborhood and in the charge of experienced people who have always honored a strong ethic of service. If the equipment for computerized reference facilities were concentrated in local libraries, or, better still for reasons of economy, if every local library were linked to a generously funded regional reference center, this would be the fastest and cheapest way for the general public to gain open access to whatever benefits the Information Age may have to offer.

Obviously, this is not the direction in which we are headed. Instead, more and more information is falling into the hands of a profit-making information industry, turning what might be a public benefit into a private business. The irony here is acute. At the very moment in history that new technology makes the distribution of information potentially cheaper and easier than ever before, interests are at work using that same technology to restrict the flow.

The contradiction shows up especially in the one area where, by principle and precedent, the public's access to basic information ought to be most open: government documents. In the past, when documents meant printed paper, the citizen's main difficulty was simply getting to where the paper was stored and finding the documents one wanted. (This was, incidentally, one of the major and most helpful specialized reference services provided by libraries.) Once located, the document was usually freely available to be copied. The computer has changed all that. Technically, it would now be possible for any citizen linked up with a local network by way of a cheap computer and a modem to track a piece of legislation through every stage of its drafting from the moment the bill was keyboarded into any official computer. Rather than waiting for a bill to appear in its final draft—when there is usually no time left to respond before the voting starts—citizens might be made participants in the legislative process. This would be an unprecedented contribution to democratic debate.

Unfortunately, the new technology lends itself just as readily to opportunistic and profiteering applications. Revenue-starved governments at all levels have found a fiscal windfall in the computer. They have decided, along with the data merchants, to treat information as a commodity and have contracted with the information industry to sell that same information in machine-readable form on a fee-for-use basis. Vendors like Mead Data Central now share handsome revenues with underfunded government agencies to sell the public's own information back to the public.

The problem is not fundamentally a technological one; it is public policy that creates such electronic bottlenecks. In California, the Legislative Data Center in the state capital has contracted to sell public documents at the rate of forty cents per kilobyte to private-sector vendors like State Net and Legi-Tech. These vendors in turn sell back their product on-line to citizens or public bodies at rates of up to $175 per hour. During the Reagan-Bush years, the federal government made similar contracts with for-profit vendors to achieve the "maximum feasible reliance" on private distribution of government information. The United States Department of Commerce estimates the earnings of the electronic information industry as of the mid-1990s at $19 billion.[4] As librarian Patricia Glass Schuman observes, thanks to this determined effort to achieve the fullest possible commodification of public information, five commercial vendors (Mead Data Services, Maxwell Communications, Knight-Ridder, West Publishing, and STN) now account for over 90 percent of the sales and use of database services.[5] John Buschman, one of the leading librarian critics of the role of information technology, observes that "we tend to think of these tools [the on-line database and the computer] as *increasing* information availability, but it is important to note that in their current economic and social contexts, privatized sources of information can block access."[6]

In France, by way of contrast, the government makes all public documents available free over the national Minitel system. The same could be true in the United States: census statistics, the maps produced by the US Geological Survey, voting data, education and welfare statistics, legislative materials—all could be placed on-line cheaply and efficiently in a variety of ways. Along with librarians, principled hackers have launched just such an effort to reclaim the data commons from its despoilers. In California in 1991, Jim Warren of Autodesk, along with Computer Professionals for Social Responsibility and with the resources of the well-known network The WELL, convened what has been called "the First Constitutional Convention of Cyberspace" to discuss the many complex issues of computers, freedom, and privacy. The demand for full and free on-line access to public documents was at the top of the agenda. The result, at least in California, has been a legal mandate, passed in 1993, to make all information about state laws and legislation in process available to the public via nonproprietary computer networks without charging fees.[7]

If campaigns like this succeed in other parts of the country, the capacity of ordinary citizens, equipped with low-cost technology, to debate, discuss, criticize, and hold their government accountable may one day match the town meetings of old. But that effort will be all the more productive if the essential technology and skills that goal demands can be provided in better ways than relying on individual citizens to buy their own machines and master them. The public needs the help of a conscientious intermediary to defend its right to know and to make that right effective, even when the technology that controls information grows bewilderingly complex. In both these respects, libraries have an excellent record of serving their society. If information technology were concentrated in the libraries of the nation, the ideal of public access would be well served.

THE LIBRARY'S HIGH-TECH IDENTITY CRISIS

■

In the era of the electronic book, the neographic text, and the virtual library, librarians have understandably begun to wonder: maybe libraries no longer need walls, maybe walls no longer need libraries, maybe librarians no longer need books, maybe libraries no longer need librarians. Maybe librarians need a hot new identity. Maybe they should become Information Managers-Scientists-Brokers, Data Surfers, Digital Gurus, Info-shamans, Cyber-hypertext-punks.

Working through their collective identity crisis is, as one might imagine, a matter of heated debate among librarians these days, but the significance of that debate reaches well beyond the profession. Precisely because the library is the public institution under the greatest competitive pressure from the new technology, one finds the most urgent questions of information technology and access being addressed more intensely and imaginatively at library conferences and in library journals than anywhere else. Once again, the demure image of the library masks the truth: librarians are at the center of this debate, often bringing more hard-won experience, intellectual breadth, and pragmatic realism to the discussion than computer enthusiasts, who tend to drift away into cyberspace fantasies.

The factions that have joined these issues within library circles illustrate some of the most bewildering cultural ambiguities surrounding information technology. To one side, we find what might at first glance seem to be the dynamic, future-oriented wing of the profession, pressing for the maximum and most rapid introduction of the new "digital information order." Here one finds heady and enthusiastic talk of revolutionary transformations in our literary culture. In an article titled "Good-bye, Dewey Decimal," *Forbes* confidently predicts that "full text retrieval, still very limited at this point, is around the corner. When it comes, the local library as we know it all but disappears. In lieu of librarians we will have programmers and database experts."[8] One librarian agrees enthusiastically. "Ultimately...libraries as we know them seem likely to disappear. People will have very little reason to visit libraries in order to gain access to information resources." Accordingly, libraries will be "disembodied" into etherealized networks composed of pure electricity.[9] A British librarian confidently announces that "the function of libraries as places which you physically visit to access information is going to be superseded." Brian Perry, director of research at the British Library, proclaims the advent of "libraries without walls." Or possibly, Charles Robinson, Director of the Baltimore County Library, speculates, instead of buildings that house books there will be "bookbanks" that operate rather like automatic teller machines: slip in your magnetized library card and out flows digitized information to be downloaded directly into personal electronic "bookplayers."[10]

On the other side of the argument are those who might initially appear to be the "conservatives," the defenders of the librarian's more traditional identity. But if one looks more closely, the perspective shifts. The "conservatives" emerge as radical, often left-wing critics of the commercial marketplace, especially of the information industry. They are conservative only in their attitude toward the heedless and premature application of technology. In short, they are neo-Luddites, as I have used the word in this study. Most often referring to themselves as "progressive librarians," this wing of the profession believes the commodification and privatization of data amounts to an insidious form of thought control by profit-based businesses that are unaccountable to any public authority. "We are," protests John Buschman, "moving far too rapidly away from our historic professional and institutional values of print literacy, social memory, and equal access to resources for an informed citizenry."[11] Those who take issue with the progressives turn out to be far more conventionally "conservative," in the sense of being more market-oriented. They tend to endorse the entrepreneurial values of the information industry as either desirable or inevitable, often defending the on-line monopolies held by private sector vendors, and perhaps even hoping to adapt the library to a fee-for-service, self-supporting model. Along these lines, libraries would become more like profit-making businesses deeply invested in the new information technology.[12]

Progressive librarians are concerned that libraries do not own the databases they use and cannot even control the fee structures. They worry that their electronic sources of information are becoming susceptible to subtle forms of manipulation by entrepreneurs who are free to decide what to include and exclude; they believe that fiscal constraints may force them to limit access to expensive on-line sources instead of permitting them to offer those sources free of charge to all who come seeking their aid. They fear that profit-making interests will take over or cream off more and more of what was once a free and universal service in ways that amount to de facto censorship for those who cannot afford the price.

> Unlike print [John Haar observes] electronic data accords its producer the means to retain and protect exclusive ownership rights. No longer are publishers confined to packaging data and selling it outright to libraries and other customers to use in perpetuity. They can treat electronic information like rental property, subdividing and leasing it to their customers on terms carefully delimited by contract.

And he makes the appeal that distinguishes the cause of progressive librarians.

> In an era when government vacillates in meeting its obligation to secure the public's information rights, libraries may be the only civic agency positioned to defend the community's stake in equal access. If we accept this essentially democratic trust, it follows that our role is to bridge, rather than widen, economic gaps in the information chain, thereby reasserting the social and political value of information that some would renounce.[13]

NREN AND THE INTERNET:
ALL THE WORLD ON-LINE
■

There is one crucial juncture at which the ideal of public access is urgently at stake. The federal government is now undertaking the construction of a national information infrastructure. At the heart of the project is NREN, the National Research and Education Network, the high-capacity, fiber-optic computer network that will link research and educational institutions, industry, and government. NREN could represent everything progressive librarians and principled hackers need to further their cause—provided the highway does not become a toll road built at the public expense for the benefit of private data and communications entrepreneurs. Some have optimistically compared the national data highway to the railroads of the nineteenth century. They overlook the fact that the railroads were a notorious government giveaway to cutthroat robber barons. The data highway could go the same way. Indeed there is no question but that it will if there are not firm legal safeguards in place to guarantee open platform services on the data highway. An open platform means users will be able to use the facility for distribution as well as reception. Not only will the highway enter their homes, but it will leave carrying whatever material users care to send along it as an open, unrestricted facility.

In designing the data highway there are better models to guide us than the railroad. During the 1930s the Roosevelt New Deal established the largest single economic enterprise the federal government has ever undertaken: the Tennessee Valley Authority. The TVA was attacked by its critics from the outset as socialistic. And it was—in the sense that its purpose was not primarily individual profit but the general good. While the TVA carried on several kinds of commerce, it did so with other values in view. It was committed to flood control, a service that makes no money. To the consternation of largely unregulated private power companies, it also functioned as a yardstick to measure the cost and the efficiency of energy production. Above all, its goal was the economic reclamation of the country's most depressed and demoralized region.

The national data highway should be that sort of project. Conveyancing information is not, of course, the same as flood control or nitrate production, but the spirit that animates the enterprise could be the same concern for the public interest. The guiding intention should be that of keeping the information economy free and open. The network should make special provisions for supplying schools, libraries, nonprofit organizations, citizens' groups, and local governments with affordable access to all it carries and with equally affordable rights of transmission. All this could happen—but there is no guarantee that it will unless every corporate interest involved in broadcast and communication and every merger dealing in these services is legally bound to provide full public access.

Hackers like to believe there is a natural law to the effect that "information wants to be free." In truth, "information" cannot *want* anything; it is a lifeless abstraction. Only *people* can want information to be free and keep it free. People can want the sources of their information, especially government-collected and generated data to be under democratic control. And, as the Internet proves, they can create the resources to do exactly that.

What—or who—is the Internet? It has been called "the mother of all computer networks": evolving out of the military-industrial ARPAnet of the early 1970s, it has expanded into an all but totally unsupervised community of communicators that, as of the mid 1990s, reaches over 15 million users in nearly 150 countries, and continues to grow rapidly. The scope of the Internet's news groups is astonishing: all human life is there. At any given moment, one can join in on globe-spanning "chat" about hobbies, passions, and amusements of every description. As with every computer bulletin board, there is a good deal of trivia: a Dan Quayle Fan Club for political satire, Fun Ways to Commit Suicide, and the inevitable, meticulously subdivided sex conferences which allow one to browse through "rape fantasies," "kinky kitchen tips," and a consumers' guide to hand-cuffs. There is also heavy intellectual discourse: book and film reviews, discussions of modern architecture, sustainable agriculture, economic policy, and constitutional law. There are also charming conversational enclaves where people loiter to talk about P. G. Wodehouse, Tolkien, English usage, sewing, surfing, and *The Simpsons*. The coffee houses of eighteenth-century London, the cafes of nineteenth-century Paris were rather like this: a gathering place for every taste and topic.

Even more remarkable than the Internet's intellectual variety is its spontaneously democratic and libertarian spirit. The Internet was created by its own users and is run without any central administration. Anybody can join. "If a network accepts the teachings of the Internet, is connected to it, and considers itself part of it, then it is part of the Internet."[14] It is just that simple. The Internet has already demonstrated that a worldwide electronic network can be operated without hierarchical domination by any state or corporate interest. If the spirit of the Internet and the technology of NREN should ally, government may need do nothing more than guarantee by law the context within which such a network runs itself: namely, that information shall be a public utility kept free because the people want it to be free. As it has always been in the free public library.

ALADDIN'S MAGIC DIGITIZED LAMP
■

There is one aspect of computer technology that is so subliminally delusionary that it often eludes critical discussion. It is a vision deeply embedded in the cult of information.

The vision is this: one sits before a brightly lit screen, stroking keys, watching remarkable things flash by on the screen at the speed of light. Words, pictures, images appear out of nowhere. Like a child, one begins to believe in magic all over again. And because one is making the magic happen, an intoxicating sense of power comes with the act. One has the culture of the entire planet there at one's fingertips! All the databases, libraries, archives, movies, art museums, bulletin boards, telephones and fax machines in the world are in this one box.

We have a name for visions like this. We call them "fairy tales." The original version of the omnipotent computer was Aladdin's miraculous lamp: rub it and a jinni appears who will grant your every wish. At least that is what Steven Levy, who has studied the lives of hackers, believes they are seeking as they work at their machines. (See page 65.) Around that dream they easily weave fantasies of omnipotence and omniscience. Eventually, they feel certain, this machine will contain *everything* anybody needs—and it will all be called "information." One need never leave that room, that desk—not to work or play, not to shop or socialize, not to be intellectually or aesthetically or sexually stimulated.

Many who subscribe to this image are knowledgeable technicians who know all the intricacies of the technology. Yet it is astonishing how naively fanciful supposedly hardheaded hackers can become where the computer is concerned. The fantasies may be innocent enough, but the image of the omnicompetent computer, like all forms of wishful thinking, masks many hard, human realities. For example, as electronic data processing is presented to the public, and especially to students, one easily forgets that behind the scenes of this technology there are ordinary and all-too-fallible human beings. There are programmers making up the rules and values by which the machine operates and who may sometimes not be all that good at their job or who may get carried away with zany projects. Similarly, the data that go into databases have to be put there by people. They are called "data-entry clerks." There is nothing glamorous about what these people do. They sit at keyboards hour after hour entering texts into the machine; they get tired, they grow distracted, they skip over and omit things, they make mistakes. The computer will never be flawless until all the mistakes have been found and corrected...someday...by somebody...probably by other bored and underpaid clerks, who will make new mistakes. The result of their labor may show up on the screen as a magical picture show of facts, figures, charts, games, and diagrams. But this is nonetheless a human fabrication. It can be wrong, it can be incomplete. It is *bound* to be incomplete if, to begin with, the people who make the rules and enter the data simply leave things out as a matter of policy, oversight, or financial limitation.

Moreover, the programmers and the clerks, like the people who assemble the chips and motherboards and (sometimes toxic) components into functioning hardware, are employees. Their labor does not come free of charge; these people expect to be compensated for what they do. Put them all together and you have what is called a "payroll," as in any other business. As time goes by, they may expect to be paid more and more, to make up for the boredom and hazards of their daily labor.

These are the kinds of real-life costs that attach to the project of creating the omnipotent computer. Computer enthusiasts who cherish the expectation that someday independent computer workstations will contain the full text collections of whole libraries seem reluctant to ask how everything that they want to have in their machines is going to get there. There are even librarians who indulge in the same fantasies; they promise "virtual libraries" without attending to the costly realities. A bulletin from the Association of College and Research Libraries predicts that "when institutions of higher education are networked and faculty members and students have individual computer workstations, the resources of the library will be accessible with just a few keystrokes." A *New York Times* report from 1990 tells us that soon "the library will not necessarily be a place to go...but rather a focal point for a variety of services. Such 'libraries without walls' are beginning to appear in schools and businesses, and the silent, musty stacks are giving way to high-technology centers, available to personal computers everywhere." Another report in the *Wall Street Journal* announces that "what you once had to go to the Library of Congress to see can be viewed at home." If there continue to be buildings called "libraries," these will be reading rooms where "you do not read books, you read terminals."

The enormous storage capacity of CD-ROM technology makes the ideal of the fully machine-readable library seem more and more feasible, just as, about a generation ago, microfilm gave rise to similar expectations. In the 1960s the prospect of ultramicrofiche led to predictions that we would soon be able to shrink the entire Library of Congress down to the size of a half dozen filing cabinets. Digitalization is doing a more convincing job of achieving that goal. Already whole bodies of literature, from voluminous legal records and public documents to the entire corpus of Greek and Latin classics, are available in full-text database form. Theologians can now do keyword searches of Thomas Aquinas and rabbis can browse through an on-line concordance to the Talmud. The Past Masters series from InteLex has digitized critical editions of the great philosophers (Locke, Hume, Mill, Spinoza, Wittgenstein) in database form and in the original language. Meanwhile, at the University of Illinois, Project Gutenberg, which began in the early 1970s, continues at one of the most ambitious electronic text production efforts yet undertaken. It is out to create an electronic library of ten thousand books by the year 2000. The texts would be available on floppy disks or CD-ROMs in a "plain vanilla" ASCII format for perhaps as little as $100, not counting the cost of the equipment. Eventually all the texts might be made machine searchable and transmittable by phone lines. The goal is worthy, though the choices being made are puzzling. As usual the Bible and the works of Shakespeare are there, along with a number of undisputed classics. But why would *Warlord of Mars* by Edgar Rice Burroughs be among the first books to be ASCII-ized? Or *Anne of Avonlea* by Lucy Maud Montgomery? Or *Amateur Radio in the U.K. and Greece* by N. Joly? The choices raise a few doubts about the project's priorities. On the other hand, when you set out to digitize everything, maybe it doesn't matter which ten thousand books come first. And, in any case, digitizing *something* is becoming one of those utterly safe, undeniably worthy projects that foundations love to finance.

Heroic databasing exercises of this kind are beginning to generate serious policy decisions. In California, a report on high-level plans for the State's college libraries promises "a bookless, electronic library." This is seen by administrators—though not by many librarians—as a practical response to budgetary constraints. In the future, we are told, university libraries will take pride in "how *few* books they contain and how much information is stored on computer disks." Someday, the headline reads, "No Books Stacks, Just Computers."[15]

It is undeniably true that computers offer valuable new information retrieval techniques that were not available before. Searches by keyword, word-truncation, and word-proximity, and searches using Boolean logic (based on logical discriminations between "and," "or," "both," "not") are powerful reference devices, especially for materials that have been entered as full text. For example, in preparing the preface to this book, I requested a search of several databases to find every use of the word "Luddite" in newspapers on file for the last five years that fell within ten words of the word "computer." Then another for every conjunction divided by twenty-five words. Scores of citations turned up; I could not have found them any other way. So impressive are results like this that some have even suggested there may soon be no need to catalog *anything*. Why not simply rely on keyword searches to find exactly the information you want?

It takes a seasoned reference librarian to know how recklessly impoverishing it would be to rely solely on techniques like these, which must perforce be limited to materials that have been fully digitized: no search can find what has not been scanned or key-stroked into a database in the first place. How likely is it, then, that the libraries of the world (including all non-English collections) will ever be totally (or largely) digitized—a recurrent computer-enthusiast fantasy?

In the judgement of Thomas Mann, general reference librarian in the Main Reading Room of the Library of Congress, not very. Mann is among the few who have thought the "computer work-station model" of the library through to its underlying assumptions and hidden difficulties. His analysis displays the realism that only a working librarian—one who deals with the flesh-and-blood public and the day-to-day hands-on problems of information retrieval—can bring to the subject.[16]

Among the problems he cites is the stubbornly intractable barrier of copyright law. More than any technical obstacle, copyright will remain a terrible buzzing fly in the data merchants' ointment—certainly for as long as information services and technology are themselves run as money-making enterprises. High-tech entrepreneurs can be strikingly Marxist when it comes to socializing other people's intellectual property. But why should authors, artists, or composers agree to let their creative property be freely stored and transmitted by vendors whose purpose is to retail that property for private gain? "We must," Mann observes, "ultimately recognize ...that copyright is not the *problem* it is represented to be by Workstation proponents; rather, copyright is precisely the *solution* to the more fundamental problem that human nature impels us to want compensation for the use of our own work."

Then there is the matter of cost. Other than brute manual key-stroking (a prospect that consumes too much time and money to take seriously when it comes to computerizing the multilingual collections of whole libraries) there are only two technologies available for digitizing existing print materials: raster scanning (or bit-mapping) and optical character scanning. The first involves taking a picture of whole pages, which can then be transferred to CD-ROM disks; the second, OCR scanning, records each character, or tries to within the limits of font recognition. Raster scanning falls far short of the computer enthusiast's ideal, since it does not permit keyword searches. Even so, the cost of producing CD-ROM editions of whole library holdings (books, periodicals, newspapers) is far beyond what most libraries could afford. It is, by one estimate, fifty times more costly than microfilming.

Optical scanning, on the other hand, necessitates expensive human proofing for the inevitable errors in machine-read fonts. As of the early 1990s, the minimal cost for proofing an OCR conversion was three dollars per page. This is why it costs so much per minute to use a commercial search service like NEXIS, which includes the full texts of only about a thousand newspapers, magazines, and wire services—and only for the last several years of coverage. A thousand is a lot, but the Library of Congress subscribes to over 50,000 newspapers, magazines, journals, and serials. By one estimate, if NEXIS had to cover the cost of providing just the LC's current serials collection on-line, it would have to charge well over $200 per minute. What would the cost be, then, of making the LC's entire hundred million items available on-line?

> In a nutshell [Mann concludes], the unfashionable truth is that entire research libraries *cannot* be reduced to the computer workstation model because of the combination of essentially unbudgeable legal, economic, preservation, and psychological impediments. . . . a skeptic can legitimately wonder if the workstation proponents have any real idea how much access to the written (and other) records of humanity is being completely lost or overlooked.

As an alternative vision for the library of the future, Mann recommends a "methods of searching model" that honors all the sources of information old and new. Electronic databases are there, and CD-ROM disks, but also high-quality cataloging that gives what are called "vocabulary-controlled, predictable systems of access." This means well-conceived classification with full standard information about each source, linking it to an agreed-upon intellectual pattern. This allows for the direct browsing of subject-grouped, full texts— that is, walking the stacks and thumbing through books, the only way to locate an enormous amount of material that shows up no other way. And as every library user knows, browsing leads to serendipity: finding something you weren't looking for. Mann's ideal library also includes "people sources," meaning outreach to organizations and individuals (hobbyists, for example) who can provide specialized advice and expertise.

Librarians who defend the continued full cataloging of print collections can assemble some impressive evidence to support their position, namely the actual searches they have performed for patrons that could not have been successful if they had been limited to digitized sources or the keyword / Boolean approach. Unless one has some familiarity with the day-to-day work of librarians and the amazing variety of questions they are asked to answer, it is difficult to appreciate the concern they show. But study any list of what librarians have been expected to find for scholars, journalists, researchers of all description, or simply for members of the general public who are pursuing hobbies or inventing things or doing crossword puzzles or dealing with difficult social problems, and you are apt to come away convinced that we are a long way from being able to bet our future on the mere fraction of knowledge that has been entrusted to computers.[17]

If people are persuaded to believe that the computer contains all that is of value, they will not look beyond the computer. Their culture will shrink to the size of what the machine can give them—especially if, as true believers in the cult of information, they have been trained to *pretend* that the computer is what it can never be: an all-knowing, infallible, totally efficient substitute for human judgment.

Compared to the glitzy magical appeal of computers, the modest efforts of reference librarians may seem stodgy, like the contrast we find in folklore between the tortoise and the hare, the hedgehog and the fox. But the same folklore teaches us that there is a great deal to be said for the tortoise and the hedgehog. Librarians, whether working with print or on-line reference materials, are trained to be thorough; they deliberate and make judgments. They have learned the shortcomings of their materials, whether a standard reference book or the latest database. At the very least they can advise patrons about the limitations and biases of the materials available. They can caution, they can warn, they can remind of human fallibility.

Librarians have good reason to worry about the naive faith and wishful thinking hackers often invest in their machines. What they see in that fascination is an overriding desire to expand the horizons of a technology rather than to serve the needs of people. And they see a woeful lack of culture. As one librarian comments:

> since *all* library-held works are unlikely to be electronically-accessible (i.e. in full text)—for reasons of expense, copyright, etc.—what will inevitably happen is what has *already* happened regarding major databases and indexing services like DIALOG: unorthodox, alternative, and non-mainstream

materials will be excluded and thus rendered less accessible, if not totally invisible. In short, the determination of what gets "full-texted" will reinforce the existing censorship-by-neglect of small press publications and various alternative/countercultural media.[18]

Anybody who allows the bells and whistles of computers to eclipse the urgency of a cultural issue like this is being philistine in the worst sense of the word. The information age may be awash in data, but the quality and variety of its sources could be drastically diminished. A universe of old, divergent, eccentric, or marginal print materials might vanish into a black hole of neglect.

The proposition is easily stated: *no* computer, *no* computer system is ever going to be enough; every humanly crafted thing will be flawed, warped, skewed. We will always need *more*, we will always need the tried, true, and well-tested. When it comes to information, we will always need print on paper and human beings to exercise discriminating judgment.

ELECTRONIC ALZHEIMER'S
∎

There is a final problem about the ideal of the virtual library that may hold little interest for most computer buffs. It has to do with history: the claims of the past upon the present. I sometimes suspect that computer enthusiasts, committed to a dynamic technology that seems always to be moving forward toward ever more spectacular breakthroughs, exist in a sort of posthistorical limbo. Perhaps this is the most appealing feature of cyberspace: it has no past, only a future. It imposes no responsibilities or obligations, only bright promises and happy diversions.

But none of this is true. Even high tech equipment ages—and not very gracefully. In fact, the technology may soon find itself bedeviled by a kind of electronic Alzheimer's disease that will cost our culture dearly.

AI scientists may not care to face the fact, but their machines are capable of mimicking not only the best powers of the human mind but some of its dysfunctional features as well. As Joseph Weizen-baum notes in our next chapter, there could be such things as "psychotic programs": programs that, over time, have been worked on by so many teams of programmers that they become internally fragmented and out of control. Not all programmers are consci-entious about annotating their work so that their successors will be able to understand why they did what they did, or to decipher the older languages in which earlier programmers worked. (Both COBOL and LOGO have been described to me as "dead" pro-gramming languages.)

Another pathology of this kind may be slowly taking shape, one that strikes at the computer's most valued characteristic: its ability to store and retrieve information. We are beginning to realize that machines can lose their memory. High-tech amnesia is still a little-discussed problem, but it begins to look like one of those modern technological disasters that is waiting to happen. Precisely because computer technology is so dynamic, it ages rapidly as "generations" of innovation replace one another, and the data these machines are storing age with them. But age takes a heavier toll of computer tapes and disks than it does of paper. Everything plastic deteriorates; magnetic particles migrate. Some hackers I know live in fear of solar storms that might erase all their disks.

The solution? It would seem simple: just keep copying the data onto fresher, more durable materials. But this is easier said than done. Not only do the materials from which computers are made grow old; so do their languages, their logic, and the mechanisms that can communicate with older storage devices. As both hardware and software drift toward obsolescence, they take along the data entrusted to them when they were state of the art. Meanwhile, the technology races relentlessly forward, losing touch with the media that hold the data. New hardware cannot always read old software. NASA, for example, owns twenty thousand seven-track data tapes from its history of space exploration that can only be read on a seven-track tape drive. In 1992, when its last seven-track drive broke, NASA was able to find only one more such drive in existence. And when that breaks. . . .

Similarly, at the Massachusetts Institute of Technology there exists a mountain of backup tapes preserving research papers and personal E-mail dating back to the 1960s. The tapes are still intact, but no computer on the campus can read them any longer. A special program has been funded to reinvent "old" computers that can once again read what the tapes contain. In Great Britain, the national electrical grid is still being run by a veteran Ferranti Argus 500 computer, one of the few in existence. The software used by the Argus is written in a language which can (as of 1993) be understood by only one surviving programmer who has made that language his special study. Asked what would happen if that lone programmer should be run over by a bus, the head of control facilities at the national grid replied, "We don't like to think about that."[19]

A study by the National Research Council in the mid-1980s concluded that anything entrusted to an electronic media format, even optical disks, has a functioning lifespan of about twenty years before it is replaced by new technology, which, as in the case of the VHS videocassette crowding out Beta or the 33 rpm record displacing the 45, may have little more going for it than a hard sell in the marketplace. At which point it may be necessary to recopy everything to ensure accessibility. This is no small expense. In the judgment of one librarian, "one cannot look to electronic devices to solve preservation problems when it is in the very nature of such devices to cause the problems in the first place."[20]

There are various clever work-arounds for dealing with "ropey" old programs and inaccessible databanks, but they are tricky and expensive. New machines can be made to emulate old machines, some of which may be engaged in services so crucial (like air traffic control) that the computerized system can never be safely shut down and rebuilt. So the new machines are redesigned to run slower and do less. We may have to keep old computers around and running in just the same way that we have had to keep old bridges and railroads in operation long after better kinds of design and materials have been created.

Large institutions and major corporations can afford solutions like this, but what about the files and databases of smaller, private users, some of which are unique repositories built up over a long period? What happens if bankrupt businesses or terminated government programs cease operation and allow their data tapes and disks to fall into disuse long enough for the software and hardware that created these files to become obsolete? Old books and paper files (especially if the paper has been deacidified) can still be consulted decades, or even centuries later; not so computer materials. Might it be that eventually whole stores of data will simply have to be consigned to electronic oblivion because it is too expensive to keep veteran technology operating or to study its arcane logic? Or will we perhaps one day need a corps of antiquarian hackers whose special skill is studying obsolete programming languages and mining the data in abandoned databases? Don Norman of Apple computer has suggested a name for the field: "cyber-archaeology."[21]

Such a solution has been seriously proposed by one student of the problem. Noting the call of the American Society for Information Science in 1993 to provide for the systematic preservation of archival material in electronic form, Fred Lerner has called for the creation of data repositories whose function would be to preserve a wide variety of storage and display media in working order, possibly at an abandoned military base: a sort of official computer cemetery. The facility, which might double as a museum of defunct computing machinery, would include old computer documentation and a group of specialists to study and maintain the equipment and to help occasional visitors to retrieve old data.[22]

IBM is the reluctant guardian of at least one massive business program that dates back to the 1960s and has undergone numerous upgrades. Recent attempts to restructure the program have produced "spaghetti code" that nobody can analyze any longer. IBM has promised to maintain the program from here to eternity, but the only practical solution has been to seal off certain old "domains" within the program so nobody can tamper with them and then hope they continue working as originally designed. Eventually, nobody may have any understanding of how those sectors function and what unforeseen results they can produce. They will become rather like the digital hieroglyphics of a dead language.

LITERACY IMPERILED
∎

There is another great issue at stake in the confrontation between the new information technology and the library: the deep meaning of "literacy" as an indispensable but now endangered faculty of the mind. I would suggest there is a quality of attention and intellectual plasticity that derives from the habit of reading—the ability to track a text from start to finish, to connect, compare, and contrast—that is essential to a significant range of issues. What we understand our culture to be, what we take democracy to be, depend on defending and enhancing that quality.

Along with teachers, librarians are the guardians of literacy; literacy is to librarianship what due process is to the practice of law and hygiene to the practice of medicine. Whatever spectacular changes our media of communication may undergo, if we diminish the importance of literacy, we lose more than we gain. Quite simply, we cheapen the art of thinking—perhaps to the point that we finally will believe that what data-processing machines do is indeed "thinking." If such a consensus ever comes to dominate our culture, it will not be because the machines have become our equals, but because we have become theirs.

There is something about all computerized activities that is worrisome in this respect, something built into the physical posture, emotional affect, and perceptual action of sitting at a video terminal, entering data, scrolling through, reading snippets of this and that. Of course, good things can come of computer literacy; it is another useful human skill—provided it does not displace real literacy to become the dominant form of intellectual exercise.

So much that comes to us out of the culture of computers, especially as the technology moves toward "edutainment" for the young, grinds away at the already diminished attention span and power of concentration. The essence, after all, of hypertextual surfing is pushing buttons and jumping around. One begins reading about Beethoven, scrolling through lots of flashy graphics; click! and one is checking a chronological time-line; click! and one gets four bars of the *Eroica* as performed by a histrionic Leonard Bernstein; click! and one is watching an excerpted movie about Napoleon; click! and one is viewing an animated map of Vienna; click! and one is keystroking notes, or click! pasting text in the clipboard, or click! accessing numerical data, or click! checking E-mail from other students around the room (and someday around the world!) and then click! back to... Beethoven? Napoleon? Leonard Bernstein?

Dazzling? Indeed it is, in the sense of endlessly distracting. What I have been most aware of in dealing with software like this is...*the software*, which is the work of technicians eager to showcase their skills. But these skills look suspiciously like the skills that go into the one-cut-per-second soft-drink commercials aimed at youthful viewers, all medium with no message deeper than the reflex association of the product with a hundred flashy images. It may finally be necessary to get this technology out of the hands of those technicians before we know how intellectually beneficial it can be within the realistic budgetary constraints of public school systems.

Whatever advantages our schools may reap from well-conceived and well-used computerized instruction, the technology reaches beyond the classroom; in its most mind-boggling applications it becomes the computer games that sell so abundantly for home or arcade use. Can there be any doubt that these obsessive amusements are radically transforming the mental life of children? They are teaching the kids—mainly the boys, it seems—how to indulge in savage martial arts without exercising anything more than two thumbs; how to zap whole galaxies; how to eviscerate dinosaurs; how to race spaceships around the universe; how to deal with goblins in the dungeon (kill them), trolls in the forest (kill them), and evil wizards in the haunted castle (kill them).

The garish animated "art" that fills the videoscreens is no worse than the comic book "art" upon which I regrettably lavished my childish time, but I suspect it is more hypnotically fixating. It moves! It beeps! It bursts into eye-popping psychedelic explosions! The "stories" that surround the beeps and the bursts have even less coherence than comic book tales and so require no expansion of the attention span. The script usually features a single figure hulking across the screen, stopping to kick, stomp, punch, shoot, stab. (The characters usually hulk from left to right, perhaps out of some minimally surviving folk memory of the activity once called "reading.") Over the course of hours, days, weeks, though heroes like Star Fox may confront every kind of cosmic entity, they are not apt to meet a single English sentence longer than "insert coin." (The most complex concept I have seen displayed in any of the games is "Run to avoid getting killed!") Industry experts and their consultants claim the games teach children all sorts of employable skills: hand-eye coordination, spatial relations, strategic planning. Reportedly they also cultivate self-esteem, logic skills, and "empowerment." As, for example: kids indulging in vicarious mayhem with Samus Aran of *Metroid II* must learn to master fourteen different futuristic weapons.[23]

Perhaps the library cannot do very much about the worst assaults the new media make upon the minds of the young. But simply by being there, by surviving, and by having as much contact with inquiring minds as possible, it can help uphold the value of literacy. If it can become one of the places where information technology is concentrated, the library might surround the computer with a greater culture that disciplines its excesses.

ECOLOGISTS OF MIND
■

> The library is special and necessary in the world of
> information because by its very nature it counters the
> decontextualization and the disembodiment that is an
> inevitable part of the electronic metamorphosis of
> information....The library and its contents...offer
> the most compelling reminder of, and the freest access
> to, the whole fabric of memory and knowledge. Infor-
> mation that is torn from that fabric is a dangerous
> medium of exchange.
> John Swan, "Information and Madness"[24]

This, I hope, is a priority that librarians can be counted upon to recognize and defend. It is a cause that comes instinctively to those who live and work among books in all their variety and those who know what a superbly designed artifact the printed volume is for leisurely reading, for browsing, for free portability, for user-friendly companionship at all times in all places. Paradoxically, it is because they are the traditional keepers of the books that I believe librarians are uniquely suited to be the public's mediators in its bewildering encounter with the new information technology.

The library is not only a socially owned, community-based in-stitution; it also happens to be staffed by men and women who are cultural generalists rather than information specialists—*book people* in the best and broadest sense of the term. Precisely for that reason, they bring to their vocation a lively and abiding respect for the hierarchical relationship between data and ideas, facts and knowledge, trivia and truth—distinctions for the lack of which the environment of mind is reduced to the same inorganic simplicity that agricultural monocultures make of the world's once highly diversified genetic commons. We cannot depend upon the information technicians, database assemblers, or (apart from a sensitive few) computer enthusiasts to recognize that fact; they relish the technical excitement and the commercial profits of the informational monoculture. The more we are left in the care of their machines to meet our intellectual needs, the more likely it is that data will displace ideas, and the life of the mind wither.

I agree that culture becomes stuffy and oppressive when we say that print literacy is the best or only exercise of the mind. It isn't; but its virtues should be obvious from even the most cursory examination of the world's culture. It belongs to a rich and necessary way of thinking that should be supplemented, not eliminated. Literacy encourages a certain ethical and psychological autonomy based upon the value of taking counsel with yourself in a quiet place namely, the privacy of your own mind. What do we stereotypically associate with libraries? "Shhh! Quiet, please." Being shushed. Why? Because people are reading. People are *thinking*. Respect their solitude. I have come to value the few remaining quiet places in the world. They remind us that there are things that must be thought about in the privacy of one's own mind, not in the presence of fragmented, graphical interfaces, or chattering printers, or beeping, blinking video displays. *Thought about*—with an investment of interpretive effort and critical skill, not simply, passively registered as a stimulus or clicked-on like a hypertext button.

Quiet places are an endangered species. Save them!

In the era of high tech, librarians have a central role to play in nourishing the art of thinking, if only because they recognize that thinking *is* an art, not a science, let alone a mechanized process. That role is in some respects an essentially conservative one—but conservative in a sense that can assume radically libertarian overtones: that of championing the enduring value of books, the importance of the ideas found in books, and the complexity of the culture built upon those books. Librarians are strategically located to defend the true nature of thought against those who would level the mind into a flat computational mechanism.

What every librarian knows, as our society's well-tested provider of information, is that reference books are only one kind of book. The reference room, with its wealth of organized data, is only one room in that mansion of intellect for which every cataloguing system is a rough blueprint. However well reference sources, whether printed or digitalized, may order the infinitude of information, librarians know there is no logic, no system, no formal process that can assemble those sources into the myriad shapes of philosophy, theology, history, literature, art, science. They know that between all the facts in the world and one good idea there is a leap of the imagination that no computer program will ever replace.

When patrons come asking for a point of information, the librarian directs them to the reference shelves. When patrons come asking for the meaning of life, the teachings of God, the nature of the universe, the rights and wrongs of a social issue—when they come in search of the Good, the True, the Beautiful—the librarian knows they must be pointed in other directions. The pointing may amount to no more than a helpful word, the phrases all of us have heard in libraries we have visited since we were children.

"Incidentally, there's a good book on that."

"You may want to browse through this section."

"That's a very big subject...we have a bibliography on it."

"Have you read this?"

Not much, it might seem. But in those few words lies the fullness of culture. They are enough to make all the difference between a question that ends with a minor point of fact, and one that opens out into a significant inquiry. *And it takes a human being to make that difference.*

In a society that seems obsessed with the self-defeating project of mechanizing everything, including its own inventive genius, librarians can provide, for those who come in search of either data or ideas, what no machine will ever offer: a living mind, a human presence.

IN THE WRONG
HANDS

■

I have seriously considered the possibility of giving up
my scientific productive effort because I know of no
way to publish without letting my inventions go to the
wrong hands.

Norbert Wiener, October 1945[1]

THE FOUNDATIONS OF
INFORMATION TECHNOLOGY

■

For the foreseeable future, the democratic uses of the home computer
are apt to remain at a rudimentary and struggling stage, burdened
by the cost of the equipment and the commercial trivia that surround
the technology in the marketplace. No doubt principled hackers,
who are still with us, will continue to find valuable political applications for computers; their efforts deserve to be supported. But
meanwhile, outside the small, still underdeveloped world of politically relevant networks and bulletin boards, the information economy does not stand still. Larger forces that have little interest in the
citizenly uses of computers are at work molding the technology to
suit their purposes. The progress they are making in that direction is
by no means an unfortunate accident, something that need not have
happened. On the contrary, the "wrong hands" which Norbert Wiener feared might capture his brainchild are precisely the hands that
brought cybernetics and information theory into existence in the first
place. For this reason, Wiener's qualms, while morally admirable,
were wholly unrealistic.

Wiener had two potential abuses of information technology in view: its military exploitation as a means of making war, and its industrial exploitation as a means of deskilling and disemploying workers. Wiener, the conscience of his much-compromised profession, did what he could to resist these evils; it was surely as much as any single person might be expected to do. With respect to the first, he resolutely refused to accept any research support that came from military sources and agitated among his colleagues to do the same, though with no success. With respect to the second, he made his services available as a consultant to the labor movement as early as 1950. In that year, he wrote to Walter Reuther, head of the United Auto Workers Union, warning him of "the very pressing menace of the large-scale replacement of labor by machines" to which automation would surely contribute. Cybernetics in the workplace, he observed, will "lead to the factory without employees" and the corresponding reduction of union power. "I do not want to contribute in any way to selling labor down the river, and I am quite aware that any labor which is in competition with slave labor, whether the slaves are human or mechanical, must accept the conditions of work of slave labor." In this prospect, Wiener saw the lineaments of nothing less than "fascism."[2]

As it turned out, these evils—the military and industrial applications of cybernation—were not two separate abuses needing to be fought on separate fronts. They have been intimately related all along. David Noble makes the case in his study, *Forces of Production*, that the government's continued heavy military investment in computers, electronics, and information theory following World War II was fully intended to alter the American industrial system radically. It was meant to advance automation as a way of offsetting the labor unrest and the assertiveness of labor unions that emerged from the war years. Automation would "rationalize" the economy by strengthening the control of management, especially the management of big firms. Techniques developed during the war, primarily in the defense industries to compensate for the wartime lack of skilled labor, would be extended to create the "factory of the future," where less and less labor would be needed. Industry could thus replace manpower with machine power and so discipline an increasingly obstreperous work force. As Charles Wilson of General Motors, vice chairman of the War Production Board and later secretary of defense, put it in 1949, America had two major problems: "Russia abroad, labor at home."[3]

This alliance of the military and the industrial for the purpose of advancing information technology continues in the era of high tech. The Defense Department remains a major source of research and development funding not only for specific weapons systems but for furthering the general use of automative methods. The program called ICAM (integrated computer assisted manufacturing) begun in 1979 by the Air Force is among the most ambitious efforts to bring capital-intensive, labor-saving high tech, including robotics, into the production process. It is the backbone of all CAD/CAM (computer assisted design and manufacturing) efforts in American industry. Other modernization programs (Techmod and Mantech) are similarly dependent on Pentagon money. As Noble observes regarding the thrust toward high tech automation, "the role of the military, with its emphasis upon performance and command rather than cost, remains primary."

> Grounded still upon an impoverished view of human beings and a systematic denial of their potential, the search for total control consists in an ever more elaborate and costly effort to construct a profitable, militarily effective, and technically elegant apparatus that is not dependent upon the cooperation and resources of the mass of the population.[4]

The ongoing military-industrial drive toward rationalizing, disciplining, and ultimately dehumanizing the workplace is among the foundation stones of information technology. This is the shop floor, board room, and marketplace reality that is so treacherously clouded over by the futurologists with their frivolous chatter about an "information economy" filled with push-button consumer gadgets and gimmicks, where, seemingly, the physical conditions of life and work will be etherealized into an electronic Shangri-La. Their superficial celebration of this great transition, like that of high tech conservatives and liberals alike who draw so freely upon them for buzz words and catch phrases, leaves out the true forces and motives behind the economic process.

If information technology is to be rescued for its most humane uses, one must at some point face the hard, unpleasant fact that the computer lends itself all too conveniently to the subversion of democratic values. This threatening liability arises precisely from what has always been advertised as the technology's greatest power: the ability to concentrate and control information. This is where the efficiency and all the promised benefits of computerized systems lie. It is what we endorse whenever we praise the computer for the speed and thoroughness of its services. That endorsement is deepened when we agree that, in providing those services, the computer is proving itself to be a "thinking machine," indeed one that thinks better than a human brain.

As we have stressed thoughout this study, the cult of information that has formed around the computer is based upon a powerfully rationalized philosophical assumption that has gained a great deal of public acceptance and is gaining more as it penetrates our schools and universities: namely, that the human mind can be fully and accurately described by the information processing model. Historically, the first important applications of that model came during and just following World War II in the areas of warfare and war-related assembly line production. Since then, such applications have steadily expanded, primarily under military auspices, into more areas of production and higher levels of skill so that more and more labor has been eliminated from the manufacturing economy, or—quite as important—credibly threatened with such elimination. The thinking that was earliest and most significantly processed into machine-readable and reproducible information was the skill of workers, the talent of their hands, the acuity of their perception, the judgment of their minds. Wherever this has happened and as often as it has happened, the result has been the transfer of power to the technicians, managers, and owners.

Once information technology had demonstrated its ability to achieve that transfer, it had found a rock-solid foundation in our economy and was in the position to attract all the prestige and money it needed. If computer science had not promised a handsome payoff to the military and corporate buyers who could afford its costly research and development, there would have been no chess-playing programs, no Pac-Man games, no NEXIS data base, no Turtle Graphics. Nor would there have been the several professions and fields of study—artificial intelligence, cognitive science, information theory—that have grown up around the technology and have become some of the most influential disciplines represented in the universities. So there have been more and more applications of the technology. A few of these, like the networking capacity and educational possibilities of the microcomputer, have been seized upon by hopeful democratic spirits like the guerrilla hackers; but such commendable uses of the computer remain outweighed by its predominant applications, many of which seriously endanger freedom and justice.

What follows is a brief checklist of those dangers.

THE SURVEILLANCE MACHINE
■

The invasion of privacy has been the single most widely publicized and discussed social issue surrounding computers. In Europe and America, there is a good-sized body of research on the subject, some of it stemming from concerned legislators and official sources and intended as the basis for law. Despite this awareness, it is all too obvious that none of these legal safeguards has any reliable force. Most of them are broad spectrum legislation filled with exceptions and loopholes and lacking any effective means of enforcement. It is very nearly a principle of nature that where law seeks to keep pace with technology, technology wins. It is like a race between an ox cart and a supersonic jet.[5]

We can see this discrepancy nowhere more dramatically than in the area of computers and telecommunications. In little more than a generation, information transfer technology has simply become too big and too dynamic to be tightly regulated. This has not happened simply because the technicians move so fast in so many unpredictable directions. That would be enough of a problem in itself. There is also the paramount fact that their efforts are fueled by the profit and power-seeking motives of those who command their skills and wares. In this area as in so many other sectors of our industrial economy, the uses of technology are shaped by the values of those who salary the technicians and own their products.

We may not be living in anything that can sensibly be called an information economy, a term that has always had more journalistic glitter than social substance; but it is the case that, within our economy, an information industry of sizable proportions has grown up over the past twenty years. It is made up not only of the computer and electronics firms who manufacture the machinery, but of ambitious new service companies—credit bureaus, data managers, direct mailers, marketing and public opinion experts. These enterprises, in turn, have helped to create a thrusting new profession of computer systems specialists whose assignment is to brainstorm more and more applications for information technology and to sell those applications to every business on the scene. The cult of information is nowhere more deeply entrenched than on this bustling, highly competitive, entrepreneurial frontier, where many of the brightest young minds of the time are hard at work merchandising the promise of the computer, cleverly maneuvering its services into every slightest need that an eager, often gullible business community might present.

Much of this was inevitable; many businesses—banking, insurance, brokerage, public administration—are inherently data intensive. But why should the phone company keep track of every number a subscriber calls? Only because it got sold a piece of equipment that can do the job; so it records the numbers, which gives it more records to keep. These days, every corner drugstore and dry cleaner confronts its customers with an electronic marvel of a machine that is a combination cash register, inventory control, credit card verification, mailing list, banking and accounting apparatus. It beeps and blinks and finally prints out a sales receipt that looks like a statistical abstract. And every inscrutable little cipher on it represents a record that is being filed somewhere.

By far the richest and most welcoming customer for the information industry is the government, still the greatest data minder of all. Major federal agencies like the Departments of Commerce, which handles the census, and of Defense, Internal Revenue, and Social Security hold somewhere between 2 billion and 4 billion overlapping files on the American public.[6] Keeping files is nothing new for governments in the modern world; but the scale on which the state now documents the lives of its citizens is unprecedented. More importantly, the files these agencies hold are no longer separate, single purpose records sealed off from one another. They are becoming interconnected by way of the more than 300 computer networks through which the government now shuttles data as part of its routine business. This integration of data makes a difference; it increases the utility of information exponentially. In the context of the networks, every scrap of data has the possibility of multiple connections and so acquires an expanding, unpredictable number of applications. For example, the networks permit, even encourage the use of "matching programs" that can relate, let us say, tax information with unpaid student loans or welfare disbursements: a promising means of clamping down on cheats and delinquents. Moreover, with minimal and feeble restrictions, all the information in the federal government's 20,000-plus computers is routinely available to federal security agencies and local law enforcement, which can then make multiple matches with data in their own files. Thus, a driver pulled over for a faulty brake light may soon have his whole life run through a battery of integrated data banks that will contain anything anybody ever cared to put on file: alimony and child support, delinquent loans, welfare violations, etc.

Beyond this, more and more official information is being coordinated with privately owned information services. The Commerce Department routinely sells census data to marketing and public relations companies. Under the Reagan administration, the Internal Revenue Service began to use private data bases, such as banking records, to catch tax evaders. Similarly, starting in 1982, the General Services Administration began to negotiate contracts to exchange records with private credit bureaus in order to identify those who default on federal loans. There are some 100 federal agencies that now freely share data with the seven major credit-reporting companies, covering such matters as liens, bank loans, divorce records, and credit cards.[7] Ironically, the justification for this integration of data resources by the Reagan administration was that, by tightening up on government programs, the president was achieving one of his prime ideological goals: getting the government off the people's back. At first sight, this may seem inconsistent. But not so. Robert Bedell, a deputy head of the Office of Management and Budget, is quoted as saying that the government would like nothing better than to protect the citizen's right to privacy. The administration's suggested way of doing this is to avoid recording information about individuals in the first place by reducing the size of government programs. "There isn't a better protection against government invading privacy than not to have the information to begin with."[8]

These are ominous words. They imply that the only way to steer clear of the sort of surveillance and intrusions which the government's matching programs produce is to stay off federal records entirely. In other words, don't apply for government assistance at all. The implicit threat can be a highly effective way of clearing the welfare rolls.

As one might expect, it is the security and law enforcement arm of government that has the largest appetite for information. At the federal level, the National Security Agency, whose budget exceeds that of the CIA, not only operates one of the government's largest computer networks, but serves as a prime funding source for some of the most advanced research in electronics and telecommunications. For example, it is the NSA which is financing pioneering work in computer voice recognition; it purportedly has devices that can pick up key words like "bomb" and "assassination" while routinely monitoring phone calls, a principal activity of the agency. Similarly, NSA's duties in the field of cryptography have led it to invest heavily in the superfast Josephson-junction switchers that may one day replace the semiconductor. NSA cooperated in setting up the FBI SEARCH program: the System for Electronic Analysis and Retrieval of Criminal History, the nation's largest data-gathering network dealing with criminal activities. SEARCH, in turn, has filtered data into the Interstate Organized Crime Index, a burgeoning data bank that, despite its title, includes political dissidents. IOCI is prominently used by police intelligence officers and has been implicated in some cases of extralegal harassment.[9]

In the private sector, the credit bureaus, with which the government now cooperates in several ways, have become major data-collecting operations in their own right. There are nearly 2,000 of these. The 5 largest (they include companies like TransUnion of Chicago and TRW of California) hold some 450 million files. It is estimated that 80 percent of Americans over the age of eighteen are in their computers somewhere. Some of these files include entries under the heading "life style"—personal habits that have to do with drinking, marriage and divorce, trouble with the police, complaints by neighbors about noise or unusual activities, anything that may satisfy the curiosity of prospective employers, financial institutions, landlords. Landlords specifically have developed "illegal detainer" data banks which keep track of court records naming anyone who ever had legal problems as a tenant. These files, too, deal in life style data. Such information is especially valuable for "block modeling," another practice made possible by the integration of data bases. Like computer matching, block models bring together scraps of information from many sources that could not have been tapped and coordinated before electronic networks existed. But block modeling adds a new twist. It runs the information through programs (they take the form of cheap, commercially available software) that compare it with generalized personality profiles. These programs are now used by employers or landlords who are on the lookout for deviant types. Block modeling allows its users to "X-ray" tenants and employees so that troublemakers and bad risks may be eliminated.

There is no limit to how much data such matching and modeling systems can absorb. Conceivably, no pool of information is too small to be sponged up by the technology. In the summer of 1984, the Selective Service dispatched a curt letter to an eighteen-year-old boy in California who was several months delinquent in registering for the draft. As it turned out, there was no boy by that name at the address used. The name was fictitious. It had been invented by two teenagers who had, some seven years before, filled out a card at a local ice cream store which was offering free birthday treats to its young customers. The name went into the store's computerized mailing list. The company which owned the store then sold its list (a common practice) to one of the country's many direct mailing businesses, which, in turn, made it available to Selective Service. Selective Service makes a practice of routinely collating such lists precisely to pin down names, addresses, and birthdays. When the fictitious boy's eighteenth birthday came round, it promptly got on his case. Or rather, the computer did, generating the warning letter it had been programmed to send.[10]

As the number of computers and computer networks used by the government mounts, some officials have expressed fears for the security of their data banks, anticipating their penetration by unauthorized parties. This is more a law enforcement officer's worry than a matter of citizenly concern. Thus, as one might guess, the government's solution to the problem is hardly encouraging. Under the terms of a 1985 National Security Directive (No. 145) which was adopted by the Reagan administration with no congressional consultation, the National Security Agency has been made solely responsible for the control and use of all federal computers and data banks. The powers contained in the directive permit the NSA to have access to all government computerized files with no provision made for the protection of privacy. The directive also implies that the NSA has the right to pursue its mandate into all private data banks linked to government operations. In late 1985, this led the NSA's National Computer Security Center into a broad investigation of the vote-counting program used in electronic polling machines in several states, an unprecedented departure for a military security service.[11]

Alvin Toffler has celebrated the computer's omnivorous appetite for data as the creation of an electronic "social memory" that will one day give us "a civilization with total recall." "An information bomb is exploding in our midst," he tells us. It is producing an "infosphere" which will provide our society with "more information and more finely organized information about itself than could have been imagined even a quarter-century ago."[12]

No doubt he is right. But I am at a loss to understand his enthusiasm for this prospect. Most of what will fill that social memory will be the dross of daily life: every phone call, every check passed, every credit card purchase, every traffic citation, every airline ticket. Of what use is this to a healthy culture and a vital political life? Obviously none. But there are those to whom just this sort of trash data is supremely valuable: the professional eavesdroppers whose infatuation with "total recall" stems from an obsessive need to keep track of everybody's least significant movement.

A survey like this of computerized surveillance by private and public sources inevitably reads like a blur of agencies, laws, programs, decked out with statistics about files and records. But one should not let the central meaning of these developments be lost among the details. Something very big, new, and threatening is permeating our political life. It makes use of the computer as its vehicle, but more important than the means is the mentality that uses the machine. However ambitiously "information" may be defined by its enthusiasts and specialists, all that the data banks and their attendants are after is data at the most primitive level: simple, atomized facts. For the snoops, the sneaks, the meddlers, data glut is a feast. It gives them exactly what their services require. They exist to reduce people to statistical skeletons for rapid assessment: name, social security number, bank balance, debts, credit rating, salary, welfare payments, taxes, number of arrests, outstanding warrants. No ambiguities, no subtleties, no complexities. The information that data banks hold is life stripped down to the bare necessities required for a quick commercial or legal decision. *Do or don't give the loan. Do or don't rent the property. Do or don't hire. Do or don't arrest.* This is human existence neatly adapted to the level of binary numbers: off/on, yes/no. What we confront in the burgeoning surveillance machinery of our society is not a value-neutral technological process; it is, rather, the social vision of the Utilitarian philosophers at last fully realized in the computer. It yields a world without shadows, secrets, or mysteries, where everything has become a naked quantity.

THE POLLING MACHINE
∎

In the 1980 presidential elections, candidate Ronald Reagan took a hard line on defense. In stern and urgent tones, he lashed out at the Soviet menace, calling for a vastly expanded military buildup. His opponent sought to use this stance to characterize Reagan as a warmonger, even a mad bomber. It was one of the weak spots in Reagan's public image.

At a certain point in the campaign, Reagan's handling of foreign and defense policy shifted noticeably. His tone became more reasoned and calm; the word *peace* began to appear more prominently in his speeches; references to "war" and the "arms race" faded. A new phrase emerged to cover his position on armaments, something bland and noncommittal, but seemingly prudent: "a margin of safety."

What caused this change of tone and rhetoric? It was done in response to a key campaign advisor, Richard Wirthlin. The advice might have been based, as such advice usually has been, on pure political instinct, which may or may not have been persuasive with the candidate and his many other counselors. Politicians always work at the center of rumors, guesswork, hunches, tested savvy, gut feelings. But in this case, Wirthlin's advice was based on something else: numbers, lots of numbers. It arose from a barrage of public opinion polling all across the nation. Wirthlin commanded statistics. That gave his advice the appearance of something more than guesswork. It looked like science.[13]

In the late 1960s, Wirthlin, a former economist at Brigham Young University in Utah, opened a market research firm in southern California called Decision Making Information. Like many such firms which measure consumer tastes, DMI easily moved into political polling, where Wirthlin was first hired on by Ronald Reagan to guide his gubernatorial campaign in California in 1970. DMI provided the usual services: voter surveys, sampling, simulations. The value of this statistical juggling is supposedly to discover where candidates are weakest or strongest—in which regions, among which ethnic, age, income groups—and then to target their campaigning accordingly. Polling can also identify which issues matter most to voters, what their likes and dislikes are, which candidates and policies have fared best or worst with them in the past.

John Kennedy was the first national candidate to make important use of polling. That was in 1960; his hired pollster was Louis Harris, who then became an independent expert. By the late 1970s, every serious candidate for office in the United States who could afford the price was following Kennedy's lead; expensive polling along with lots of media exposure had become the prevailing campaign style. But by then, the top dollar figures in the business, like Wirthlin, had gone on to new heights of push-button statistical precision. DMI had developed important connections. Its clients included government agencies like Health and Human Services, the Department of Labor, the Office of Education. In turn, the firm was tapped into nearly forty federal data banks that make their information publicly available. Wirthlin, with the aid of a large staff—as many as 300—was able to mobilize this wealth of data through an intricate computer method called PINS, Political Information Service. He had put together the most ambitious electronic sampling and simulating service ever developed, a new standard for the profession. His telephone surveys—which included automated, tape-recorded polls—were larger, more intense, and constant. He developed "tracking" techniques that involved nightly phone interviews with between 500 and 1,000 randomly selected voters toward the end of the campaign. There were even devices which allowed the phone interviewer to enter answers directly into computers, assuring results within milliseconds. Wirthlin's carefully prepared interviews and computer programs, which divided the U.S. population into 108 demographic categories, could neatly single out any item of the candidate's platform or personal image—"the nice guy factor," "the meanness factor," "the dangerous and uncaring factor"—and rapidly assess its "trend line" fluctuations in specific voter groups, providing overnight reactions to a speech, a debate, a press conference, even an offhand remark. The same refined and prompt polling could be done to assess the progress of the opposition, and the campaign could be adjusted as the numbers dictated: more of this, less of that, push harder here, lay off there, smile more, keep your left side to the camera.[14]

With each election, the influence and the visibility of the pollsters grows. Some, like Wirthlin and Patrick Caddell, have assumed a good deal of personal prominence in the public eye as the new generation of political strategist. Having honed the business of polling and simulation to a fine methodological edge in the marketplace, they can employ the same skills to sell candidates as they do to sell commodities. The secret of their success is the mystique of computerized information, their ability to generate and confabulate with prodigious quantities of data, and so to come up with "hard numbers" on any issue, any policy, any incident, gesture, turn of phrase. Wirthlin, for example, was able to present his presidential client with a dizzying array of computerized quantities. By the time the election took place in 1980, his PINS program had run 400 simulations based on every conceivable combination of assumptions about what candidate Reagan should and should not do. Nor need the pollster's services end with the election. Wirthlin remained on the Reagan administration payroll after the candidate's victory, continuing to provide public opinion research and advice at a cost of up to $1 million a year.

The pollsters are available to anyone who can afford them; they have been used by groups of every political persuasion. But they obviously bias elections in favor of those who can spend the most for the best services. Congressional incumbents, who have access to government-financed computers and free mailing privileges, also have an edge. Their franking privilege can be nicely combined with the services of another booming new information business: the direct mailers. These are the people who stand behind the rising tide of junk mail that now arrives in American mailboxes at the current rate of some 10 million pieces a day. The direct mailers deal in lists. They accumulate computerized lists of names and addresses from hundreds of sources, then analyze and refine them so that they will target specific populations for advertising, fund raising, political campaigns. The largest of these firms (Metromail of Lincoln, Nebraska, R. L. Polk Company of Detroit, the Donnelley Marketing Service of Stamford, Connecticut) routinely enter whole city directories, phone books, county records, motor vehicle data into their computers, integrating the information with census and zip code data. This has resulted in some 70 million of the country's 85 million households being on file to be arranged in custom-tailored mailing lists.

Do the pollsters make that much difference for the candidates? They are, of course, quite expert at selling their own services and so, as one might imagine, ready to insist that no candidate can do without them—even though (obviously) at least half the candidates who run for office, even with their aid, will always lose. But the question is largely beside the point. What matters is that the candidates *think* the pollsters make a difference and now plan their campaigns in response to computerized information. The result is a dismal style of politics that grows more and more obsessively focused on imagery, sloganeering, rhetorical legerdemain—in fact, on the huckstering skills of the marketplace.

To be sure, politics has always been dogged by these vices in America, but the pollsters only ingrain the corruption deeper by claiming they can maneuver their candidates with pinpoint accuracy. No doubt a great deal of the advice the pollsters offer candidates is sheer nonsense: shallow discussions of ephemeral public perceptions, illusory projections, statistical figments. For of course, none of the information is any better than the assumptions that program it. But it is nonsense garbed in quantities, quantities in intricate combinations that have been flushed out of computers. Such "demographics" —or better still, "psychographics," a new public relations fad that purports to integrate quantified consumer/voter values and aspirations—have come to hold the same authority for politicians that spreadsheets hold for the business community. The numbers lend enchantment. They make it *look* as if the pollsters know what they're talking about, and they give the pollsters an intimidatingly scientistic air. "I am primarily a scientist," says pollster Jonathan Robbin. "That is my calling. By scientist, I mean I am interested in the problems of measurement and interpretation and the concept of understanding how things work." Robbin is the inventor of a computer-based marketing method called Geodemographics based on zip codes and social statistics. He has done polling for Sears, for General Motors, for the Army, and for labor unions during elections.[15]

In fact, there may sometimes be a certain cunning effectiveness to the advice such experts give, experienced as they are at the media-mediated level of fickle public preferences, whims, prejudices, insecurities. After all, their marketing techniques do succeed in selling a lot of worthless merchandise the public never knew it wanted. More to the point: there exists a pollster, Richard Wirthlin, who succeeded in making Ronald Reagan president. Any technique that can make a winner out of such unlikely material is bound to look impressive to the rest of the field.

As so often happens when the computer's narrow mechanical powers are applied to a complex problem, the success that results comes mainly by way of downgrading the task into something the computer can do—and then cheering loudly enough to drown out the sensible reservations. What pollsters claim for their methods results from a drastic cheapening of the democratic process. In effect, they deflect attention from issues of substance by turning debate and electoral judgment into a vacuous statistical game. That, of course, is the one best use they can make of their computers: they poll to see who's "ahead." Not just ahead in an overall sense, but in ever more meticulously refined measures: with this group, in that area, on this issue. And they poll repeatedly and elaborately—perhaps even on a daily basis. The result is a steady stream of distracting numbers which are now normally released to the public as newsworthy items. The pollsters are followed in this effort by the media, which have also become highly computerized. So the polls and the surveys and the simulations are matched up and compared and debated. Pollsters are pitted against pollsters; computers are pitted against computers —as if the principal issue in the election were the reliability of polls. This is not even politics reduced to the level of a horse race; it is a contest between racing touts comparing their track records.

Over the past decade, as computers have become more proficient and prominent, we have developed a popular culture obsessed with rankings and ratings. Even beauty contests are now elaborately tabulated on esoteric programs that flash the totals across the television screen from second to second. Sports and athletics have become a morass of instant statistics. The newspapers feature the latest ratings of television shows; movies and records are ranked by their weekly earnings. In the business world, we have day-to-day printouts of corporate performance. It was inevitable that this ethos of quantitative competition should finally assimilate politics.

In recent elections in the United States, the main question under feverish discussion, in the media and in the camps of the candidates, has become: *who's winning*. Who's winning in California . . . in

Florida . . . among the senior citizens . . . among the yuppies . . . among the blue collar ethnics. The campaign itself, as it is measured by these ratings, becomes the obsessive concern of the commentators and experts—not the issues for which the campaign presumably serves as a vehicle. Issues are, after all, matters of subjective judgment. But the state of the campaigns, as reflected in the polls, is a matter of hard numbers, and hard numbers allow for easy evaluations. A candidate is a "good" choice if he is "ahead"; he is a "bad" choice if he is "behind." Candidates who are "out front" are treated with the respect and admiration due to winners; their campaigns are in "good shape." Candidates who are "falling behind" are "in trouble." They look like losers and are treated with a wised up skepticism. Their campaigns are "in disarray," "falling apart," "going broke." A point made in a debate is "good" if it scores high in the next day's polling, even though it may have been no more than a joke or a clever comeback. A slip of the tongue, a show of temper or fatigue may be a "mistake"; it is at once identified as a major item for polling. Did it "hurt"? Can the candidate "recover" and "catch up"? Voters are encouraged to pay close attention to how candidates look or sound. Do they seem relaxed, in command, ill at ease?

Such are the transient trivialities that register in computerized polling. They have nothing to do with thought or conviction; asking about them does not encourage thought or conviction. These are nothing more than low-grade verbal reflexes, ephemeral emotional twitches. But once the queries have been collected, totaled up, computed, printed out, they take on the authority of exact numbers. The media report them solemnly. The public and the candidates read the numbers and ponder them. Pundits draw sober conclusions. But more and more what everybody is responding to is the polling itself. The polls are measuring the polls.

None of this stops when the elections are over. It now continues as a full-time professional activity. On each issue that comes along, on each incident that breaks into the news, the public is polled. It learns that other members of the public "like" or "don't like," "approve" or "don't approve." We are encouraged to believe that politics is about "opinions"—not the *forming* of opinions, but their mere tabulation. This can be made to seem admirably democratic. After all, *everybody* has an opinion, and isn't one opinion as good as the next? If you ask the right question, you can whittle that opinion down to a single word: yes or no. Everybody can say yes or no. What validates an opinion? The act of polling itself, which fuses all the opinions together, counts them, and then serves them up as significant findings for public consideration. The electorate is placed in the absurd position of becoming spectators to their own predicted political behavior.

Perhaps one day an author with the involuted surrealist touch of the Argentine Nobel laureate Jorge Luis Borges will write a story about this bizarre state of affairs. It will begin with a poll asking people if they approve of the way the polls have been handling the president's approval rating. Then there will be a poll measuring the public's opinion about the results of that poll. Then there will be a poll about the poll about the poll. At last there will be an election in which the public will vote for the poll that it thinks most accurately reflects the public's opinion.

Politics in the Information Age.

THE WAR MACHINE
■

In the absence of a second superpower, it is impossible to imagine how the balance of terror, which dominated international relations for forty years from the end of World War II, could again become a factor in political affairs. As I noted in the Introduction, lesser, but still genocidal nuclear dangers remain in the area of regional conflicts; there a glitch in an antiquated computer program could cost the lives of millions. But nightmarish policies like Mutual Assured Destruction and Launch On Warning seem to have faded from our lives. The temptation is to expunge the fearful memory from our minds. We shouldn't. It has something of immense value to teach us. We now know what lies we were told about the reliability of these weapons, especially about the trillion-dollar Strategic Defense Initiative that would have pledged our national treasury to the infallibility of computer programs as inscrutable as the will of God. We have learned that the record of computer and human error that marked our nation's experience with nuclear weapons pales by comparison to that of the former Soviet Union, where command and control were shot through with criminal negligence and incompetence. I have, therefore, decided to let this section stand with minor corrections, mainly in the tense of verbs, as a kind of grim monument on the grave of the Cold War, reminding us what mad risks we were once persuaded to run. The facts and figures I mention here belong to the past, but we do well to remember that once upon a time *we were willing to bet the survival of the human race on what we were told computers can do.*

If the measure of political power is the magnitude of the decisions one makes, then we may once have been only inches away from entrusting the computer with our society's supreme governing authority. In the course of the Cold War, both in the United States and the Soviet Union, more and more control over the world's thermonuclear arsenal was steadily lodged in computerized systems, along with the programmed scenarios that would determine how, when, where that arsenal was to be used. This was nothing less than the power over our collective life and death.

The Pentagon maintains that the United States never had the capability for LOW. But this was not for lack of trying. In the final stage of the Cold War between 1985 to 1990, the Department of Defense spent $600 million on a highly touted strategic computing initiative meant to explore the military uses of the most advanced computer systems with a view to creating fully automated weapons, possibly including new additions to the deterrence system. The weapons that can do the job are no longer referred to as "smart," but as "brilliant."[18] Military technology based on AI would have to process millions of times more data through vastly more complicated programs than anything now in existence. The military always contended that research for these weapons systems would have unlimited economic spinoff. The Defense Advanced Research Project Agency assured Congress that "the domestic commercial applications of this new technology will certainly complete the transformation of U.S. society to the information age."[19]

For example, in the "Star Wars" strategic defense initiative, antimissile defense was to be based upon multilayered computer systems of dazzling complexity, all of which would have to operate in combat (with no significant prior testing beyond computer simulations) free of human supervision. Former Secretary of Defense Caspar Weinberger described the task of SDI (optimistically) as the ability to "reliably identify, track, and destroy several thousand targets in a very, very short space of time." How short? About two to three minutes. The programs meant to orchestrate the amalgamation of such advanced technologies would have to anticipate hundreds of combat contingencies that might arise in the heat of battle: evasive tactics, equipment failure, mishap, climatic changes. No human brains could process so much information rapidly enough. The SDI programs would have had to run to tens of millions of lines of coding—a thousand times more than the most complex programs that now exist. They would require teams of programmers working for years.[20]

Even short of SDI, the military's computer dependence eventually did become well advanced. The Strategic Air Command's nuclear deterrence strategy was masterminded by the world's largest single information processing and telecommunications complex: the Worldwide Military Command and Control System. WIMEX refers to a global network of sensors, satellites, and computer facilities that tied together twenty-six major American command centers around the world. From the mid-1970s, WIMEX was the subject of frequent and urgent criticism for its many vulnerabilities, which included some questionable original computer purchases.[21] The doubts were well founded; the system malfunctioned repeatedly. In 1977, during a systemwide test, more than 60 percent of its messages failed to get transmitted. During one eighteen-month period in the late 1970s, the North American Air Defense reported 150 "serious" false alarms, 4 of which resulted in B-52 bomber crews starting their engines; missile crews and submarine commanders were placed on high alert.

Most of these mistakes were traced to improper identifications on radarscopes, or to faulty parts, sometimes small, cheap electronic components. In one instance in November 1979, a training tape of a simulated Soviet attack was played by mistake and was read by the system as a real alert. All these crises were finally corrected by the intervention of military commanders who simply knew this *had* to be a mistake. Fortunately, they had the time—at least several minutes—to make up their slow-moving human minds and to stop the alert. But as the response time allowed by the weapons grows shorter, the system will have to become more hair-triggered and autonomous.

Before the Cold War ended, the key locus for advanced military automation was not the nation's intercontinental missile system but the more limited European theater. There, Soviet intermediate-range missiles and the American Pershing II and Cruise missiles were based within a few minutes' flight time of one another. On both sides, the weapons had first strike capability, meaning the accuracy or undetectability necessary to destroy the other side's weapons by a preemptive attack. The situation became so touchy that the Pentagon finally sought to develop an artificial intelligence expert system to be placed in full control of the weapons. The project was contracted with TRW Defense Systems of California.[22] TRW's feasibility study took the approach that has become standard in the design of expert systems: it examined the way experts do things, in this case generals making war. Superior generals were identified and their "judgmental ability" was then translated into a computer program, in the same way that the experience of several superior doctors might be compiled into an expert medical diagnostic program. Of course, there is a difference. No general has ever waged thermonuclear war, let alone proven himself a winner. So where were such "experts" to be found? They were selected by their performance at war games, computerized simulations of battle, which were presumably based upon somebody's nonexpert conception of what a thermonuclear war would be like. Thus, the computer programs of this expert system were not based on hard-won and tested experience but upon evaluations made by other computer programs.

The goal of research like this was (in the words of the Defense Department) to achieve "completely autonomous land, sea, and air vehicles capable of complex, far ranging reconnaissance and attack missions.... In contrast with previous computers, the new generation will exhibit human-like intelligent capabilites for planning and reasoning."[23]

Information technology is the child of military necessity; it has been part of the war machine from the very beginning, when the first primitive computers were used during World War II to assist with ballistics and gunnery and to make the calculations for the atomic bomb. In the United States, the nation's most ambitious research and development effort was to be the Microelectronic and Computer Technology Corporation in Austin, Texas,[24] a twelve-company consortium that clearly violated the antitrust laws. As Jonathan Jacky observed in 1985, "The Department of Defense is now subordinating computer science to military needs as completely as nuclear phsyics, aeronautics, and rocketry were subordinated in the 1940s." He estimated that by 1990, the Pentagon would be spending over $30 billion a year on software programming alone, 10 percent of the entire defense budget.[25] Only the collapse of the Soviet Union altered that projection.

No doubt every computer enthusiast would dismiss video games like *Space Invaders* as among the most trivial uses of this remarkable technology that so cleverly counterfeits human intelligence. But there is an intimate connection between these childish amusements and the Promethean extensions of information technology that we find in the SDI. That connection is the psychology of warrior bravado, the chauvinist foundation of the nation-state system. This fascination with manly violence first emerges in the agonistic rough-and-tumble of adolescent boys, where one might wish it would soon exhaust itself. But too many of the boys never grow up; their passion for combat simply becomes more disciplined, more regimented. And at last the nerds of the world have presented the soldier boys with the biggest video arcade of all—the planet Earth.

Had the Cold War continued, the split-second speed of modern weapons would surely have ended the last, tentative political constraints upon the thermonuclear war machine. Even the residues of fear, compassion, and self-doubt that may survive in the souls of soldiers would finally be eliminated. The weapons would have gravitated into the province of machines whose artificial intelligence would be an unfeeling, one-dimensional caricature of soldierly will. The honor, the daring, the personal heroism that were the only redeeming qualities of the military vocation would have vanished. The final, most decisive act of war conceivable would have come down to the logic of numbers processed coldly and swiftly through the inscrutable silicon cells of a machine.

MACHINE À GOUVERNER

■

As far back as 1950, when the "ultra-rapid computing machine" was still a clumsy beast, Norbert Wiener speculated upon the eventual social and political applications of cybernetics. He confronted the question:

Can't one imagine a machine to collect this or that type of information, as for example information on production and the market, and then to determine as a function of the average psychology of human beings and of the quantities which it is possible to measure in a determined instance, what the most probable development of the situation might be? Can't one even conceive a State apparatus covering all systems of political decisions . . . ? We may dream of the time when the *machine à gouverner* may come to supply—whether for good or for evil—the present obvious inadequacy of the brain when the latter is concerned with the customary machinery of politics. [26]

At the time these words were written, they might have been taken for science fiction. Even among the cybernetic experts, there would have been few who believed that matters possessing the moral complexity of international conflict or economic planning would ever be entrusted to machine intelligence. Wiener himself, after scrutinizing the prospect from several angles, finished with the warning:

Woe to us if we let it decide our conduct, unless we have previously examined the laws of its action, and know fully that its conduct will be carried out on principles acceptable to us!

But Wiener's restraint was not shared by all of his colleagues, especially not by those who were busily opening the fields of artificial intelligence and later cognitive science. As early as 1960, Herbert Simon was confidently looking forward to the day "much less than twenty-five years" in the future when "we shall have the technical capability of substituting machines for any and all human functions and organizations," including those that require "emotions, attitudes, and values." [27]

This forecast, like so much of the opportunistic self-advertising that issues from the artificial intelligence community, has of course not come to pass; its fulfillment is nowhere in sight. Nonetheless, buoyed up by exuberant, professional promises like this, the province of information technology has expanded aggressively into several areas of our political life, including the highest levels of policy and decision making.

The beginnings of this development were small and scattered, reaching back to the systems (or operations) analysis teamwork of World War II. Following the war, applied systems theory found a new home in military think tanks like RAND and Mitre, where social scientists were often allied with physicists and strategists to work on ad hoc research projects like assessing the effects of thermonuclear war or civil defense planning. During the Kennedy years, counterinsurgency warfare was a hot focus of social science research, drawing upon teams of political scientists, anthropologists, and psychologists. By that time, the dominant form of social science in the universities was behavioral and heavily statistical, an ungainly caricature of the physical sciences. The style cried out for computerization, but at the universities the social scientists tended to be treated like second-class citizens when it came to sharing time on the few machines available.

It was not until the later 1960s that the breakthrough came— and then on two fronts. In 1967, the International Institute for Applied Systems Analysis was established in Vienna. IIASA was a well-financed, computer-equipped center supported by both the Eastern and Western blocs. It has served to pioneer several efforts in the area of "world" or "global modeling" for long-range social planning. [28] A few years later, in 1969, social scientists at Harvard and MIT teamed up to organize what they saw as a Manhattan Project for their disciplines. They succeeded in drawing a five-year, $7.6 million grant from the Defense Department to explore new programming techniques. The grant set up Project Cambridge, whose research was supposed to be of the most general kind, and therefore useful for a variety of social science studies. The effort was advertised as a search for "neutral computer tools." [29] But Defense Department funding inevitably linked Project Cambridge to the needs of the Pentagon, which expected value for its money. As a result, the project soon became involved in Cold War–related assignments like developing "indications and warnings" programs for military intelligence. Another of its studies sought to construct computer models of friendly and hostile villages in Thailand and then to recommend policy accordingly. A similar form of modeling used computers to select bombing targets in Vietnam during the war years. Villages that met the parameters of the friendly model were left standing; those that modeled hostile were marked for obliteration. Computerized social science had at last found its way into a life-and-death application.[30]

A 1971 report on Project Cambridge makes clear its wide-ranging political intentions:

> With these techniques, it would be possible in a few days to consider all possible strategies for an invasion of Cuba or North Vietnam. Probably further off, but still in the foresee-able future, such techniques could be used to decide whether or not to intervene in a foreign revolution or election.[31]

Perhaps the most ambitious effort at applying information technology to the art of government took place in Chile in the early 1970s. Then President Salvador Allende brought in the British cybernetics expert Stafford Beer to develop and administer an optimum economic order for the country. Working from the formula "information is what changes us; information constitutes control," Beer had brainstormed an intricate computerized system which he quaintly called the Liberty Machine. Its purpose was to concentrate every scrap of data available from a national, or even from the world economy, and from this to fashion a "cybernetic model." The computers governing the model would "receive real-time data from the systems which they monitor, and they would distill the information content." It would then be possible to "formulate hypotheses, undertake simulations, and make predictions about world trajectories." Between 1971 and 1973, Beer, working in secret for the Ministry of Finance, sought to establish something like the Liberty Machine in Chile. The effort was a serious one, installed at great expense in a central control room (the "Opsroom") in Santiago, where it succeeded at the height of its powers in bringing 60 percent of the Chilean economy into its data gathering and governing network.[32] The system included the ability to anticipate and break strikes. Beer has reported: "We used every scrap of relevant scientific knowledge in designing the place—neurocybernetic knowledge of brain processes, knowledge from applied and group psychology, knowledge from ergonomics."[33] The exercise entailed an interesting new conception of "freedom." "Liberty," Beer decided, "may indeed be usefully redefined for our current technological era. It would say that competent information is free to act—and that this is the principle on which the new Liberty Machine should be designed." It is a definition that makes the computer an integral part of the concept.[34]

Beer's great project collapsed with the fall of the Allende government in a CIA-sponsored coup, but even in its aborted form it is a measure of how much a true-believing cybernetic utopian is willing to take on. Schemes of this magnitude should be viewed as simply the most ambitious projections of research that has been seeking ways to computerize a variety of human services and institutions: medicine, law, psychiatry, counseling, public administration. All these efforts are based on one root assumption: that human thought, even at its most subtle and intricate levels, is a kind of information processing; therefore, the more data and the faster the processing, the better.

Currently, many of the computerized modeling techniques developed by social scientists since the days of Project Cambridge have found their way into government under the catch phrase *crisis management*. In 1983, the Reagan administration gave this new discipline a special dignity by setting up a highly computerized Crisis Management Support and Planning Group within the National Security Council. The operation was entrusted to Richard Beal, a political scientist from Brigham Young University in Utah, who had been an employee of Richard Wirthlin, Ronald Reagan's political pollster. Beal's assignment was to create computer data bases for some twenty global trouble spots. One of the proudly publicized achievements of the operation was its capacity to generate information in a "composite video form" using "state of the art graphics." The graphics included maps, bargraphs, and symbols depicting such activities as negotiations and warfare. The objective of these clever computer and video inventions was to offer the president, on short notice, a simple graphic representation of an international crisis with supposedly all the data he might need in a televised form for choosing a line of policy. Perhaps it looked something like a video game, plotted upon a map of the world.[35]

The facility was far from a purely academic experiment. It was the headquarters from which President Reagan and his key advisors worked during the Grenada invasion of October 1983.[36] The result of that exercise, which included careful censorship of the press as part of managing the crisis, was deemed a success. (Wirthlin's polling after the event vouched for that.) Perhaps in part this was what influenced the National Security Agency a year later to make one of the largest single computer purchases by the government in its history: several hundred machines bought from AT&T for nearly a billion dollars. The computers will be distributed to NSA outposts worldwide and tied into crisis management headquarters in Washington.

The Joint Chiefs of Staff have also decided to invest in computerized modeling and simulating. Their project, begun in 1984, is called FORECASTS and is designed to use "country-specific information" to project probable futures in over 130 nations up to a distance of twenty to thirty years hence. The data base for FORECASTS reviews over a thousand indicators for each country, "most of them consisting of a time series of values for each indicator for each of the years from 1960 to 1980." FORECASTS can then extend the trend lines of these data into the future and can simulate "the interplay between variables over time." The project is regarded as a major "tool for decision making," primarily in a "heuristic" sense, "helping to suggest the range of possible shapes the future may assume."

> Forecasts will be useful in considering how the United States will relate to the rest of the world, what U.S. interests might be, where conflict is likely to originate, and to what extent U.S. capabilities will depend on external sources of energy, materials, and manufactures. . . . There is also a data base management system which enables the data to be queried and updated.[37]

AT THE LIMITS OF SANITY:
THE PSYCHOTIC MACHINE
■

Attempts to install the day-to-day, on-line, computerized equivalent of government on the scale of Stafford Beer's Liberty Machine are apt to be rare experiments. But efforts like the Crisis Management Center of NSA and FORECASTS are likely to become more prominent—and more dangerous—applications of computer power at high decision making levels. The danger lies in the discrepancy that exists between the seemingly rational expectations with which such projects are launched and the situation in which they may finally be required to do their job. For when they are at last called upon by political leaders to perform as advertised in a true crisis, when time is racing by and the peace of the world may hang in the balance, the machines may have drifted out of touch with their users' reality principle. They may literally have gone crazy: minds—albeit artificial ones—that have become a chaos of conflicting imperatives. How can this come about?

At the outset, when a project like the Crisis Management Group is initiated, the leaders involved are likely to regard the effort as the pursuit of a defensible, high priority objective in the contemporary world: the simple act of gathering data, lots of data. The cult of information presses in that direction with its full force; the opportunity to use state-of-the-art computers for that purpose is apt to make the undertaking all the more attractive by lending it an aura of precision and futuristic sophistication.

As more and more machines and networks go into operation, the kind and amount of data they gather begins to expand exponentially. It is like a hunger that cannot be satisfied. Indeed, it becomes one of the favored ploys of the computer virtuosos who mastermind the system to seek out unlikely and exotic kinds of data, the sort that no unaided human intelligence could have taken into account. For example, Paul Bracken tells us that the COMINT program of the National Security Agency once collected "millions of messages that flow through the Soviet military and political bureaucracies" by tapping the phone lines of the Soviet Union. And this was only one of several surveillance programs pouring data into the NSA computers. As of the 1980s, Bracken observes, "the aggregate collection and comparison of information from hundreds of programs across an enemy's entire command has been made possible using computers." He suggests the possibilities might have been extended still farther, to such fine points as monitoring the laundry facilities at Soviet ports, information that may give "excellent strategic warning of when surface and submarine forces were about to put to sea."[38] Imagine, then, somewhere in the depths of the Pentagon's war machine, a computer tabulating the dirty underwear of the Soviet Navy, analyzing the meaning of this key indicator, working it up graphically into a dynamic decision making model, perhaps a multi-media, interactive video on which the peace of the world depends.

In type and amount, the data that is concentrated in the government's computers is far beyond anything a single human brain can process. The leaders who use the machines in time of crisis may have no idea why certain forms of information have been collected at all or assigned the weight they carry. Nevertheless, those who sit before the scintillating video screens, stroking keys, calling up authoritative charts and graphs and simulations, are bound to feel briskly in step with the times. They are masters of the world's data, working at the leading edge of the Information Age. What easily drops out of sight is the fact that all the machines they confront are operating in obedience to programs that are based upon assumptions and values. What they have before them is not, in some purely neutral sense of the term, "raw data" that are being offered up for their judicious consideration—though that is how the crisis managers tend to describe the matter, with total professional detachment. They purport simply to be providing objective information on demand. But this information has been edited, shaped, weighted, and ordered; it reflects priorities perhaps of a highly ideological kind. The more simplified and graphic the computerized representations become, the more densely interpretive they will have to be. A summary, after all, condenses more tightly, shapes more arbitrarily. Thus, the graphics that were presented to President Reagan by his crisis managers during the Grenada invasion must have been shot through with assumptions about Caribbean politics, worldwide Communist intentions, America's role in the Western hemisphere. Values must have been at play balancing diplomatic against military options. Was it clear to the president at every point where the data left off and these values and assumptions began? Was it clear whose assumptions and whose values they were? Could the programs that shaped the information be traced to the minds responsible for creating them? Will presidents in the future be dealing with the same crisis programs that were created when the project began under Ronald Reagan's auspices?

As time goes on in the history of every computer system, questions like these become more difficult to answer. To begin with, large computer programs are rarely the work of a single, identifiable individual; they are put together by teams of programmers and researchers. At any given time, the team will be a mix of styles and preferences; there will be different approaches, different levels of competence. Not many of these personal quirks will be apparent; the programmers are likely to present a façade of professional objectivity and uniformity. Nevertheless, they are fashioning an intellectual artifact that reflects the tastes, choices, judgments of its makers.

In time, the system needs updating and adjustments; other programmers who may reflect the standards of a later generation will bring their judgment to bear as they take up the job. In just this fashion, the programs that now govern the Pentagon's weapons systems have been stitched and patched together over the course of several presidential administrations. There have had to be major overhauls that were rough compromises with existing, antiquated hardware. The system is not simply a technical, but an historical artifact shaped by a vast number of programmers, most of whose contributions could no longer be identified, and many of whom would probably not be able to reconstruct the work of the team on which they served. What assumptions about strategy and world politics were foremost in the minds of those who were on the job in 1962 . . . 1968 . . . 1974? What theories and methods were in fashion among computer scientists in those years?

Joseph Weizenbaum has raised the point that many super-scale computer systems are now governed by "incomprehensible programs," electronic palimpsests for which no one can any longer be held responsible.

> These often gigantic systems are put together by teams of programmers, often working over a time span of many years. But by the time the systems come to use, most of the original programmers have left or turned their attention to other pursuits. It is precisely when gigantic systems begin to be used that their inner workings can no longer be understood by any single person or by a small team of individuals. [39]

The near disaster at the Three Mile Island nuclear plant is an example of just this sort of incomprehensible program at work in a single, only medium-sized facility. It took the plant's operators several fateful hours before they could understand the meaning of computer-controlled alarm signals whose governing program was beyond their immediate comprehension. Situations like this may soon become even more densely impenetrable. Techniques are now being developed that allow computers *to program themselves* without any human intervention. These techniques—self-programming programs that supposedly "learn" from their own operations—are among the latest applications of artificial intelligence research. One of them, IBM's Query-By-Example programming language, is making its way into the business community as a way of saving the costs of certain forms of programming. One expert in the field, Donald Michie of Edinburgh University, has warned that such automatic programming procedures could lead to a "technological black hole" in which "humans will not be able to understand the reasoning behind computer results that make key decisions."[40] While self-programming programs must still be programmed by a human mind, they further remove the machine that uses them from human responsibility.

Machines that run by incomprehensible programs are approaching a kind of technological madness. They are on their way to becoming disintegrated intelligences, split and fragmented, a psychotic stew of assumptions and standards that can no longer be given a rational order. Yet, if the machine is part of a crisis management project, it will continue to process data, packaging it neatly into charts, graphs, simulations, giving the surface appearance of rationality. Computers are gifted with such a facade of impersonal precision; they have no way to look or sound or act crazy. Of course, the true madness would be that of the decision makers and the society at large that elected to become dependent on mechanical systems that bring these liabilities with them. And yet that act of delivering over one's responsibility to a supposedly infallible mechanism can be a real temptation, one that is deeply rooted in our culture.

The effort to build a *machine à gouverner* stems from an article of faith that has long been part of Western society's scientific tradition: the belief that all the secrets of nature can be fully understood by reductive analysis and mechanistic modeling. Translated into a program of research and development, this conviction has yielded striking results along many lines in our time. The organs of the body are being replaced by mechanical substitutes, though with varying degrees of success. Genetic engineering is finding ways to rebuild, and supposedly improve, living structures by rearranging the mechanisms of heredity. The human mind has been on the agenda of the mechanists since the first crude clockwork models of mentality appeared in the eighteenth century. Now that paradigm of intelligence has matured along with our technology into the data processing model of thought. The mind in all its aspects can now be seen as "nothing but" a rather complicated information-shuffling machine that works up its highest powers from simple, formal procedures that organize data points. And just as the ultimate proof of the mechanistic model in medicine is the invention of a mechanical heart or kidney that will sustain life, so in cognitive science the effort is to invent a machine that will convincingly imitate the highest functions of the minds—its power to reason, to judge, to decide.

It would be one thing if AI and cognitive science claimed, more humbly, that computer models might help us understand certain, limited applications of the mind. Even this would be a dubious proposition, based upon the assumption that two things which perform roughly the same function, the biological brain and the mechanical computer, must be equal in nature. But it would at least exhibit a becoming modesty. There are people in the field who claim no more than this; there may even be those who are prepared to reach a more self-effacing conclusion: that the real significance of the computer model is that it tells us how much we *don't* understand about the mind and *cannot* understand on the terms of that model.[41]

But modesty of this kind draws no professional plaudits; it attracts no grants and awards. It makes a poor showing alongside the dramatic advances being registered in other sciences. It will not build a rich career. Where corporate money and military-industrial power offer stunning rewards, it is difficult to hold back from making the claims these sources invite one to make. The cult of information has many members; not the least of these are the academic professionals who have committed themselves to mastering the mind. The data processing model is all they have to work with; they will push it as far as it can go.

That may not be very far. There is no possibility that computers will ever equal or replace the mind except in those limited functional applications that do involve data processing and procedural thinking. The possibility is ruled out in principle, because the metaphysical assumptions that underlie the effort are false. But it *is* possible to redefine the mind and its uses in ways that *can* be imitated by machines. Then we have a mechanical caricature which levels the activity down to a lower standard. That is what the *machine à gouverner* would be should it ever be built. We can see the outline of that caricature already in the social applications of computer power reviewed in this chapter. In each case, a complex social phenomenon has been reduced to something brutally simple that falls within the province of the machine. Politics is revised to become opinion mongering; war is revised to become the calculation of velocities and trajectories, throw weights and megadeaths.

It is important to realize, however, that these foolish simplifications, just as they stand, even without the hope of eventual elaboration, are useful to certain forces in our society. The bureaucratic managers, the corporate elite, the military, the security and surveillance agencies are able to make good use of computerized data to obfuscate, mystify, intimidate, and control. Because they overwhelmingly own the sources and machinery of data, the cult of information lends a mystique to their dominance.

The reason they can exploit the information they control so effectively should be obvious. These social elements have deeply rooted, long-standing interests to which information can be assimilated and from which programs can be deduced. In military affairs, they work to preserve the nation-state system; in economics, they work in response to the entrepreneurial ethic; in politics, they work to further Utilitarian managerialism. All these are well-rationalized commitments, never questioned by those who hold them, never needing public avowal or discussion. From them, a clear and simple political agenda arises: to concentrate more profit and power in the hands of those who already have profit and power. As long as that agenda can be conveniently kept out of sight, the massive collection of information into ever larger data banks and its ever more efficient processing through global networks can be made to seem necessary, even socially beneficial. It is simply the unfolding of a technological imperative. It is the coming of the Information Age, dawning upon us like a change of season.

But no matter how high the promise of that age is pitched, the price we pay for its benefits will never outweigh the costs. The violation of privacy is the loss of freedom. The degradation of electoral politics is the loss of democracy. The creation of the computerized war machine is a direct threat to the survival of our species. It would be some comfort to conclude that these liabilities result from the abuse of computer power. But these are the goals long since selected by those who invented information technology, who have guided it and financed it at every point along the way in its development. The computer is *their* machine; its mystique is *their* validation.

DESCARTES'S ANGEL

∎

Reflections on the
True Art of Thinking

On the night of November 10, 1619, René Descartes, then an aspiring philosopher still in his early twenties, had a series of three dreams which changed the course of his life and of modern thought. He reports that in his sleep, the Angel of Truth appeared to him and, in a blinding revelation like a flash of lightning, revealed a secret which would "lay the foundations of a new method of understanding and a new and marvelous science." In the light of what the angel had told him, Descartes fervently set to work on an ambitious treatise called "Rules for the Direction of the Mind." The objective of his "new and marvelous science" was nothing less than to describe how the mind works. For Descartes, who was to invent analytical geometry, there was no question but that the model for this task was to be found in mathematics. There would be axioms ("clear and distinct ideas" that none could doubt) and, connecting the axioms in logical progressions, a finite number of simple, utterly sensible rules that were equally self-evident. The result would be an expanding body of knowledge.

Descartes never finished his treatise; the project was abandoned after the eighteenth rule—perhaps because it proved more difficult than he had anticipated. He did, however, eventually do justice to the angel's inspiration in the famous *Discourse on Method,* which is often taken to be the founding document of modern philosophy. [1] Descartes' project was the first of many similar attempts in the modern world to codify the laws of thought; almost all of them follow his lead in using mathematics as their model. In our day, the fields of artificial intelligence and cognitive science can be seen as part of this tradition, but now united with technology and centering upon a physical mechanism—the computer—which supposedly embodies these laws.

The epistemological systems that have been developed since the time of Descartes have often been ingenious. They surely illuminate many aspects of the mind. But all of them are marked by the same curious fact. They leave out the Angel of Truth—as indeed Descartes himself did. For he never returned to the source of his inspiration. His writings spare no time for the role of dreams, revelations, insights as the wellsprings of thought. Instead, he gave all his attention to formal, logical procedures that supposedly begin with zero, from a position of radical doubt. This is a fateful oversight by the father of modern philosophy; it leaves out of account that aspect of thinking which makes it more an art than a science, let alone a technology: the moment of inspiration, the mysterious origin of ideas. No doubt Descartes himself would have been hard pressed to say by what door of the mind the angel had managed to enter his thoughts. Can any of us say where such flashes of intuition come from? They seem to arise unbidden from unconscious sources. We do not stitch them together piece by piece; rather, they arrive all at once and whole. If there are any rules we can follow for the generation of ideas, it may simply be to keep the mind open and receptive on all sides, to remain hospitable to the strange, the peripheral, the blurred and fleeting that might otherwise pass unnoticed. We may not know how the mind creates or receives ideas, but without them—and especially what I have called the master ideas which embody great reserves of collective experience—our culture would be unimaginably meager. It is difficult to see how the mind could work at all if it did not have such grand conceptions as truth, goodness, beauty to light its way.

At the same time that Descartes was drafting his rules of thought, the English philosopher Francis Bacon was also in search of a radical new method of understanding. Bacon, who was a mathematical illiterate, preferred to stress the importance of observation and the accumulation of facts. He too was a man with a revolutionary vision —the intention of placing all learning on a new foundation of solid fact derived from the experimental "vexing" of nature. Before the seventeenth century was finished, these two philosophical currents —the Rationalism of Descartes, the Empiricism of Bacon—had formed a working alliance to produce the intellectual enterprise we call science: observation subjected to the discipline of an impersonal method designed to have all the logical rigor of mathematics. As Bacon once put it, if one has the right method, then "the mind itself" will "be guided at every step, and the business be done as if by machinery."

Since the days of Descartes and Bacon, science has grown robustly. Its methods have been debated, revised, and sharpened as they have thrust into new fields of study; the facts it has discovered mount by the day. But the angel who has fired the minds of great scientists with a vision of truth as bold as that of Descartes has rarely been given her due credit, and least of all by the computer scientists who seem convinced that they have at last invented Bacon's mental "machinery" and that it can match the achievements of its human original without the benefit of unaccountable revelations.

The gap that has so often been left by philosophers between the origin of ideas and the subsequent mechanics of thought—between the angel's word and the analytical processes that follow—simply reflects the difference between what the mind can and cannot understand about itself. We can self-consciously connect idea with idea, comparing and contrasting as we go, plotting out the course of a deductive sequence. But when we try to get behind the ideas to grasp the elusive interplay of experience, memory, insight that bubbles up into consciousness as a whole thought, we are apt to come away from the effort dizzy and confounded—as if we had tried to read a message that was traveling past us at blinding speed. Thinking up ideas is so spontaneous—one might almost say so *instinctive*—an action, that it defies capture and analysis. We cannot slow the mind down sufficiently to see the thing happening step by step. Picking our thoughts apart at this primitive, preconscious level is rather like one of those deliberately baffling exercises the Zen Buddhist masters use to dazzle the mind so that it may experience the inutterable void. When it comes to understanding where the mind gets its ideas, perhaps the best we can do is to say, with Descartes, "An angel told me." But then is there any need to go farther than this? Mentality is the gift of our human nature. We may use it, enjoy it, extend and elaborate it without being able to explain it.

In any case, the fact that the origin of ideas is radically elusive does not mean we are licensed to ignore the importance of ideas and begin with whatever we *can* explain as if that were the whole answer to the age-old epistemological question with which philosophers have struggled for centuries. Yet that, I believe, is what the computer scientists do when they seek to use the computer to explain cognition and intelligence.

The information processing model of thought, which has been the principal bone of contention in these pages, poses a certain striking paradox. On the basis of that model, we are told that thinking reduces to a matter of shuffling data through a few simple, formal procedures. Yet, when we seek to think in this "simple" way, it proves to be very demanding—as if we were forcing the mind to work against the grain. Take any commonplace routine of daily life —a minimal act of intelligence—and try to specify all its components in a logically tight sequence. Making breakfast, putting on one's clothes, going shopping. As we have seen in an earlier chapter, these common-sense projects have defied the best efforts of cognitive scientists to program them. Or take a more extraordinary (meaning less routine) activity: choosing a vocation in life, writing a play, a novel a poem, or—as in Descartes's case—revolutionizing the foundations of thought. In each of these exercises, what we have first and foremost in mind is the whole, global project. We *will* to do it, and then —somehow, seemingly without thinking about it—we work through the matter step by step, improvising a countless series of subroutines that contribute to the project. Where something doesn't work or goes wrong, we adjust within the terms of the project. We understand projects: whole activities. They may be misconceived activities, but they are nevertheless the ends that must come before the means. When we get round to the means, we remain perfectly aware that these are subordinate matters. The surest way any project in life goes wrong is when we fixate on those subordinate matters and lose sight of the whole. Then we become like the proverbial centipede who, when he was asked to explain how he coordinated all his parts, discovered he was paralyzed.

What I am suggesting is that, in little things and big, the mind works more by way of gestalts than by algorithmic procedures. This is because our life as a whole is made up of a hierarchy of projects, some trivial and repetitive, some special and spectacular. The mind is naturally a spinner of projects, meaning it sets goals, choosing them from among all the things we might be doing with our lives. Pondering choices, making projects—these are the mind's first order of activity. This is so obvious, so basic, that perhaps we are only prompted to reflect upon it when a different idea about thinking is presented, such as that thought is connecting data points in formal sequences.

Now, of course, the mind takes things in as it goes along. We do register data. But we register information in highly selective ways within the terms of a project which, among other things, tells us which facts to pay attention to, which to ignore, which deserve the highest and which the lowest value. Thinking means—most significantly—forming projects and reflecting upon the values that the project involves. Many projects are simply given by the physical conditions of life: finding food, clothing the body, sheltering from the elements, securing help in time of danger. But all of us at least hope we will have the opportunity in life to function at a higher level than this, that we will spend as much of our time as possible beyond the level of necessity, pursuing what John Maynard Keynes once called "the art of life itself." Forming projects of this kind is the higher calling that comes with our human nature. Teaching the young how to honor and enjoy that gift is the whole meaning of education. That is surely not what we are doing when we load them down with information, or make them feel that collecting information is the main business of the mind. Nor do we teach them the art of life when we ask them "to think like a machine." Machines do not invent projects; they are invented by human beings to pursue projects. What Seymour Papert calls "procedural thinking" surely has its role to play in life; but its role is at the level of working out the route for a trip by the close study of a road map. It is an activity that comes into play only after we have chosen to make a journey and have selected a destination.

The substance of education in the early years is the learning of what I have called master ideas, the moral and metaphysical paradigms which lie at the heart of every culture. To choose a classic model in the history of Western pedagogy: in the ancient world, the Homeric epics (read or recited) were the texts from which children learned the values of their civilization. They learned from adventure tales and heroic exemplars which they could imitate by endless play in the roadways and fields. Every healthy culture puts its children through such a Homeric interlude when epic images, fairy tales, *chansons de geste,* Bible stories, fables, and legends summon the growing mind to high purpose. That interlude lays the foundations of thought. The "texts" need not be exclusively literary. They can be rituals—as in many tribal societies, where the myths are embodied in festive ceremonies. Or they may be works of art, like the stained glass windows and statuary of medieval churches. Master ideas may be taught in many modes. In our society, television and the movies are among the most powerful means of instruction, often to the point of eclipsing the lackluster materials presented in school. Unhappily, these major media are for the most part in the hands of commercial opportunists for whom nobility of purpose is usually nowhere in sight. At best, a few tawdry images of heroism and villainy may seep through to feed the hungry young mind. The rudiments of epic conduct can be found in a movie like *Star Wars,* but the imagery has been produced at a mediocre aesthetic and intellectual level, with more concern for "effects" than for character. At such hands, archetypes become stereotypes, and the great deeds done are skewed with an eye to merchandising as much of the work as possible.

Those cultures are blessed which can call upon Homer, or Biblical tales, or the Mahabharata to educate the young. Though the children's grasp of such literature may be simple and playful, they are in touch with material of high seriousness. From the heroic examples before them, they learn that growing up means making projects with full responsibility for one's choices. In short, taking charge of one's life in the presence of a noble standard. Young minds reach out for this guidance; they exercise their powers of imagination in working up fantasies of great quests, great battles, great deeds of cunning, daring, passion, sacrifice. They craft their identities to the patterns of gods and goddesses, kings and queens, warriors, hunters, saints, ideal types of mother and father, friend and neighbor. And perhaps some among them aspire to become the bards and artists of the new generation who will carry forward the ideals of their culture. Education begins with giving the mind images—not data points or machines—to think with.

There is a problem, however, about teaching children their culture's heroic values. Left in the hands of parents and teachers, but especially of the Church and the state where these institutions become dominant, ideals easily become forms of indoctrination, idols of the tribe that can tyrannize the young mind. Heroism becomes chauvinism; high bright images become binding conventions. Master ideas are cheapened when they are placed in the keeping of small, timid minds that have grown away from their own childish exuberance.

In the hands of great artists like Homer, images never lose the redeeming complexity of real life. The heroes keep just enough of their human frailties to stay close to the flesh and blood. Achilles, the greatest warrior of them all, is nevertheless as vain and spoiled as a child, a tragically flawed figure. Odysseus can be more than a bit of a scoundrel, his "many devices" weakening toward simple piracy. It is the fullness of personality in these heroes that leaves their admirers balanced between adulation and uncertainty. The ideal has more than one side; the mind is nagged with the thought "yes, but. . . ." Where such truth to life is lost, the images become shallow; they can then be used to manipulate rather than inspire.

The Greeks, who raised their children on a diet of Homeric themes, also produced Socrates, the philosophical gadfly whose mission was to sting his city into thoughtfulness. "Know thyself," Socrates insisted to his students. But where else can self-knowledge begin but with the questioning of ancestral values, prescribed identities?

Here is the other significant use of ideas: to produce critical contrast and so to spark the mind to life. Homer offers towering examples of courage. Ah, but what is *true* courage? Socrates asks, offering other, conflicting images, some of which defy Homer. At once, idea is pitted against idea, and the students must make up their own minds, judge, and choose. Societies rarely honor their Socratic spirits. Athens, irritated beyond tolerance by his insistent criticism, sent its greatest philosopher to his death. Still, no educational theory that lacks such a Socratic counterpoint can hope to free the young to think new thoughts, to become new people, and so to renew the culture.

In a time when our schools are filling up with advanced educational technology, it may seem almost perverse to go in search of educational ideals in ancient and primitive societies that had little else to teach with than word of mouth. But it may take that strong a contrast to stimulate a properly critical view of the computer's role in educating the young. At least it reminds us that all societies, modern and traditional, have had to decide *what* to teach their children before they could ask *how* to teach them. Content before means, the message before the medium.

The schooling of the young has always been a mixture of basic skills (whether literacy and ciphering or hunting and harvesting) and high ideals. Even if our society were to decide that computer literacy (let us hope in some well-considered sense of that much-confused term) should be included among the skills we teach in the schools, that would leave us with the ideals of life still to be taught. Most educators surely recognize that fact, treating the computer as primarily a means of instruction. What they may overlook is the way in which the computer brings with it a hidden curriculum that impinges upon the ideals they would teach. For this is indeed a powerful teaching tool, a smart machine that brings with it certain deep assumptions about the nature of mentality. Embodied in the machine there is an idea of what the mind is and how it works. The idea is there because scientists who purport to understand cognition and intelligence have put it there. No other teaching tool has ever brought intellectual luggage of so consequential a kind with it. A conception of mind—even if it is no better than a caricature—easily carries over into a prescription for character and value. When we grant anyone the power to teach us *how* to think, we may also be granting them the chance to teach us *what* to think, where to begin thinking, where to stop. At some level that underlies the texts and tests and lesson plans, education is an anatomy of the mind, its structure, its limits, its powers and proper application.

The subliminal lesson that is being taught whenever the computer is used (unless a careful effort is made to offset that effect) is the data processing model of the mind. This model, as we have seen, connects with a major transition in our economic life, one that brings us to a new stage of high tech industrialism, the so-called Information Age with its service-oriented economy. Behind that transition, powerful corporate interests are at work shaping a new social order. The government (especially the military) as a prime customer and user of information technology is allied to the corporations in building that order. Intertwined with both, a significant, well-financed segment of the technical and scientific community—the specialists in artificial intelligence and cognitive science—has lent the computer model of the mind the sanction of a deep metaphysical proposition. All these forces, aided by the persuasive skills of the advertisers, have fixed upon the computer as an educational instrument; the machine brings that formidable constellation of social interests to the class-rooms and the campus. The more room and status it is given there by educators, the greater the influence those interests will have.

Yet these are the interests that are making the most questionable use of the computer. At their hands, this promising technology— itself a manifestation of prodigious human imagination and inven-tiveness—is being degraded into a means of surveillance and control, of financial and managerial centralization, of manipulating public opinion, of making war. The presence of personal computers in mil-lions of homes, especially when they are used as little more than trivial amusements, does not in any meaningful way offset the power the machine brings to those who use it for these purposes.

Introducing students to the computer at an early age, creating the impression that their little exercises in programming and game playing are somehow giving them control over a powerful technol-ogy, can be a treacherous deception. It is not teaching them to think in some scientifically sound way; it is persuading them to acquiesce. It is accustoming them to the presence of computers in every walk of life, and thus making them dependent on the machine's supposed necessity and superiority. Under these circumstances, the best ap-proach to computer literacy might be to stress the limitations and abuses of the machine, showing the students how little they need it to develop their autonomous powers of thought.

There may even be a sound ecological justification for such a curriculum. It can remind children of their connection with the lively world of nature that lies beyond the industrial environment of ma-chines and cities. Sherry Turkle observes that, in times past, children learned their human nature in large measure by comparing them-selves to the animals. Now, increasingly, "computers with their in-teractivity, their psychology, with whatever fragments of intelligence they have . . . bid to take this place."[2] Yet it may mean far more at this juncture in history for children once again to find their kinship with the animals, every one of which, in its own inarticulate way, displays greater powers of mind than any computer can even mimic well. It would indeed be a loss if children failed to see in the nesting birds and the hunting cat an intelligence as well as a dignity that belongs to the line of evolutionary advance from which their own mind emerges. It is not the least educational virtue of the traditional lore and legends that so much of it belongs to the preindustrial era, when the realities of the nonhuman world were more vividly present.

How much ecological sense does it make to rush to close off what remains of that experience for children by thrusting still another mechanical device upon them?

There is a crucial early interval in the growth of young minds when they need the nourishment of value-bearing images and ideas, the sort of Homeric themes that open the adventure of life for them. They can wait indefinitely to learn as much as most schools will ever teach them about computers. The skills of unquestionable value which the technology makes available—word processing, rapid computation, data base searching—can certainly be saved for the later high school or even college years. But once young minds have missed the fairy tales, the epic stories, the myths and legends, it is difficult to go back and recapture them with that fertile sense of naive wonder that belongs to childhood. Similarly, if the taste for Socratic inquiry is not enlivened somewhere in the adolescent years, the growing mind may form habits of acquiescence that make it difficult to get out from under the dead hand of parental dominance and social authority.

As things now stand, there is a strong consensus abroad that our schools are doing a poor to mediocre job of laying these intellectual foundations. The reasons for the malaise of the schools are many. Teachers are often overworked and underappreciated; many students come to them bored, rebellious, distracted, or demoralized. Some of the children in our inner cities are too disadvantaged and harassed by necessity to summon up an educative sense of wonder; others may have been turned prematurely cynical by the corrupted values of commercialism and cheap celebrity; many, even the fortunate and affluent, may be haunted by the pervasive fear of thermonuclear extinction that blights all our lives. The schools share and reflect all these troubles; perhaps, at times, the troubles overwhelm the best efforts of the best teachers, driving them back to a narrow focus on basic skills, job training, and competitive grading. But it is at least worth something to know where the big problems lie and to know there is no quick technological fix for them. Computers, even when we reach the point of having one on every desk for every student, will provide no cure for ills that are social and political in nature.

It may seem that the position I take here about the educational limits of the computer finishes with being a humanist's conservative appeal in behalf of the arts and letters. It is that. Scientists and technicians, whose professional interests tend to make them computer enthusiasts, may therefore see little room for their values in the sort of pedagogy I recommend. But as the story of Descartes's angel should remind us, science and technology at their highest creative level are no less connected with ideas, with imagination, with vision. They draw upon all the same resources of the mind, both the Homeric and the Socratic, as the arts and letters. We do not go far wrong from the viewpoint of any discipline by the general cultivation of the mind. The master ideas belong to every field of thought. It would surely be a sad mistake to intrude some small number of pedestrian computer skills upon the education of the young in ways that blocked out the inventive powers that created this astonishing technology in the first place. And what do we gain from any point of view by convincing children that their minds are inferior to a machine that dumbly mimics a mere fraction of their native talents?

In the education of the young, humanists and scientists share a common cause in resisting any theory that cheapens thought. That is what the data processing model does by closing itself to that quality of the mind which so many philosophers, prophets, and artists have dared to regard as godlike: its inexhaustible potentiality. In their search for "effective procedures" that can be universally applied to all aspects of culture, experts in artificial intelligence and cognitive science are forced to insist that there is nothing more to thought than a conventional mechanistic analysis will discover: data points shuffled through a small repertory of algorithms. In contrast, my argument in these pages has been that the mind thinks, not with data, but with ideas whose creation and elaboration cannot be reduced to a set of predictable rules. When we usher children into the realm of ideas, we bring them the gift of intellectual adventure. They begin to sense the dimensions of thought and the possibilities of original insight. Whether they take the form of words, images, numbers, gestures, ideas unfold. They reveal rooms within rooms within rooms, a constant opening out into larger, unexpected worlds of speculation.

The art of thinking is grounded in the mind's astonishing capacity to create beyond what it intends, beyond what it can foresee. We cannot begin to shape that capacity toward humane ends and to guard it from demonic misuse until we have first experienced the true size of the mind.

NOTES

■

In Defense of the Naked Mind:
Introduction to the Second Edition

1. Marvin Minsky, *The Society of Mind* (New York: Simon & Schuster, 1985).

2. Minsky quoted in Raymond Kurzweil, ed., *The Age of Intelligent Machines* (Cambridge, Mass.: MIT Press, 1992), pp. 216–217. For Hubert Dreyfus' latest views on Artificial Intelligence, including an illuminating critique of neural networks, see the Introduction to *What Computers Still Can't Do* (Cambridge, Mass.: MIT Press, 1993).

3. Searle, who calls his school of epistemology "Biological Naturalism," raises telling points along this line in his book *The Rediscovery of the Mind* (Cambridge, Mass.: MIT Press, 1992), a good, witty, and hard-hitting survey of AI research.

4. Bart Kosko, *Fuzzy Thinking: The New Science of Fuzzy Logic* (New York: Hyperion, 1993).

5. See the report in *Bay Area Computer Currents*, September 7–20, 1993, p. 18.

6. See the report in *The Washington Post*, May 10, 1991. Holocaust games, which come in over one hundred varieties, circulate underground in Germany, where they are technically illegal. But such clever electronic sabotage of the system is a political ideal in certain "cyberpunk" circles.

7. Daniel Ellsberg, "Manhattan Project II: To End the Threat of Nuclear War," *Harvard Journal of World Affairs*, Summer 1992. On Ellsberg's project to achieve a "zero-nuclear-weapons world," also see "Undoing the Doomsday Machine," *Outlook: The Washington Post*, May 10, 1993, and "Manhattan Project II," *The Progressive*, August 1993.

8. Scott Sagan, *The Limits of Safety: Organizations, Accidents, and Nuclear Weapons* (Princeton, N.J.: Princeton University Press, 1993), pp. 9–10, 266.

9. James McCollom, *The Continental Affair* (New York: Dodd, Mead and Company, 1987), pp. 78–80, 127–129, 315–317.

10. For a typical ever-so-carefully balanced report on computers in the marketplace as of the mid-1980s, see "Manic Market," *Time*, November 10, 1986. The article observes that "as a practical matter, small investors

can't compete in program trading." Still it concludes, "The stock market may be faster, rougher and more complicated than ever before, but for all its painful perils and uncertainties, it is still the best game of its kind in town."

11. Joel Kurtzman, *The Death of Money: How the Electronic Economy Has Destabilized the World's Markets and Created Financial Chaos* (New York: Simon & Schuster, 1993), p. 19. This is one of the few incisively critical analyses of finance in the computer age.

12. Jonathan Laing, "The Next Meltdown? Fears Grow that Derivatives Pose a Big Threat," *Barron's*, June 7, 1993, pp. 10–34.

13. Quoted in Laing, "The Next Meltdown?" p. 10.

14. Kurtzman, *The Death of Money*, pp. 12, 202–203, 205.

15. Donald Ely and Tjeerd Plomp, "The Promises of Educational Technology: A Reassessment," in Tom Forester, ed., *Computers in the Human Context: Information Technology, Productivity, and People* (Cambridge, Mass.: MIT Press, 1989), pp. 248–261.

16. C. A. Bowers, *The Cultural Dimensions of Educational Computing: Understanding the Non-Neutrality of Technology* (New York: Teachers College Press, Columbia University, 1988), p. 36.

17. Doris K. Lidtke and David Moursund, "Computers in Schools: Past, Present, and How We Can Change the Future," *Technology in Education*, May 1993, pp. 84–86. For a balanced, critical discussion of Seymour Papert's ongoing work with LOGO, see Allison Bass, "Computers in the Classroom," in Forester, ed. *Computers in the Human Context*, pp. 237–247.

18. The estimate appears in Michael W. Apple, "Computers in Schools: Salvation or Social Disaster?" *The Education Digest*, February 1992, pp. 47–52.

19. For a good recent statistical survey of "How Computers Are Used in United States Schools," see Henry Jay Becker's article by that title in *Journal of Educational Computing Research*, vol. 7 (4), 1991, based on data from the 1989 International Association for the Evaluation of Educational Achievement Computers in Education Survey.

20. Charles Piller, et al., "America's Shame: The Creation of the Technological Underclass in America's Public Schools," *Macworld* Special Issue on Personal Computers in Education, September 1992.

21. Charles Piller and Liza Weiman, "America's Computer Ghetto," *The New York Times*, August 7, 1992.

22. The assessment is that of Stewart Brand in *The Media Lab: Inventing the Future at MIT* (New York: Viking, 1987).

23. On Software Toolworks, see the report by John Eckhouse, "Computer Age Goes Hollywood," *San Francisco Chronicle*, August 30, 1993.

24. Other recent titles that betray the same hostility: *Windows for Non-Nerds; I Hate Word for Windows; Murphy's Laws of DOS: Getting the Best of Your Computer before Your Computer Gets the Best of You; Help! WordPerfect Six; Windows for the Rest of Us; This Is the Mac, It's*

Supposed to be Fun; and *Fear Macs No More.* There is even a *Black Computer Survival Guide,* by Eno Essien (Emigrant MT, Blackk Inkk Research Group, 1992) for "anyone who feels left out of the computer boom"—especially African-Americans.

1. "Information, Please"

1. For a survey of the early history of the computer industry, see Joel Shurkin, *Engines of the Mind* (New York: Norton, 1984). Shurkin details the first use of UNIVAC at CBS in 1952 (pp. 250–253).

2. Norbert Wiener, *The Human Use of Human Beings: Cybernetics and Society* (Boston: Houghton Mifflin, 1950). A much-revised paperback edition appeared from Doubleday Anchor Books in 1954.

3. Newell and Simon, quoted in Joseph Weizenbaum, *Computer Power and Human Reason* (San Francisco: W. H. Freeman, 1976), p. 169.

4. Ibid., p. 138.

5. Simon, quoted in John Pfeiffer, *The Thinking Machine* (New York: Lippincott, 1962), p. 174.

6. Warren Weaver, "The Mathematics of Communication," *Scientific American,* July 1949, p. 12.

7. Fritz Machlup, "Semantic Quirks in Studies of Information," in *The Study of Information,* ed. Fritz Machlup and Una Mansfield (New York: Wiley, 1983), pp. 653, 658. Machlup's prologue and epilogue to this anthology are incisive surveys of the many strange meanings the word *information* has acquired since Shannon's work was published.

8. Weaver, "The Mathematics of Communication," p. 12.

9. Pfeiffer, *The Thinking Machine,* p. 186. The book is based on Pfeiffer's television documentary.

10. Steven Rose, *The Chemistry of Life* (Baltimore: Penguin Books, 1970), pp. 17, 162.

11. For Barbara McClintock's work, see Evelyn Fox Keller, *A Feeling for the Organism* (New York: W. H. Freeman, 1983).

2. The Data Merchants

1. All the quotations in this chapter from Naisbitt and Toffler are from their books: *Megatrends* (New York: Warner Books, 1982); and *The Third Wave* (New York: Morrow, 1980), respectively.

2. U.S., Congress, Office of Technology Assessment, *Information Technology and Its Impact on American Education* (Washington, D.C.: Government Printing Office, 1982); National Committee on Excellence in Education, *A Nation at Risk* (Washington, D.C.: Government Printing Office, 1983).

3. Newt Gingrich, *Window of Opportunity* (New York: TOR Books, 1984), p. 68.

4. For literature on the Conservative Opportunity Society, write to its headquarters at 106 North Carolina Street, S. E., Washington, D.C. 20003. Gingrich reviews the origins and membership of the group in his postscript to *Window of Opportunity*. Also see *Conservative Digest* for August 1984.

5. Paul Craig Roberts, *The Supply-Side Revolution* (Cambridge: Harvard University Press, 1984), p. 310.

6. Kevin P. Phillips, *The Emerging Republican Majority* (New Rochelle, N.Y.: Arlington House, 1969).

7. Herman Kahn, *The Coming Boom* (New York: Simon & Schuster, 1982).

8. See "Defense Men Take Control of America's Computers," *New Scientist* (London), May 26, 1983, p. 526.

9. The statistics for 1985 defense expenditures come from a report on National Public Radio by David Malthus, July 8, 1985.

10. See Henry Levin and Russell Rumberger, "The Low-Skill Future of High Tech," *Technology Review*, August–September 1983. Also see James Fallows, "America's Changing Economic Landscape," *Atlantic*, March 1985, for an optimistic assessment of the rise of the Sunbelt and high tech, but one which does not question the fact that the low-paying service sector is where most displaced industrial workers now have to look for jobs. For the AFL-CIO reading of the situation, see *Deindustrialization and the Two Tier Society*, Industrial Union Department (AFL-CIO) Publication (Washington, D.C., 1984).

11. Rogers and Larsen, *Silicon Valley Fever: Growth of High Technology Culture* (New York: Basic Books, 1984), p. 189.

12. Annette Fuentes and Barbara Ehrenreich, *Women in the Global Factory* (Boston: South End Press, 1983), pp. 48–56.

13. The novel was *Bugs* (New York: Doubleday, 1981; New York: Pocket Books, 1983).

14. Tim Eiloart and Nigel Searle, "Business Games off the Shelf," *New Scientist* (London), September 28, 1972, p. 579. Also see Jon Stewart, "The Electronic Office of the Future," *San Francisco Chronicle*, special report, September 18, 1979, and M. David Stone, "The Intelligent Desk," *Science Digest*, March 1985, pp. 78–79.

15. See Toffler's *The Third Wave*, ch. 14.

16. Myron Krueger, *Artificial Reality* (Menlo Park, Calif.: Addison-Wesley, 1983), p. 230.

17. *The Futurist*, quoted in *Epiphany*, Fall 1983, p. 17.

18. Steven Jobs interviewed in *Playboy*, February 1985, p. 17.

19. Edward Feigenbaum and Pamela McCorduck, *The Fifth Generation* (Reading, Mass.: Addison-Wesley, 1983), pp. 92–93.

20. The scientist is Roger Schank, quoted in Frank Rose, *Into the Heart of the Mind: An American Quest for Artificial Intelligence* (New York: Harper & Row, 1984), p. 208.

21. Robert Jastrow, "Toward an Intelligence Beyond Man's," *Time*, February 20, 1978, p. 59.

22. Jesse H. Shera, as quoted in Machlup, *The Study of Information,* p. 649.

23. Avron Barr, "AI: Cognition as Computation," in Machlup, *The Study of Information,* p. 261.

24. Toffler, *The Third Wave,* pp. 172, 183, 190.

25. Christopher Evans, *The Mighty Micro* (London: Gollancz, 1984); I. G. Good, "Machine Intelligence," *Impact* (UNESCO publication), Winter 1971.

26. Minsky, quoted in Patrick Huyge, "Of Two Minds," *Psychology Today,* December 1983, p. 34.

27. Sherry Turkle, *The Second Self: Computers and the Human Spirit* (New York: Simon & Schuster, 1984), p. 313.

28. Pfeiffer, *The Thinking Machine,* pp. 20–21.

29. John Kemeny, *Man and the Computer* (New York: Scribners, 1972).

30. Minsky, quoted in William Stockton, "Creating Computers To Think Like Humans," *New York Times Magazine,* December 7, 1980, p. 41.

31. Gordon Pask and Susan Curran, *Micro Man: Computers and the Evolution of Consciousness* (New York: Macmillan, 1982), pp. 2–3.

32. Robert Jastrow, *Time,* February 20, 1978, p. 59. Also see Geoff Simons, *The Biology of Computer Life* (London: Harvester, 1985).

3. The Hidden Curriculum

1. The numbers on computers in American schools come from the following sources: a three-part series by Edward Fiske and Richard Vevero in the *New York Times,* December 9, 10, 11, 1984; Alfred Bork, "The Computer in Education," *Education Network News,* March–April 1984; Cathy Castillo, "Computers in California Schools," *This World (San Francisco Chronicle* Education Special), April 29, 1984; and Ian Anderson, "California Schools Reap Bumper Harvest of Apples," *New Scientist* (London), March 3, 1983.

2. On computers in Japanese schools, see *Electronic Learning,* March–April 1982, p. 12. For Great Britain and France, see "Classroom Computing: A European Perspective," *Personal Computing* (September 1984): 70; and John Lamb, "Programming the First Generation," *New Scientist* (London), March 28, 1985, p. 34.

3. The figure $700 million per year was the estimated cost of Representative Timothy Wirth's Computer Literacy Act of 1984. For a survey of the views and proposals before Congress, see "Will Legislation Help?" *Personal Computing,* September 1984, pp. 72–73.

4. Beth Ann Krier, "Planning the Schools of the Future," *Los Angeles Times,* December 18, 1984, pt. 5, p. 1.

5. Rogers and Larsen, *Silicon Valley Fever,* p. 259.

6. Barbara Deane, "User-Friendly Learning," *California Living Magazine,* August 18, 1985, p. 11. The British educator is quoted in Liza Loop, *ComputerTown* (Reston, Va.: Reston/Prentice-Hall, 1983), p. 10. Computer-Town is the name of a computer literacy campaign funded by the National Science Foundation in 1979.

7. See *The Education Digest,* February, 1992, p. 49.

8. See Scarola's introduction to the "Learning" section of *The Whole Earth Software Catalog* (New York: Doubleday, 1984), pp. 175–177. This section of the catalog offers a good survey of some of the best educational software on the market.

9. This reading of the job market, based on Bureau of Labor Statistics data, comes from Henry M. Levin and Russell W. Rumberger, "The Educational Implications of High Technology," Report of the Institute for Research on Educational Finance and Governance, Stanford University, February 1983, p. 5.

10. Linda Watkins, "On Many Campuses, Computers Now Are Vital and Ubiquitous," *Wall Street Journal,* November 30, 1984, p. 1.

11. For a survey of computers in the universities, see Donna Osgood, "A Computer on Every Desk," *Byte,* June 1984. Also see Judith A. Turner, "A Personal Computer for Every Freshman," *Chronicle of Higher Education,* February 20, 1985, p. 1.

12. "AT&T Donates $7 Million in Computer Labs to 61 Schools," *Business Wire,* June 23, 1993.

13. *Teaching and Technology: The Impact of Unlimited Information Access on Classroom Teaching,* Proceedings of a National Forum at Earlham College, (Ann Arbor, MI.: The Pierian Press, 1991).

14. "How Multimedia Computer Technology is Reshaping the Way Students Learn and Professors Teach," *U.S. News & World Report,* September 28, 1992.

15. Thomas DeLoughry, "EDUCOM Hopes to Demonstrate How Computers Can Improve Instruction and Save Money," *The Chronicle of Higher Education,* July 14, 1993.

16. Cyert, quoted in *Wall Street Journal,* November 30, 1984, p. 18.

17. Ernest L. Boyer, "Education's New Challenge," *Personal Computing,* September 1984, pp. 81–85.

18. The quotes from Melmed and Cyert come from Stephen L. Chorover, "Cautions on Computers in Education," *Byte,* June 1984, pp. 22–24.

19. The quote is from Steven Levy, *Hackers: Heroes of the Computer Revolution* (New York: Anchor Press/Doubleday, 1984), p. 284. In this section, I am following Levy's excellent and entertaining history of the early hackers.

20. Turkle, *The Second Self,* p. 218.

21. Melvin Berger, *Computers* (New York: Coward, McCann & Geohegan, 1972).

22. Kalaghan, quoted in *New York Times,* January 13, 1985, p. A1.

23. Levy, *Hackers*, pp. 289–290.

24. Software that simulates Mendelian genetics is available in Control Data's PLATO series and in the CATLAB program from the University of Iowa's CONDUIT series.

25. On this aspect of Mendel's work, see Robin Dunbar, "Mendel's Peas and Fuzzy Logic," *New Scientist* (London), August, 30, 1984, p. 38.

4. The Program Within the Program: The Case of Logo

1. For a report on Papert's work at the Centre Mondial Informatique, see *New Scientist* (London), February 10, 1983, pp. 358–361.

2. The quotations from Papert in this chapter are from his book, *Mindstorms: Children, Computers, and Powerful Ideas* (New York: Basic Books, 1980). Also see Papert, "Misconceptions About Logo," *Creative Computing,* November 1984, pp. 229–230.

3. Margaret Boden offers a good chapter on such problem-solving programs in *Artificial Intelligence and Natural Man* (New York: Basic Books, 1981), pp. 370–389. She uses the examples of meal planning and baking a cake.

5. Of Ideas and Data

1. Machlup and Mansfield, *The Study of Information*, p. 644.

2. Vladimir Nabokov, "The Art of Literature and Common Sense," *Lectures on Literature* (New York: Harcourt Brace Jovanovich, 1980).

6. Computers and Pure Reason

1. Bertrand Russell, *A History of Western Philosophy* (New York: Clarion Books, 1945), p. 37.

2. Boden, *Artificial Intelligence and Natural Man*, pp. 15, 16–17.

3. Machlup and Mansfield, *The Study of Information*, p. 671.

4. Robert Jastrow, *The Enchanted Loom: Mind in the Universe* (New York: Simon & Schuster, 1984), pp. 166–167.

5. Boden, *Artificial Intelligence and Natural Man*, pp. 6–7.

6. *Science Digest*, June 1984, p. 94.

7. Jane Bryant Quinn in the financial section of the *San Francisco Chronicle*, May 14, 1985.

8. Steven Levy, "A Spreadsheet Way of Knowledge," *Harper's*, November 1984.

9. See "The Apple Connection" column in *Bay Area Computer Currents*, November 20–December 3, 1984, p. 29.

10. Ariel Dorfman, "Evil Otto and Other Nuclear Disasters," *Village Voice*, June 15, 1982.

11. Weizenbaum, *Computer Power and Human Reason,* p. 213.

12. Quoted in ibid., p. 138.

13. *Life,* November 20, 1970, p. 586.

14. For a survey and critique of AI in America, Europe, and Japan, see the three-part series in *New Scientist* (London), November 15, 1984, pp. 18–21; November 22, 1984, pp. 17–20; November 29, 1984, pp. 12–15.

15. See Fred Hopgood, "Computer Chess Bad, Human Chess Worse," *New Scientist* (London), December 23/30, 1982, pp. 827–830. Also see M. David Stone, "Electronic Chess Experts," *Science Digest,* March 1985, p. 8.

16. The newspaper-raincoat program is detailed in Rose, *Into the Heart of the Mind,* ch. 4.

17. Minsky, quoted by Muyghe, *Psychology Today,* December 1983, p. 34.

18. David Noble, *Forces of Production: A Social History of Industrial Automation* (New York: Knopf, 1984). Noble offers a critical survey of the ICAM program and several similar efforts to eliminate the human factor from industrial technology. See especially his final chapter, "Another Look at Progress," which I am drawing upon in this section.

19. On problems with new highly computerized weapons systems, see Ernest Canine, "Weapons: Quality vs. Quantity," *Los Angeles Times,* August 8, 1982, pt. 2, p. 5. Also the report in *New York Times,* May 12, 1985, p. 3-1.

20. Feigenbaum and McCorduck, *The Fifth Generation,* p. 40.

21. Alexander Besher, financial section, "Pacific Rim" column, *San Francisco Chronicle,* July 15, 1985, p. 31.

7. The Computer and the Counterculture

1. For the history of the computer industry from the 1960s through the 1980s, see Shurkin, *Engines of the Mind;* Rogers and Larsen, *Silicon Valley Fever;* Levy, *Hackers;* and Paul Freiberger and Michael Swaine, *Fire in the Valley* (Berkeley, Calif.: Osborne/McGraw-Hill, 1984).

2. Quoted in Levy, *Hackers,* p. 165.

3. *Resource One Newsletter,* no. 2, April 1974, p. 8.

4. Michael Rossman, "What Is Community Memory?" mimeo, 1979.

5. Jim Warren, quoted in Freiberger and Swaine, *Fire in the Valley,* p. 99.

6. Freiberger and Swaine, *Fire in the Valley,* p. 37.

7. Jerry Brown, quoted in *Esquire,* February 1978, p. 65.

8. The poem appears in *The Pill Versus the Springhill Mine Disaster* (New York: Dell/Laurel, 1973).

9. Hugh Gardner, *The Children of Prosperity* (New York: St. Martin's Press, 1978), pp. 35–48.

10. For O'Neill, see his book, *High Frontier* (New York: Doubleday,

1982), and the fall 1975 issue of *Co-Evolution Quarterly* featuring his project. For Soleri, see his *Arcology* (Cambridge: MIT Press, 1970).

11. Levy, *Hackers*, p. 251.

12. Chester Anderson, *San Francisco Oracle*, November 6, 1967.

13. Brand, quoted in *San Francisco Focus Magazine*, February 1985, p. 107.

14. Joel Kotkin, "IBM Takes on the Mantle of America's Champion," *Washington Post* Special, reprinted in *San Francisco Chronicle*, October 14, 1985, p. 26.

8. The Politics of Information

1. G. M. Young, *Victorian England: Portrait of an Age*, 2d ed. (Oxford: Oxford University Press, 1964), pp. 11, 32–33.

2. For a sampling of the materials available from government sources, see Matthew Lesko, *Information USA*, a guide and manual available from 12400 Beall Mt. Road, Potomac, MD 20854. Also see Susan Osborn and Jeffrey Weiss, *The Information Age Sourcebook* (New York: Pantheon, 1982), which was compiled from some 500 government agency books and brochures.

3. John Lamb, "Confusion Among the Databases," *New Scientist* (London), February 21, 1985, p. 23. Lamb also deals with the problem of incoherence among the many data bases (different codes, protocols, and command languages) as well as the increasing expense of subscriptions and access charges. It should be mentioned that the U.S. government is one of the largest operators of data bases, many of them cheap or free. For a guide to this veritable jungle of information, see *The Federal Database Finder*, also available in Lesko, *Information USA*.

4. As early as January 1982, military experts were questioning the simulations on which Ronald Reagan had campaigned. See the report by Ian Mather in *The Observer*, January 24, 1982. Both the CIA and the Arms Control Association eventually challenged the figures used by Reagan on the Soviet arms buildup. See *New York Times*, March 3, 1983, p. 1, March 9, p. 23; and the Knight News Service report, *San Francisco Examiner*, June 18, 1984, p. 1.

5. For a discussion of Papert's idea of computer cultures, see James Dray and Joseph Menosky, "Computers and a New World Order," *Technology Review*, May–June 1983. Also see Papert's first chapter in *Mindstorms*.

6. For a review of services like EIES and Compuserve as well as data base resources, see the "Telecommunicating" section in Brand, ed., *Whole Earth Software Catalog*. This section also offers some bibliographic guides on the subject.

7. Mike Cane, *The Computer Phone Book* (New York: New American Library, 1983), surveys a few hundred computer bulletin boards. On net-

working generally with or without computers, see *The Networking News-letter* (Box 66, West Newton, MA 92165).

8. Associated Press report, *San Francisco Chronicle,* June 12, 1985, p. 11.

9. On the ARPAnet, see *The Networking Newsletter* 1, no. 3 (1984): 15.

10. For a report on the services available from SCAN, see Evelyn Greenwald, "Reference Power," *American Libraries,* November 1984, p. 698.

9. Ben Franklin's Information Service

1. Fay Blake, "Information and Poverty," in *Proceedings of the Congress for Librarians* (Ann Arbor, Mich.: Pierian Press, 1988), pp. 9–12.

2. On the gendered image of librarianship, see Dee Garrison, *Apostles of Culture: The Public Librarian and American Society, 1876–1920* (New York: Macmillan, 1979).

3. The services that I am using as models here are primarily those of my own university library and of SCAN, the Southern California Answering Network, which operates out of the Central Library of the Los Angeles Public Library. SCAN dates back to the early 1970s as a federally funded project and is very much the model I am advocating here. It is, in fact, almost too good to be true that the government should have put our tax money to use in so enlightened a way. Among the database vendors to which SCAN subscribes are NEXIS, Dialog, and Orbit. It also draws upon numerous specialized CD-ROM databases, such as Health Index, Phone Disc, and Moody's Company Data. Vendors of this kind provide access to hundreds of databases; Dialog alone includes some three hundred databases, Orbit another two hundred or so. This range of information as well as the expense is far greater than the ordinary home computer user could handle. There are always those in official positions who protest that such services are too costly to be provided for the relative few who use them. But information can hardly be budgeted that way; the teachers, writers, journalists, scholars do not consume information like food and drink for their own benefit. They have only one thing to do with it: pass it along. The help I received in researching this book is in these pages for all to see. It has become as much the property of every reader as it is mine.

4. For a discussion of these developments, see Henry Blanke, "Libraries and the Commercialization of Information: Towards a Critical Discourse of Librarianship," *Progressive Librarian,* Winter 1990–1991, pp. 9–15.

5. Patricia Glass Schuman, "Reclaiming Our Technological Future," *Library Journal,* March 1, 1990, pp. 34–38.

√ 6. John Buschman, "A Critique of the Information Broker: Contexts of Reference Services," *Reference Librarian* 31 (1990), 131–151.

7. For a review of Jim Warren's commendable effort to establish a

national standard of citizen access in California, see Jim Warren, et al., eds, *Computers, Freedom and Privacy* (Los Alamitos, California.: IEEE Computer Society Press, 1991). Also see the report on California's AB 1624 in *Microtimes,* November 15, 1993 p. 24.

8. David C. Churbuck, "Good-Bye, Dewey Decimal," *Forbes,* February 15, 1993, p. 204.

9. F. W. Lancaster, "Future Librarianship: Preparing for an Unconventional Career," *Wilson Library Journal,* May 1983, p. 749.

10. On these possibilities, see Mike Holderness, "Time to Shelve the Library?" *New Scientist,* December 5, 1992, pp. 22–23, and Charles Robinson, "The Public Library Vanishes," *Library Journal,* March 15, 1992, pp. 51–54. For a discussion of new electronic publishing techniques and their impact on libraries, see The Andrew W. Mellon Foundation, *University Libraries and Scholarly Communications* (Washington, D.C.: Association of Research Libraries, 1993), and Chuck Creesy, "The New Digital Information Order," *The AAUP Computer Newsletter,* May 1993.

11. John Buschman, "Information Technology, Power Structures, and the Fate of Librarianship," *Progressive Librarian,* Winter/Spring 1993, p. 15. This journal speaks for radical wing of the profession. It can be ordered from Empire State College, 330 W. 42nd Street, 4th floor, New York, NY, 10036.

12. For a review of these developments, see Carolyn Gray, "The Civic Role of Libraries," in an excellent volume edited by John Buschman, *Critical Approaches to Information Technology in Librarianship* (Westport, Conn.: Greenwood Press, 1993), pp. 151–172.

13. John Haar, "The Politics of Electronic Information: A Reassessment," in Buschman, *Critical Approaches,* pp. 203, 208.

14. Ed Kroll, *The Whole Internet User's Guide and Catalogue* (Sebastapol, Calif.: O'Reilly and Associates, 1992) is one of several good guides. Order via 1-800-998-9938. The Internet Society holds annual conferences (off-line...in hotels) and issues a print-on-paper newsletter. Write to The Internet Society, Suite 100, 1895 Preston White Drive, Reston, VA 22091. Phone: (703) 648-9888.

15. *San Francisco Chronicle,* July 15, 1993.

16. Thomas Mann, *Library Research Models: A Guide to Classification, Cataloging, and Computers* (New York: Oxford University Press, 1993) is required reading for all those who seek a comprehensive treatment of information storage and retrieval.

17. Mann provides an instructive list of such queries in *Library Research Models,* pp. 115–120.

18. Private communication from Sanford Berman, head cataloger at Hannepin County Library, Minnesota, and co-editor of *Alternative Library Literature: a Biennial Anthology* (McFarland and Company Inc.).

19. For a discussion of electronic amnesia, see Steve Homer, "Battling on with Veteran Computers," *New Scientist,* November 14, 1992, pp. 32–35.

20. Mann, *Library Research Models,* p. 138. Also see Simson Garfinkel, "Making Sense of Computer Gibberish," *Los Angeles Times,* November 15, 1992, and Brian Hayes, "The Electronic Palimpsest," *The Sciences,* September/October 1993, pp. 10–13.

21. Don Norman, "Will Tomorrow's Computer Be Able to Read Today's Files?" *AppleDirections,* October 1993, p. 14.

22. Fred Lerner, "Arsenals into Data Stores," *New Scientist,* January 9, 1993, p. 47–48.

23. For a severely negative assessment of the impact of videogames on children, see David Sheff, *Game Over: How Nintendo Zapped an American Industry, Captured Your Dollars and Enslaved Your Children* (New York: Random House, 1993).

✓ 24. John Swan, "Information and Madness," *Library Journal,* February 1, 1988, p. 28.

10. In the Wrong Hands

1. Wiener, quoted in Noble, *Forces of Production,* p. 73.

2. See Noble, *Forces of Production,* pp. 71–76, for a full account of Wiener's heroic efforts to defend cybernetics from misuse.

3. Wilson, quoted in Noble, *Forces of Production,* p. 21. See especially his chapters 2, 3, and 4 on automation in the immediate postwar period.

4. Noble, *Forces of Production,* p. 328. For a fuller description of these programs, see the epilogue to *Forces of Production.*

5. For a survey of the legal and political problems that arise from computerized forms of surveillance, see James Rule et al., *The Politics of Privacy: Planning for Personal Data Systems as Powerful Technologies* (New York: Elsevier, 1980); and David Burnham, *The Rise of the Computer State* (New York: Random House, 1983).

6. For a survey of government and private use of data banks, see the series by Scott Winokur, "Nowhere to Hide," *San Francisco Examiner,* October 7–12, 1984.

7. Associated Press report, "Credit Records Open to U. S. Security Soon," *San Francisco Chronicle,* April 11, 1984.

8. Quoted by Winokur, "Nowhere to Hide," October 7, 1984, p. 14.

9. On the activities of the NSA, see Loring Wirbel, "Somebody Isn't Listening," *The Progressive,* November 1980, pp. 16–19.

10. The incident is recounted in Winokur, "Nowhere to Hide," October 11, 1984, p. B-4.

11. Comprehensive NSA control of data banks was reported on National Public Radio's "Morning Edition," July 1, 1985. Also see the report in *New York Times* for September 24, 1985, reprinted in *San Francisco Chronicle,* September 25, 1985, p. 12.

12. Toffler, *The Third Wave,* pp. 192–194.

13. For a somewhat overdramatized account of Richard Wirthlin's ser-

vices in the 1980 Reagan campaign, see Roland Perry, *Hidden Power* (New York: Beauford Books, 1984). The general outlines of Perry's narrative are confirmed by a report, "The Marketing of a Candidate," *Advertising Age,* December 15, 1980, and in accounts given below.

14. For discussions of Wirthlin's methods, see Mark Levy, "Polling and the Presidential Election," *Annals of the American Academy of Political and Social Sciences,* March 1984; and Wirthlin's own account of the 1980 campaign, "The Republican Strategy and Its Electoral Consequences," in *Party Coalitions in the 1980s,* ed. Seymour Lipset (San Francisco: Institute for Contemporary Studies, 1981). On polling generally, see Dom Bonafede, "Campaign Pollsters—Candidates Won't Leave Home Without Them," *National Journal,* May 26, 1984; Bruce E. Altshuler, *Keeping a Finger on the Public Pulse* (Westport, Conn.: Greenwood Press, 1982); and Steven J. Rosenstone, *Forecasting Presidential Elections* (New Haven: Yale University Press, 1983).

15. Robbin, quoted in Burnham, *The Rise of the Computer State* (p. 90), which gives an illuminating account of how a labor union used Robbin's technique to defeat right-to-work legislation.

16. See the report, "Nuclear War and the Computer," *Datamation,* February 1984, pp. 50–51, and in *New Scientist* (London), October 25, 1984.

17. See the report in *New Scientist* (London), October 25, 1984, p. 7. Also see the report in *San Francisco Chronicle,* July 11, 1985, p. 17. A news item on Computer Professionals for Social Responsibility appears in *Datamation,* February 1984, pp. 58–60, and a discussion of their lawsuit appears in Laura Fraser, "Can a Computer Declare War?" *This World* magazine, *San Francisco Chronicle,* November 24, 1985, p. 19.

18. On the Strategic Computing Initiative, see reports in *New York Times,* June 18, 1984, p. 17, October 23, 1984, p. C-1; and *Washington Post,* November 4, 1983, p. 1, and September 5, 1984 p. F-1. Also see "Military Computing: DARPA's Big Push in AI," *Datamation,* February 1984, pp. 48–50.

19. U.S., Congress, House Appropriations Committee, Department of Defense Appropriations for 1985, pt. 5, 98th Cong. 2d sess., p. 495.

20. On the strategic defense initiative, see Jonathan Jacky, "The Star Wars Defense Won't Compute," *Atlantic,* June 1985, pp. 18–29; Jeff Hecht, "Star Wars: An Astronomical Bribe for Scientists," *New Scientist* (London), June 20, 1985, pp. 14–18; "Reagan's Star Wars," Report by the Union of Concerned Scientists, *New York Review of Books,* April 26, 1984, pp. 47–52.

21. On WIMEX and the computer problems of the U.S. early warning system generally, see Daniel Ford, *The Button: The Pentagon's Strategic Command and Control System* (New York: Simon & Schuster, 1985).

22. See "General Computer Takes Charge," *New Scientist* (London), April 21, 1983, p. 153.

23. DARPA Report, *Strategic Computing,* quoted by Jacky, "The Star

Wars Defense Won't Compute," p. 20.

24. See John Lamb, "Defense Men Take Control of America's Computers," *New Scientist* (London), May 26, 1983, p. 526.

25. Jacky, "The Star Wars Defense Won't Compute," p. 26.

26. Wiener, quoting Pere Dubarle, in *The Human Use of Human Beings*, pp. 178–180.

27. Quoted in Weizenbaum, *Computer Power and Human Reason*, p. 244.

28. On IIASA, see the report in *New Scientist* (London), July 19, 1973, p. 27.

29. Judith Coburn, "Project Cambridge: Another Showdown for Social Sciences?" *Science*, December 5, 1969, pp. 1250–1253.

30. On computerized bombing in Vietnam, see Weizenbaum, *Computer Power and Human Reason*, pp. 238–240.

31. Joseph Hanlon, "The Implications of Project Cambridge," *New Scientist* (London), February 25, 1971, pp. 421–423.

32. See the report on Beer's project in *New Scientist* (London), October 25, 1973, p. 260. Also see "Economy by Computer," *This World* supplement, *San Francisco Chronicle*, January 21, 1973, p. 15.

33. Beer quoted in John Adams, "Everything Under Control," *Science for the People*, April–May 1973, p. 4. This article as a whole is a good critical review of Beer's theories.

34. Stafford Beer, "The Liberty Machine," *Futures*, December 1971, pp. 338–348.

35. See "Crisis Management Under Strain," *Science*, August 31, 1984, pp. 907–909, which describes Richard Beal's basic plans for the project and his video-graphics innovations.

36. Ralph K. Bennett, "Grenada: Anatomy of a 'Go' Decision," *Reader's Digest*, February 1984, pp. 72–77. There is also a somewhat fictionalized reconstruction of the computerized assault on Grenada in Roland Perry, *Hidden Power*, ch. 22.

37. This description of FORECASTS comes from a personal letter from the Public Affairs Office of the Joint Chiefs of Staff, July 29, 1985.

38. Paul Bracken, *The Command and Control of Nuclear Weapons* (New Haven: Yale University Press, 1983), pp. 39–41.

39. Joseph Weizenbaum, "On the Impact of the Computer on Society," *Science*, May 12, 1972, pp. 612–613. Also see his chapter "Incomprehensible Programs," in *Computer Power and Human Reason*.

40. "Computers That Learn Could Lead to Disaster," *New Scientist* (London), January 17, 1980, p. 160.

41. Joseph Weizenbaum would be the most prominent example of a computer scientist who takes this position. It is also the position taken by Hubert Dreyfus, *What Computers Can't Do* (New York: Harper & Row, 1973); and John Searle, *Minds, Brains and Science* (Cambridge: Harvard University Press, 1985).

11. Descartes's Angel: Reflections on the True Art of Thinking

1. Jacques Maritain offers a lengthy analysis of Descartes's fateful dream in *The Dream of Descartes* (New York: Philosophical Library, 1944).

2. Turkle, *The Second Self*, p. 313.

INDEX

■

ABOUT THE AUTHOR

Theodore Roszak is Professor of History at California State University, Hayward. He is the author of several works of fiction and non-fiction, including *The Making of a Counterculture*. His most recent books include *The Voice of the Earth: An Exploration of Ecopsychology,* and the novel *Flicker.* He has been a Guggenheim Fellow and has been twice nominated for the National Book Award. His writing has appeared in *The New York Times, Sierra, The Nation, The New American Review, Newsday, The Atlantic Monthly, Harper's, The Michigan Quarterly, The Denver Quarterly, Ethics,* and in Great Britain *New Scientist, The Guardian,* and *The Times Educational Supplement.*